Ua Mau Ke Ea O Ka'aina I Ka Pono

"The Life of the Land is Perpetuated in Righteousness"

—King Kamehameha III,
Royal Coat of Arms, 1843

HAWAII THE BIG ISLAND TRAILBLAZER
Where to Hike, Snorkel, Surf, Bike, Drive

third edition
text by Jerry Sprout
photographs, design, production by Janine Sprout
technical consultant, Michael Sagues

For: John and Patty Brissenden, Paula Pennington and Jimmy Dunn, John and Suzanne Barr, Greg Hayes and Joan Wright, Joseph Stroud and Ellen Scott, Rich and Kate Harvey, Linda Kearney, John Manzolati, Carol Mallory, Jim Rowley, Barbara and Gary Howard, Barry and Alice Zacherle, Jack and Sandy Lewin, Rob Moser, Mark and Vicki Hyde, the Michael Sagues family, the Matthew Sagues family, and the Rickford family

Diamond Valley Company, Publishers
89 Lower Manzanita Drive, Markleeville, CA 96120

www.trailblazertravelbooks.com
www.trailblazerhawaii.com (blog)
Facebook: trailblazertravelbooks
trailblazertravelbooks@gmail.com

ISBN: 978-0-9786371-8-7
ISBN E-book: 978-0-9786371-9-4
Library of Congress Catalog Card Number 2002096351

Printed in the United States of America
Copyright ©2003, 2005, 2007, 2008, 2009, 2011, 2013, 2014
by Jerry and Janine Sprout

proofreader: Gregory Hayes
cover: Hula platform, Kilauea Caldera

Mahalo Nui!

Linda Elliott, Hawaii Wildlife Center; Kerry Balaam and Brett Lajala at ʻIole Foundation; Bobo Tabayoyon, Carlsmith Beach Park; Cole Figeuria and Tara at Dolphin Quest; Susan Carlile, Umauma Falls; Smiley Burrows, Green Lake; Keska Burns and Sean, Hawaii Tropical Botanical Gardens; Emily Catey, Volcano Art Center; Miguel Salmoiraghi; Mark and Vicki Hyde; Tim and Jan Gillespie; John Barnes, Mauna Loa; Anne Kern, Kona Historical Society; Virginia Branco at Mokupapapa Center; Les, Loraine, and Freckles Miller; Kona Gayle; Lynn and the late Paul Gephart, Hawaiian Artifacts; Kay Kammerzell, New Moon; Elizabeth Buffy Pickett, Ocean Warriors; Barbara and Gary Anderson, Shipman House; Lorna and Albert Jeyte, Kilauea Lodge; Dave Griffin and Chris Kaluau, Blue Hawaiian; Manny Vincent Kawihae Canoe Club; Doug Arnott and Susan Keris at Arnott's Lodge; Michael Tuttle, Hawaii's Best Bed & Breakfast; Donna Saiki, Pacific Tsunami Museum; Daniel Kaniela Akaka, Jr., Mana Lani Resort; Luana A. B. Neff, Hawaiian Force; Laura Aquino, Current Events; David Nardin and Paul Fukumura-Sanada, Mauna Loa Observatory; Keoki Paʻaoao, Mauna Lani; Laura Craft, Barbara Bower, Keck Observatory; Longboarder T. J. Street; Mountain biker Rick Solomon, Kamuela; Gary Rothfus; Roz Roy, Bayview Farms; Albert Kehaulani Solomon, Jr.; Gil Kaheli at Miloliʻi; Martha Zacho at Puukohola Heiau; Nancy and Greg Gerard; Nalani and Moira at Hawi Post Office; Edie Paulson and Tim Pemberton; John Kitchen, Ipo, Garry, and all at Hawaii Forest & Trail; Kia in Waipio Valley; Elaine Carlsmith; Patty from the Hokuleia; Aunty Lei at the Waikaloa Mariott; Ed and Loni Kuhl at the Four Seasons; Lily Anne, Lele, and Richard at Kaloko Park; Mervin et. al. at Hoʻokena; Janet at Volcano Winery; Molly at Isaacs Art Center; Elaine Christianson; Christine Reed, Basically Books; Yumi at Mokupapaa Center;

Chris at Hapuna Beach; Darren at Wapio Valley; Lani, Alamo; Shannon at Jaggar Museum; Kawika and Enoka at Wawaioli Beach Park; Arnold at Hawaii Volcanoes Observatory; Larry at White Sands Beach; Tom Dequiar, Puʻuhonua O Honaunau; Kaleolani Standley and Keahi, Kaupulehu Cultural Center; Staff at the Department of Land and Natural Resource; Kumu Nani Lim Yap, Hula Halai; Hikoʻula Hanpai, Storyteller; Bo and Patrick at Kalopa State Park; Lorrie at the Hilton; Vivian Steeley, Big Island Visitors Bureau; Chef James Cassidy at the Four Seasons; Steve at Ahalanui Beach Park; sailors Koca and Casey; Patty McCarthy, Waipio Valley; Auntie at Keauhou Beach Hotel; Marie at Kealakekua Bay; Jana and Jevon Kaʻaloa and Jarren Moeoge, Super J's; Kamuela Moraes, Richardson Ocean Park; Reed Harmon, Kohala Divers; Lynne Kreinberg, Kealia Ranch Store; Momi Subiono, Greenwell Ethnobotanical Garden; County of Hawaii, Parks Department; Fanny Au Hoy, Huliheʻe Palace; Tailiko Scarbrough at Kahaluʻu Beach; James Kimo Pihana and Kelani, Mauna Kea; Rob Ely, Kupono McDaniel, and Andrea Kaʻawaloa, Hawaii Volcanoes National Park; Ken Pacchio at Kihilo Bay; Joann Bragalone, Ululani Gallery; Suga' Daddy; and to everyone else whose name we didn't get!

PUʻU Oʻo STEAM PLUME, HAWAII VOLCANOES NATIONAL PARK

HAWAII TRAILBLAZER is an offering to the strong and beautiful and intelligent people of the Big Island. May your message of Aloha spread to the farthest reaches of the earth and live on forever.

HAWAII

THE BIG ISLAND

Trailblazer

WHERE TO
HIKE, SNORKEL, SURF, BIKE, DRIVE

JERRY AND JANINE SPROUT

DIAMOND VALLEY COMPANY

PUBLISHERS

MARKLEEVILLE, CALIFORNIA

TABLE OF CONTENTS

ALOHA AND WELCOME
TO THE BIG ISLAND OF HAWAII

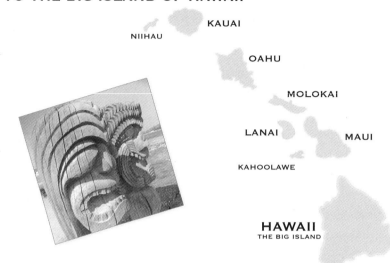

KAUAI

NIIHAU

OAHU

MOLOKAI

LANAI

MAUI

KAHOOLAWE

HAWAII
THE BIG ISLAND

Forget the movie version of Hawaii and prepare yourself to see another planet altogether when you journey to the Big Island. Yes, you'll find white-sand beaches arranged around turquoise coves, whose warm, clear waters are packed with fish and coral as colorful as a bag of gum drops, and, yes, deep green valleys are laced with waterfalls, and birds as colorful as the fish will flitter through exotic forests. Even so, these are just a few predictable elements of this strange and wonderful new land.

Usually, after taking an initial spin around the island, visitors are struck by its diversity—and for good reason. The Big Island is comprised of five separate volcanoes that have joined together over a million years, making it about twice as large as the rest of the Hawaiian Islands combined. On the slopes and shores of these oceanic peaks you will find 11 of the world's 13 climatic environments. No place is more diverse. Yet, after taking another spin or two, visitors begin to appreciate the singular nature of this land, and to realize that the notion of island-as-planet is more than just a metaphor.

Creation enfolds here, right before your eyes. Enough new lava—molten earth batter—has erupted in the last twenty years alone to pave five round-trip roads to the moon. The newest of earth is nearly barren, fields of rock glistening smooth or heaped in jagged piles. At the coastline of these barren fields, coconut palms and ohia trees sprout after just years. At other eruption sites, just a century into the light of day, new other trees and shrubs take hold. And at older flows, exposed to the elements for thousands of years, full forests have established. On the island's oldest eruptions sites in the north are tropical jungles with beaches and valleys that hardly hint of their fiery origins. Recipe for Eden: Squirt a zillion tons of molten earth into the sea, add rain, air, sun, and time—*et voila!*

The new-planet idea is most apparent from a perspective atop the Big Island's mammoth twin peaks, Mauna Kea and Mauna Loa. Although both stand *only* about 14,000 feet above sea level (at 13,796 feet Mauna Kea bests its sister by 119 feet) the real story is below the waterline, where the mountains descend another 40,000 feet to the seafloor, making them easily the largest on earth. Surrounding these unearthly bodies is a universe of water, about 2,500 miles of open sea in every direction, the most-isolated landmass on the planet. This was the last land discovered by human beings, the Polynesian argonauts some 2,000 years ago. Western culture didn't set foot here until nearly 1800.

If history can foretell the future, then the fate of this new planet is sealed. All the Hawaiian Islands in the archipelago—130 of them, stretching over 1,600 miles—are moving with the earth's crust in a northwesterly direction, like the shell of an egg turning around its magma yolk. As they move, erosion and sea action wear away the

HAPUNA BEACH, SNOW-CAPPED MAUNA KEA SUMMIT

land, and the highest peaks are submerged into the ocean. Some 5-million years ago, Kauai, the farthest north of the eight major islands, was where the Big Island is now, sitting over the molten Hot Spot. Maui, just north, used to be one huge island, but is now eroded away to four separate islands. The Big Island will slowly be worn down, its joined volcanoes becoming separate islands, and, finally, sea-washed coral atolls. Unless, of course, history is not a predictor, and the Hot Spot changes its nature and volume so that Loihi, the seamount brewing 20-miles offshore the Big Island today, does not simply herald a new island, but the beginning of a new Pacific continent.

PUʻUHONUA O HONOUNOU, WAIPIO VALLEY

Fortunately, NASA technology is not required to explore this planet—just a car, a swimsuit, and some flip-flops. In the north are the Kohala Mountains, whose high green pastures are home to Parker Ranch, the largest ranch in the U.S. On the seaward slopes of Kohala, the Big Island's oldest land, are the lush valleys of Waipio, 'Iole, and Pololu that call forth romantic images of the South Pacific. Sightseers will be attracted to the quaint plantation towns and history parks in Kohala, and hikers will love walking on some of the state's best tropical trails.

South from Kohala, on the west side of the island, are vast, barren lava fields. This is land only a lizard would love at first sight. But drive toward the ocean a mile or two along the almost-always-sunny coastline and you'll discover Hawaii's best beaches. Hidden in the wild sections, and well marked on resort grounds, are ancient petroglyphs and village ruins that speak of an earlier time. Trails connect long stretches of coastline, both through the gardenscapes of the resorts and the natural lands.

The Kona coast, the Big Island's most recognizable place name, covers the southwest side of the island. While rightly known for sunshine, Kona gets enough moisture at its 1,000- to 2,000-foot level to yield its famous coffee and macadamia orchards. Kailua-Kona, just south of the airport, is a strip of modest resorts and condos, a few miles long. Snorkeling and surfing spots are interspersed along this coast, where Kamehameha the Great chose to live his final decade.

Midway on the Kona coast is Kealakekua Bay, where Captain James Cook made landfall and was heralded as a god, only to be slain later along its shores. Some of

MAKALAWENA

the best snorkeling in the Hawaiian Islands is in this bay. The coast gets steep in the south of Kona, but you can duck down at Ho'okena and Miloli'i for snorkeling and remote coastal hiking. At Manuka State Park, farther south just before forests give way to desert lava fields, are native forests with both nature trails and wilderness treks.

At South Point, Mauna Loa's 60-mile-long southwest rift zone slopes gently into the sea. This most-southerly land in the United States was the most northerly for the Polynesians, who are thought to have made first landfall here. Going northward along the east side, the land rises steadily to the 4,000-foot level, 30 miles away, at Hawaii Volcanoes National Park. On the way up, you pass the rain forests of the Kau Forest Reserve, which are home to Wood Valley, a botanical wonderland that most visitors miss.

One of America's treasures, the quarter-million acre national park is centered around Kilauea Caldera, where volcanology became a science. Eruptions of this "lava lake," have occurred as recently as the 2008. Pu'u O'o, where current flows meet the sea in a towering plume of toxic steam, is a short drive from park headquarters, down Chain of Craters Road. The upcountry of the park and its adjoining state lands are hardly volcano-like, with ferns the size of trees in thousands of acres of native rain forests.

A half-hour down the mountain to the north of the park is Hilo, which gets a bum rap because of its yearly rainfall. With many square blocks of vintage storefronts that survived two tsunamis—set in an arboretum of banyans and beach trees, and enveloped by a greenbelt of bay-front parks—Hilo is the Hawaiian Island's best-kept secret. It does get monsoon rains, feeding the Wailuku River that rushes down from the saddle of the island's twin peaks and through the town. Then after the rains comes the preternatural brilliance of the tropical sun. Within a few miles of the historic part of town are two state parks, Waiola and Wailuku, with a large lake and waterfalls. Also near Hilo is a run of four beach parks that offer snorkeling lagoons and surfing waves.

The Puna coast is a short trip from Hilo, but too far away for a reasonable day trip from Kona. Many visitors miss this coast which features views of the current eruption at the national park and the unheralded but fantastic Kehena-Poihiki Scenic Coastal Drive. In Puna, you'll also find several excellent snorkeling tide pools and natural thermal ponds in which to take a soak. Cape Kumukahi gets practically no play, in spite of being the island's dramatic east point, where you can breathe the freshest sea-level air in the world, and walk the historic pasture lands of Green Lake. This coastline was moved a half-mile seaward by a 1960 eruption of Kilauea's east rift zone. On the uplands of Puna grow most of the exotic flowers exported around the world.

The center of the island is Mauna Kea—Ka Piko Kaulana o Ka Aina—"The Famous Summit of the Land." Near the summit, in the Mauna Kea Ice Natural Area Reserve, is one of the highest lakes in America, Lake Waiau, which the ancients considered the

HAMAKUA COAST, KOHALA COAST RESORT

"umbilical cord to the heavens." Fittingly, also near the summit, are a dozen of the world's most powerful celestial observatories, including the Keck and the Subaru. Tours take people to the top, or you can make the trip in your own four-wheel drive vehicle.

Hamakua is Mauna Kea's east coast, going north from Hilo. Dozens of streams cleave this windward side, issuing forth in waterfalls at Akaka State Park and Umauma. The old highway intertwines with the new, creating a scenic drive through wild tree tunnels and the fanciful Hawaii Tropical Botanical Gardens. Hamakua's rolling shoulders were former sugar cane fields, a history that is told by the plantation towns tucked away along the coast. Above the former fields are a run of forest reserves, with old-growth koa and other trees, most easily seen at Kalopa Native Forest State Park.

The high plains of Mauna Kea are reachable through Mana Road, a cowboy trail, as well as several trailheads off the streamlined Saddle Road. Set above 6,000 feet between the two big mountains, these locales will have you asking, Where am I? Saskatchewan? Africa? No, you're on the Big Island of Hawaii, a planet unto itself in the middle of the Pacific. If you can find the time to at least hit the highlights, hither and yon, the place will leave your head spinning in sync with the earth.

GETTING TO AND AROUND ON THE BIG ISLAND

AIRLINES

Most flights to either the Kona or Hilo airports include a stopover and change of terminals in Honolulu. Most international airlines service Honolulu. Some airlines have non-stop flights to the Big Island (unless schedules have changed): United flies from San Francisco and Los Angeles, and American from Los Angeles.

CAR RENTAL

All the major companies, plus a few local companies, service the Big Island. Book early and phone around to get the best deals. Some companies offer mini-leases, if you're planning to stay longer. Tour companies and shuttle taxis are widely available. Public buses are also available. For independent travelers, a car is essential. Numbers for car rental agencies and bus companies are in *Resource Links*. See *Free Advice & Opinion,* page 214 for driving conditions and advice on renting a four-wheel drive vehicle.

WHEN TO COME

High season on the Big Island is when school's out during the summer, and also briefly around Christmas and New Year's. Visitation doesn't drop off much during any month. Unlike the other Hawaiian Islands, the Big Island's tourists are spread over lots of country, and you will not feel the crush at any time—except for traffic snarls either side of Kailua-Kona. But if you'd like a slack time, early autumn and mid-to-late winter are the best bets. Room occupancy rates vary from 60 to 80 percent. See *Strategies for Visiting the Big Island* on page 198 for trip planning help.

DRIVING TIMES ON THE BIG ISLAND

See *Driving Tours,* page 184 for specific road descriptions and routes.

KAILUA-KONA TO:

Kona Airport, 7 mi. (15 min.)
Kawaihae, 32 mi. (35 min.)
Hawi, 52 mi. (1.25 hr.)
Pololu Lookout, 61 mi., (1.5 hrs.)
Waimea, 40 mi. (50 min.)
Waipio Valley, 63 mi. (1.5 hrs.)
Middle Saddle Rd., 58 mi. (1.25 hr.)
Hilo via Hwy. 19, 94 mi. (2 hrs.)

Captain Cook, 15 mi. (30 min.)
Miloli'i, 42 mi. (1 hr.)
South Point, 68 mi. (1.5 hrs.)
Volcanoes National Park, 98 mi. (2 hrs.)
Hilo via Hwy. 11, 124 mi. (2.5 hrs.)
Puna Coast via Hwy. 11, 143 mi. (3 hrs.)

HILO TO:

Volcanoes National Park, 28 mi. (35 min.)
South Point, 78 mi. (1.5 hrs.)
Middle Saddle Rd., 30 mi. (40 min.)
Waipio Valley, 41 mi. (1 hr.)
Waimea, 55 mi. (1.25 hrs.)

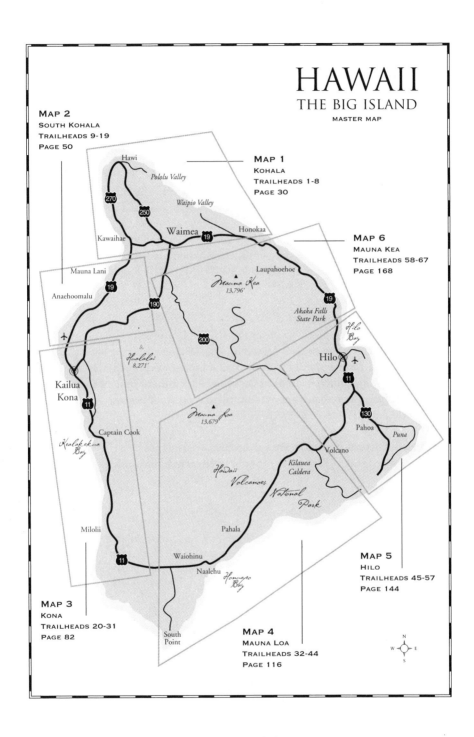

HAWAII
THE BIG ISLAND
MASTER MAP

MAP 2
SOUTH KOHALA
TRAILHEADS 9-19
PAGE 50

MAP 1
KOHALA
TRAILHEADS 1-8
PAGE 30

MAP 6
MAUNA KEA
TRAILHEADS 58-67
PAGE 168

Hawi

Pololu Valley

270

250

Waipio Valley

Kawaihae

Waimea 19

Honokaa

Mauna Lani

Laupahoehoe

Mauna Kea
13,796'

Anaehoomalu

19

190

Akaka Falls
State Park

19

Hilo
Bay

200

Hualalai
8,271'

Hilo

11

Kailua
Kona

11

130

Mauna Loa
13,679'

Pahoa

Puna

Captain Cook

Volcano

Kealakekua
Bay

Kilauea
Caldera

Hawaii
Volcanoes

National
Park

Milolii

Pahala

MAP 5
HILO
TRAILHEADS 45-57
PAGE 144

Waiohinu

11

Naalehu

Honuapo
Bay

MAP 3
KONA
TRAILHEADS 20-31
PAGE 82

South
Point

MAP 4
MAUNA LOA
TRAILHEADS 32-44
PAGE 116

N
W — E
S

HOW TO USE THIS BOOK

Use the INDEX to locate a trail or place that you've already heard about. Use the TABLE OF CONTENTS and MASTER MAP to find a part of the island you'd like to explore. Then use the TRAILHEAD MAP for each region to focus on a particular spot, and go to the trailhead descriptions to pick out an activity that sounds good. Trailheads include hikes of varying lengths, as well as snorkeling and surfing spots.

Use the ACTIVITIES BANNER in the TRAILHEAD DIRECTORY to see which recreational opportunities are available and where. Go to the BEST OF section to locate a hike or other activity that suits your interests, mood, and the day.

Use RESOURCE LINKS to find listings and phone numbers for public agencies, museums and attractions, tours and outfitters, accommodations and restaurants, and all other visitor information. Also see STRATEGIES FOR VISITING THE BIG ISLAND, which will aid in planning your trip.

CALCULATING HIKE TIMES

Hikers in average condition will cover about 2 mph, including stops. Groups and slower-movers will make about 1.5 mph, or less. Well-conditioned hikers can cover 3-to-3.5 mph. Everyone should add about 30 minutes for each 800 feet of elevation gain. Also add 60 minutes or longer to daylong hikes, for a margin of error, and just because this is Hawaii—trails are not generally easy and people tend to look around more.

To check your rate of speed: 65 average-length steps per minute, equals about 2 mph; 80 steps per minute is about 2.5 mph; 95 average steps per minute comes to about 3 mph.

KEY TO READING TRAILHEAD DESCRIPTIONS

23. TRAILHEAD NAME   **ACTIVITIES BANNER**

   What's Best:
   Parking:

HIKE: Hike Destination (distance, elevation)
         Hike descriptions.
Be Aware:
More Stuff: (S A M P L E)
Talk Story:

SNORKEL: SURF: Snorkeling and surfing descriptions.

"23." Trailhead Number: These correspond to the numbers shown on the six Trailhead Maps. Numbers begin with Map 1, Kohala and continue to Map 6, Mauna Kea. In most cases, trailhead numbers that are close together numerically will be close geographically. There are 66 trailheads, listed sequentially in the text of the book, divided into six sections. The Trailhead Directory is a complete list, including activities.

Trailhead Name: Each trailhead offers one or more recreational activities—hiking, snorkeling, and surfing. (Mountain biking is mapped and described in a separate section.) Some trailheads offer one parking place and a single activity. Other trailheads have several parking places, all close together, and several recreational activities. Some trailheads take a whole day, or more, to explore, while others can be combined with nearby trailheads to fill out a day of adventuring.

Activities Banner: This shows which of the three recreational activities are available at this trailhead. Included are one or more of the following, always listed in the same order:
> HIKE: Hikes, ranging from long treks to easy strolls.
> SNORKEL: Snorkeling and swimming, including freshwater pools.
> SURF: Surfing with boards, sails, kites, bodyboards, and bodies.

What's Best: A thumbnail description of what to expect when visiting this trailhead.

Parking: Gives specific directions from the nearest highway to the parking spot for the trailhead's primary hike destination. Secondary *Driving* directions are also given, for nearby hikes. Directions usually include the nearest mile-marker, which is abbreviated as "mm." For the island's main highways, the mile markers start at "0" in Hilo and increase as you drive around toward Kona. Roadside signs mark every mile.

Mauka means to turn or head inland, toward the mountains. *Makai* means to go seaward, toward the coast. These are island-style directions.

HIKE: The first paragraph after the Hike: symbol lists each Hike Destination available at the trailhead, followed by the (distance, and elevation gain) for each hike in parentheses. Distances are given to the nearest .25-mile. Only elevation gains of 100 feet or greater are noted. All hiking distances in parentheses are ROUND TRIP.

Paragraphs following the Hike: symbol give trail descriptions. The first reference to a **Hike Destination** is boldfaced. Trail descriptions include junctions with other trails, the type of terrain and walking surface, as well as elevation changes and landmarks . **Second Destinations** follow in subsequent paragraphs, boldfaced and described in the order they are listed in the first Hike paragraph.

Be Aware: Notes special precautions and difficulties associated with a hike or other activity. Also read *Free Advice & Opinion* for listings of rules and hazards that apply to adventuring on the Big Island.

More Stuff: Gives other hikes and activities available at this trailhead that are not among the primary listings. Normally these are out-of-the-way spots, sometimes with difficult access and terrain. Fewer visitors will be at these places.

Talk Story: Gives historical or cultural background. Rooted in the islands' oral tradition, 'talk story' is the term locals use for reminiscing about the old days.

SNORKEL: SURF: Descriptions for snorkeling and surfing follow, in order, after the hike paragraphs. Descriptions include where to go for these water sports, as well as notations for precautions. Parking directions for these activities will be included in the descriptions—unless they have already been listed in the parking directions or hike descriptions above. For example, parking directions for a snorkel or surf spot will most often be among those already given for a beach walk. **Snorkel** and **Surf** locations are boldfaced. One trailhead may describe several nearby locations for each activity.

okay, you now have your feet wet, time to jump in . . . .

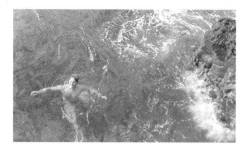

THE BIG ISLAND

WHAT DO YOU WANT TO DO TODAY?

Best Of lets you pick an activity to suit your whims and the weather. The picks are listed by trailhead number, with the lowest number first. The 'best among the best' attractions are **boldfaced**.

TH = TRAILHEAD
DT = DRIVING TOUR

HIKING

TROPICAL CLIFFS AND VALLEYS

VOLCANO AND CRATER HIKES

HISTORICAL PARKS & PLACES

GARDENS

COAST WALKS TO
HIDDEN BEACHES

POINT BREAKS
Beach 69, TH10, page 54
Kua Bay, TH18, page 72
Pu'umoa Point, TH34, page 122
Keokea Point (3-Miles),
   TH49, page 156
Hakalau Bay, TH59, page 172

CARRY THE BOARD
Pololu Beach, TH4, page 37
Mahaiula Bay, TH19, page 74

OFFSHORE BAY BREAKS
Kaunaoa Bay, TH9, page 52
Pinetrees, TH20, page 84
He'ei Bay, TH26, page 96
Honoli'i Beach Park, TH57, page 163

REEF BREAKS
South Puako Beach (Ruddles),
   TH11, page 56
Kaloko Pond, TH21, page 87
Banyans, TH24, page 91
Richardson Ocean Park (4-Miles),
   TH49, page 156
Pohoiki Bay-Bowls, TH52, page 158

PICNIC PLACES
Keokea Beach Park, TH4, page 37
**Holoholokai Beach Park, TH11,
   page 54**
Kekaha Kai Beach Park, TH19, page 72
Manuka State Park, TH31, page 108
Waiakea Fishpond, TH47, page 149
Moku Ola, TH48, page 151
Ahalanui County Park, TH53, page 158
Waikaumalo Park, TH60, page 172
Laupahoehoe Park, TH61, page 174
Kalopa State Park, TH62, page 174

RAINBOW FALLS

TRAILHEAD DIRECTORY

MAUNA LOA

*Hawaii Volcanoes National Park

HILO

MAUNA KEA

Kohala

POLOLU VALLEY LOOKOUT

TRAILHEAD PREVIEWS

That the Big Island actually is made up of five volcanoes mashed together is evidenced most clearly in Kohala, the green nub in the north that points toward Maui. The mile-high Kohala Mountains are long-since-dormant volcanoes, about a million years older than other parts of the island. They have reached the erosion stage, beginning their losing battle with waves, rain, and gravity. The topographical result is what many visitors come to Hawaii to see: The northeast coast, which receives the trade wind's wet weather, is creased by three dozen streams, creating valleys one- to two-thousand-feet deep, adorned with tropical greenery and ribbony waterfalls.

No roads travel the entire coast. But hikers can explore the valleys and beaches on several trails that are among the most exhilarating in the state. Waipio Valley is the best-known, accessible via a four-wheel road—or a 20-minute walk. The beach and lagoon, also known as Valley of the Kings, was young Kamehameha's favorite surfing hangout. Kaluahine and Hi'ilawe falls, as well as others, rain down from jungly cliffs, and the Muliwai Trail climbs from Waipio to Waimanu Valley, a wilderness to the north. You can explore the upper part of Waipio on the White Road trail into the Kohala Forest Reserve, leading from near Waimea to a spectacular diving-board lookout, although—bad news—this trail may still be closed due to an access dispute. To see the other end of Kohala's fissured coast, you need to drive around to the other side, to the Pololu Valley—another fabulous foray into a deep green crease with a wild beach.

SPENCER BEACH PARK

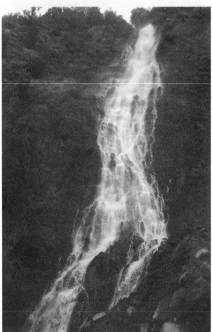

MULIWAI TRAIL BOUND, KALUAHINE FALLS

The south end of Kohala is a reminder that it is not a separate island. Here, instead of beaches, are rolling plains at 3,000 feet and higher, the sprawling pastures of the Parker Ranch, which is the largest privately held cattle ranch in America. Flows from Mauna Kea, none more recent than 4,000 years ago, have piled up against the Kohala Mountains.

The west side of Kohala is another story altogether. In the 25-mile drive from Waipio on the east to Kawaihae on the west coast, you go from forests getting 200 inches of rain yearly to kiawe deserts receiving about 15 inches. A similar shift in climate occurs when driving the 20 miles north from Kawaihae to road's end at Pololu Valley. Nature's sprinkling system has provided nicely for outdoor adventurers, since you can always retreat from a storm to find sunshine.

For seekers of Hawaiian history and culture, Kohala is a garden of abundance. Start with the Kamehameha Statue, in Kapa'au, a monument that was lost at sea before finding its home. Nearby is 'Iole Foundation, site of the Bond Estate, the second-oldest structures on the island and home to a lush stream valley with trails. Then continue west to King Kamehameha Birthplace and the Mo'okini Heiau, on a windswept shore where the echoes of history are palpable—no kidding. Just down the coast from this remarkable site is Mahukona Beach Park, where a decrepit mill and dock tell of more recent history, that of the sugar industry of the late 1800s and early 1900s. The old wharf at Mahukona is Kohala's best snorkeling spot, and among the best on the island.

MAU'UMAE BEACH

You can hike a wild coast from Mahukona to Lapakahi State Historical Park (or drive there) to hark back again to ancient times at a village that was Hawaii's first to be preserved. Craft workers ply their trades on-site, furthering the traditions of Old Hawaii. A self-guided trail winds through the village, passing a cove that also doubles as a snorkeling venue, in a marine conservation district.

The Big Island's newest temple, the Pu'ukohola Heiau is at the southern end of west Kohala. Now a national historical site, it was built in 1790 by Kamehameha the Great and was where he vanquished his rivals to gain control of the island. Surfing and snorkeling are popular at several locales nearby, including Kawaihae and Spencer Beach Park. The choicest spot around is a short hike down the coast from Spencer to Mau'umae Beach. You might stake out some sand and hang for awhile at this semi-secret snorkelers' cove.

BIG ISLAND ECO ADVENTURE, 'IOLE

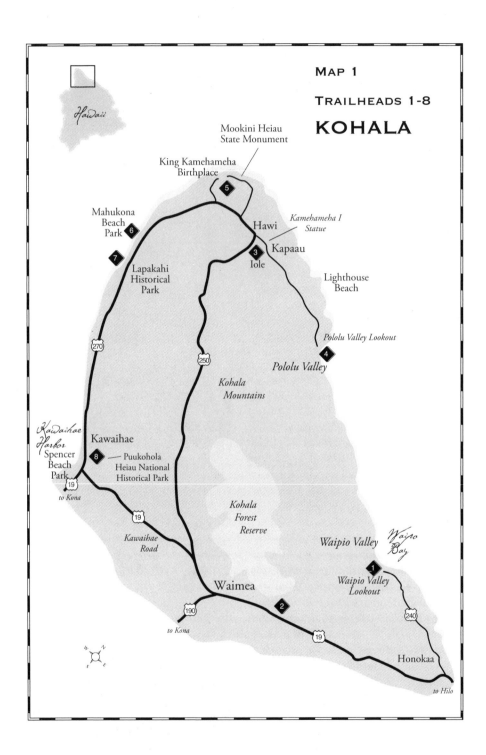

MAP 1

TRAILHEADS 1-8

KOHALA

Hawaii

Mookini Heiau
State Monument

King Kamehameha
Birthplace

Mahukona
Beach
Park **6**

Hawi   *Kamehameha I Statue*

Kapaau

3
Iole

7

Lapakahi
Historical
Park

Lighthouse
Beach

5

270

Pololu Valley Lookout

250   **4**

Pololu Valley

*Kohala
Mountains*

*Kawaihae
Harbor*
Spencer
Beach
Park   Kawaihae   **8**   — Puukohola
Heiau National
Historical Park

19
to Kona

19

*Kawaihae
Road*

*Kohala
Forest
Reserve*

Waipio Valley   *Waipio Bay*

1
*Waipio Valley
Lookout*

Waimea

190   **2**

to Kona

19   240

Honokaa

to Hilo

T R A I L H E A D S

TH :	TRAILHEAD
HIKE :	HIKES AND STROLLS
SNORKEL :	SNORKELING, SWIMMING
SURF :	BOARD, BODYBOARD, BODYSURF
MM :	MILE MARKER; CORRESPONDS TO HIGHWAY SIGNS
MAKAI :	TOWARD THE OCEAN
MAUKA :	INLAND, TOWARD THE MOUNTAINS

ALL HIKING DISTANCES IN PARENTHESES ARE ROUND TRIP. ELEVATION GAINS OF 100 FEET OR MORE ARE NOTED. SEE RESOURCE LINKS FOR CONTACTS AND TELEPHONE NUMBERS.

1. WAIPIO VALLEY   HIKE, SURF

WHAT'S BEST: Here's a tropical fantasy land with cliffs spewing waterfalls into a lush valley—taro fields, calm lagoons, and a surfer's beach. Waipio is a marquee attraction.

PARKING: Take Hwy. 19, the Mamalahoa Hwy., east from Waimea. Near mm44, take Hwy. 240 toward Honoka'a. Continue for 9 mi. Parking is at the end of the road. *Be Aware:* The road down is is steep and narrow. Only 4WD is allowed.

HIKE: Waipio Valley Lookout (.25-mi.); Waipio Beach and Kaluahine Falls (3 mi., 525 ft.); Muliwai Vista (4.5 mi., 975 ft.); Waipio taro fields (4 mi., 550 ft.)

Talk Story: The ali'i of ancient times favored verdant Waipio for both agriculture and leisure, and it became known as the **Valley of the Kings**. Taro, bananas, guava, coconuts, and other fruits grow amid exotic and native trees. In 1780, **Kamehameha the Great,** who had spent his youth surfing here, chose this valley to receive his commission as guardian of the war god, Kukailimoku. Several heiaus that predated Kamehameha graced the valley, including the massive Honuaula Heiau. Tunnels connected some of the heiaus, one of which was said to be the entranceway to a ghostly underworld. The entire valley used to be protected by a 50-foot high sand dune, called Lalakea, or "white fin," but the 1946 tsunami took out the dune, and many ancient sites. *Be Aware:* Bring plenty of drinking water. Plan on getting your shoes wet on the taro fields hike.

The **Waipio Valley Lookout** is a short stroll to a pavilion and railed viewing area. This is a postcard shot, taking in about half the beach below and the 1,200-foot cliffs a mile away. To **continue to the valley**, walk down the paved road. The blacktop soon crosses the stream on its headlong pursuit of the falls. **For the beach and Muliwai Trail**, turn right at the bottom of the main road. Shaded by exotic trees, you'll soon reach the black sand and rocks of **Waipio Beach**. To your right is **Kaluahine Falls**, making a straight shot down the cliff to the surf. Hug the bouldered shore to reach the bottom of the falls. *Be Aware:* Heads up for falling rocks.

For the **Muliwai Trail Vista**, walk to your left through the ironwoods, formerly a campground. You'll see the trail's long switchback (the "zig-zag") etched into the cliff at the far end of the beach; the seaward crook of the trail is your destination. You need to cross **Waipio Stream**, which is usually best accomplished where the water riffles, just inland from the surf. *Be Aware:* Don't cross if the stream is running swiftly. The Muliwai Trail was damaged in the 2006 earthquake; some interior sections may be closed.

After the stream, veer left into the ironwood trees along a path that skirts the margin of the beach. As you reach the cliff, to the left is a private cottage, with a barbed-wire fence on the cliff side of its driveway. The **Muliwai Trail**, probably still marked by a tattered and unreadable sign, heads up the hill to the right. You'll make several short switchbacks before beginning the long ramp to the vista—which is about a third of Muliwai's 1,200-foot climb. A shaded spot affords a penthouse look down at Waipio Beach. On the way back down you'll get fabulous views up the valley. *More Stuff:* The Muliwai Trail is a backpackers' odyssey. It ascends another 800 feet from the vista and continues another 6 miles to the verdant wilderness of **Waimanu Valley**. Along its entire course, the rugged Muliwai dips into a half-dozen stream valleys. Even seasoned trekkers need to suck it up to make this a day hike.

For the sublime hike into the **upper Waipio taro fields**, go left at the bottom of the paved road. You'll pass a fishpond, **loku puʻuone**, its slack waters mirroring the valley's towering cliffs. Continue past rustic homes on the left, set beneath the twin silvery ribbons of 1,200-foot **Hiʻilawe Falls**, the flows of which are controlled by the agricultural ditch above. About .5-mile into the valley hike is a major stream crossing, on the other side of which is the horse outfitter. Continue another .25-mile to *just before* a second crossing—go left on a trail that goes up the stream, which is actually a water-washed roadway. You need to walk in the water for a bit. (The main road continues across the valley, crossing several streams and ending where newly arrived home-buyers have fenced off access.) The up-valley road, which achieves dry ground, continues under a canopy of bird-filled trees, passing taro fields. Rising above the fields are Waipio's green cliff faces, often accented by ribbony waterfalls. This unusually dramatic, Old-Hawaii scenery continues for about a mile, ending at a homestead gate. *More Stuff:* The homestead owner is hiker-friendly, but ask before proceeding. The trail gets steeper and overgrown, the habitat for wild pigs and adventure hikers.

SURF: With a many-tiered shore break, **Waipio Beach** is the most popular surfing spot on a rugged coast. About half of Maui is visible from the beach, and it's easy to imagine the fleet of war canoes that Kamehameha launched here in 1791 to thwart invaders from Oahu and Kauaʻi. *Be Aware:* Riptide generated by surf makes Waipio usually unsafe for swimming. The shallow shore break is also a hazard for bodysurfers.

WAIPIO VALLEY

2.   KOHALA FOREST RESERVE   HIKE

WHAT'S BEST: A thrilling precipice over Waipio Valley and a waterfall vista are down the trail from this rural neighborhood. When open, this hike is among the best in Hawaii.

PARKING: Take Hwy. 19, the Mamalahoa Hwy., east from Waimea. After mm54, pass in quick succession of roads and then turn left on White Road. Go .6-mi. and park off-street near a locked metal gate. *Be Aware*: To reach the forest reserve, hikers must cross a short road leased out by Hawaiian Homelands. This access has been 'closed' for several years. Some people have been using the trail again in spite of 'no trespassing' signs.

HIKE: Kohala Forest Reserve to: **Alakahi Falls Lookout (3 mi., 175 ft.)**, or **Waipio Bamboo Altar (5.75 mi., 350 ft.)**

For both hikes, get by the gate and follow the road up and to the right around **Waimea Reservoir**. Then the road curves left around the green hillock of Pu'u Ka'ala, reaching a **Kohala Forest Reserve** gate. The road ascends in a garden of ferns, flowers, and leafy trees, and then levels and crosses the **Hamakua Ditch**. Bamboo and other exotics buffer the waterway. After about a mile, the trail narrows as you curve to the right through a lush gully and cross a short stretch of boardwalk. Say goodbye to the irrigation ditch for awhile. The trail is shaded by a sparse overstory of huge native trees, plus a few surprises like towering sequoias—though storm wind trim the top of the forest in places. And just when you start to marvel at the forest, the trail abruptly reaches the ledge of **Waipio Valley**. The drop-off is nearly 2,000 feet. Across the half-mile width of the valley, **Alakahi Falls** tumbles in several pitches toward Waipio Stream far below.

For the **Waipio Bamboo Altar**, which is at the head of valley, continue left from the falls lookout. After about 100 feet you'll pass a cave and then reach a viewpoint. The trail dips into the ripples of the cliff and rejoins **Hamakua Ditch**, flowing at times on raised trestles and then into mysterious tunnels. Near the head of the valley, the ditch is unleashed in a water slide, above which the trail climbs to the swampy plateau. Continue several hundred feet on the trail to enter the darkness of a bamboo thicket. Soon, an opening will appear to your right, the **Bamboo Altar**, where you can stand at a 2,000-foot cliff and look down the green barrel of Waipio Valley to see waves crashing at the black sand beach, 6-miles distant. To your left is **Waimanu Gap**, a slot in the fissured cliffs. The trail, overgrown and not well-traveled, continues for several miles toward Waimea. *Be Aware:* The trail to the head of the valley can get washed out and is one-person wide in places. Cliffs are vertical and extreme caution is advised.

More Stuff: Some locals use a different access to the Kohala Reserve, but permission from Parker Ranch may be required. Go west from Waimea on Highway 19 (Kawai-hae Road). Turn right on **Opelu Road** just before mm58 at Merriman's Restaurant, continue .3-mile to a gate, where Opelu ends at the right turn. Also, **Hawaii Forest & Trail** offers a hike in the area, past White Road on Mud Lane; give 'em a call.

3. HAWI   HIKE, SURF

WHAT'S BEST: Stroll the former sugar towns of Hawi and Kapa'au. Nearby are 'Iole Foundation, offering miles of lush trails amid historic sites, and the new Hawaii Wildlife Center. Top it off with a walk on the wild side to rugged Lighthouse Beach.

PARKING: Take Hwy. 19 north from Kailua and veer left toward Kawaihae on Hwy. 270 past mm21 to Hawi; Kapa'au is 2 mi. east. (From Waimea, take Hwy. 250 to Hawi.) *For 'Iole Foundation:* Pass Kapa'au, turn right just before mm24 on 'Iole Road. *For Hawaii Wildlife Center and Lighthouse Beach:* Pass 'Iole Road. At mm24.5 (opposite Maulili Loop) turn left on a wide, dirt Lighthouse Road. The center is .1-mile in on the right. *For Lighthouse Beach,* continue .3-mile, go straight on the potholed dirt road, and turn right at defunct sugar mill buildings. Park .6-mi. from the highway, near gate at Aina Koa.

HIKE: ʻIole Foundation (up to 9 mi., 500 ft. on choice of trails); Hawaii Wildlife Center (.25-mi.)' Lighthouse Beach (2.25 mi., 250 ft.)

With weatherworn wood-frame buildings dating from the 1800s, **Hawi** and **Kapaʻau** are just right for town strolls while on a trip through historic Kohala (see page 186 in *Driving Tours*). The tranquil road to **ʻIole Foundation** is bordered by tropical trees and penetrates a large organic macadamia nut orchard, part of the 2,400 acres managed by the nonprofit organization. *Note:* All visitors must check in at the office (.4-mile up the road on your right) to get a free permit and hiking information. Staff will fill you in on the options. Six different trails interconnect through profuse flora around the lush stream valley set 1,500 feet above the coastline—and reflect centuries of Hawaiian history.

During the times of **Kamehameha the Great**, ʻIole (ee-oh-lay) was the food basket for the king's armies and retinue, supplying taro, bananas, sweet potatoes, and other Polynesian staples. Called an ahupuaʻa (ah-hoo-poo-ah-ah), this traditional division of land had become overgrown over the decades, but in 2013 a group of young men (The Protectors for the Children of the Land) cleared the stream and planted taro and other crops in the manner of their Hawaiian ancestors. The group teaches the traditions to local school children. This same land in 1841 became the homestead for Protestant Congregationalist missionary **Elias Bond** and his wife Ellen Mariner Howell. "Father and Mother" Bond dedicated **Kalahikiola Church** in 1855 (faithfully restored in 2010 after damages caused by an earthquake in 2006) and **Kohala Girls School** in 1874 (which is being restored to be turned into a conference center). You are free to roam ʻIole, but guided walking tours, available by reservation, really do bring history to life.

ʻIOLE FOUNDATION GROUNDS

More Stuff: **Big Island Eco Adventures** (next to the office) operates a zipline that crosses the jungled stream gulch in breathtaking lifts that drop about 1,000 feet overall. Beginning the adventure is a 200-foot-long suspension bridge that crosses over a waterfall. All along the way, artful interpretive signs impart a sense of place and natural history. Safety features and skilled guides take all the work and worry out of the experience for participants, making this zip first-class.

While not a tourist attraction, the **Hawaii Wildlife Center** warmly welcomes visitors. The brainchild of Linda Elliott, the center opened in 2013 and is the state's (and Pacific Ocean's) only hospital for injured and ill birds, from the sea, shore, and forest. On the grounds of the architecturally attractive building are a native plant garden and interpretive area featuring real-time videos of what's going on inside.

Not on the tourist circuit, **Lighthouse Beach** is just the ticket if you want solitude on green coastal bluffs with a view of Maui. Proceed on unsigned Lighthouse (Old Kohala Mill) Road through the unlocked Surety Kohala gate, on a route cut through a broadleaf and ironwood forest. After about .25-mile, you'll reach open country and gain a view of **Kauhola Point**, a parklike protrusion into the ocean. Less than .25-mile before reaching the point is a left-forking road that leads to a turnstile and the short trail to **Keawaeli Bay**. The bay's beach is rocky, but the treed backshore will inspire daydreamers. (The Kauhola Lighthouse, a classic white cylinder nearly 100 feet in height, was undermined by both wave action and the 2006 earthquake, and was taken down in 2009. It had stood since 1933.)

SURF: Local guys four-wheel to **Lighthouse Beach** to surf the right-break into Keawaeli Bay. A rough road provides access at the lighthouse site. An easier (but not easy) ride is to be found on the offshore tiers in the center of **Keawaeli Bay**. The bluffs above the bay provide a great viewing spot. *Be Aware:* Watch for submerged rocks. These surfing venues are definitely not for beginners.

POLOLU BEACH

4.   POLOLU VALLEY   HIKE, SNORKEL, SURF

WHAT'S BEST: Lush seacliffs and rugged beach lure sightseers and shutterbugs. Trekkers will find a tropical wilderness experience on the trail from the far end of the beach.

PARKING: Take Hwy. 19 north from Kailua and veer left toward Kawaihae on Hwy. 270. (Or take Hwy. 250 down from Waimea to Hawi.) Continue east through Hawi. The highway ends past mm28. Park before the end (past the shack) on busy days.

HIKE: Pololu Valley Lookout to: Pololu Beach (1.25 mi., 425 ft.), or Honokane Nui Valley view (4 mi., 900 ft.); or Honokane Nui Valley ruins (5.5 mi., 1,850 ft.)

The surreal view of emerald sea cliffs and pounding surf from the **Pololu Valley Lookout** will sell most visitors on this hike. **For all hikes**, start down the steep cobblestone trail, once **Old Government Road**, making switchbacks to taro farms in the valley. At the bottom, veer to the right to get a view of the valley, looking over the large freshwater pond. Then backtrack through a stand of ironwoods, and cross the stream (or rock dam) near the shore at **Pololu Beach**. Black sand and driftwood front a near-constant shore break.

For the **Honokane Nui Valley** hikes, find a trail that runs toward the far end of the beach, between an ironwood-covered sand dune and the driftwood of the beach. Stones and a fence mark the trail's border in places. Nearly at the end of the beach, the soft-dirt trail veers to the right, through lush ground cover and heads toward a crease in the sand dune. Go up this crease and then veer left to begin a series of switchbacks that climb the cliff. *Note:* If your route becomes uncertain, then you are wandering on one of the false trails in the dunes. Under a ceiling native trees, the trail jogs out to the sea bluffs, before heading inland through often-muddy gouges. Near the top, you'll pass through a haggard gate. A few minutes later the trail pops out to open, low-lying scrub and reveals a view of the mile-deep **Pololu Valley**. You continue inland on a moderate climb for another .25-mile or so, penetrating a tunnel of vegetation, before coming to the chest-pounding **view of Honokane Nui Valley**. Turtle-shaped, tiny **Paoakalani Island** lies just offshore.

For the **Honokane Nui Valley ruins**, follow the trail inland on its steep, switchbacking descent through dense foliage. A garden of ti, ferns, and tropical broadleafs awaits at the bottom. When you reach flat ground, look carefully for an unmarked opening on the ocean-side of the trail, before reaching the stream. Under a towering overstory of trees, a path wanders amid mossy rock walls and enclosures, part of an ancient village that was partially destroyed during tidal waves of the late 1900s. You'll reach a boulder beach, which is about ten minutes from the trail. *Be Aware:* Rockfall and downed trees can be hazards on the descent. Also, always note your return route when leaving the main trail. This trail is rugged and sometimes not maintained.

More Stuff: Trekkers can continue on the trail as it crosses the stream (be mindful of flash floods) and ascends 400 feet to the next ridge, through one of the prettiest pandanus forests in Hawaii. You'll look into the next valley, **Honokane Iki**, site of more ruins, an old chimney, cabins (upstream), and a wild cove. To see it, you'll need to suck it up for another 400-foot descent. The trail continues all the way to **Waimanu** and **Waipio valleys**, over about 20 rough miles crossing more than a dozen streams.

The **Kohala Ditch Trail** is reachable via a road across from the ranch shack—the last building before the end of the highway. Permission is needed from Surety Kohala Corporation in Hawi. Your best bet is to set up a tour with **Hawaii Forest & Trail**, which has an office in Kona. They'll take you on a wild van ride a couple miles up the steep pasturelands and into lush forests. Guides fill you in on the exotic flora and the remarkable engineering of the Kohala Ditch during the five-hour adventure. *Note:* The Kapioloa Falls hike was wiped out by an earthquake in 2006, but a new falls hike is available.

SNORKEL: Snorkeling is usually iffy at **Keokea Beach Park**, but take a ride down for a picnic and a view from the park's elevated pavilion. To get there, turn makai at mm27.5 and continue a mile down to rugged **Keokea Bay**. Originally a retreat for sugar cane workers, the 7-acre site was made a county park in 1975. To your right is a small keiki pool, created by a boulder breakwater, that is normally safe for swimming.

SURF: Experienced surfers carry their boards down to ride the break at **Pololu Beach**, but conditions are not for beginners. If surf is mild and you feel like playing in the water, avoid the center of the beach, where rip current is notorious. **Kokea's** onshore break attracts bodyboarders.

HONOIPU LANDING CANOE RACE FINISH

5. KING KAMEHAMEHA BIRTHPLACE   HIKE

WHAT'S BEST: Yes, you *can* hear the heartbeat of history on these windswept slopes by the sea, where the great king was born and a sacrificial heiau remains intact.

PARKING: Take Hwy. 19 north from Kailua and veer left toward Kawaihae on Hwy. 270. Go .75-mi. past mm18 and turn makai on Old Coast Guard Rd., also called Birthplace Rd.; the first left past the guard station at Puakea Bay Dr. Drive down 1.5 mi. to the coast and park on the left in an unpaved area. See *More Stuff* below for an alternate access.

HIKE: Kamehameha Birthplace (1.25 mi.); Moʻokini Heiau (1.75 mi., 100 ft.)

For both hikes, pass around the fence on the ocean side and go to the right. Stay in the grassy area and then, beyond the first few homes, veer right up to the red-dirt road. You'll pass by abandoned Coast Guard buildings and reach a berm where the road has been closed to vehicles. The road continues along a wild seascape. From a rise you'll be able to see **King Kamehameha Birthplace.** A commemorative sign fronts a double-walled enclosure about 100 yards square. In the center are the birthstones. *Talk Story*: During a nighttime storm in the fall of 1758, the infant prophesied to rule the kingdom, "the Lonely One," was born. This isolated spot was chosen to protect the future king from early assassination by High Chief Keawemauhili of Hilo, an uncle who had other ideas about who should rule the island. Kamehameha's birthdate was pinpointed by oral chants from the time telling of a mysterious celestial object that passed overhead, which astronomers have since pegged as Haley's Comet.

To moody **Moʻokini Heiau**, continue up the dirt road less than .25-mile, until reaching a signed junction. The heiau, with walls 25-feet high and nearly 100-yards long, is a short walk up the hill. No other heiau in Hawaii has quite the timeless presence. *Talk Story*: The heiau dates from around 500 AD, constructed by early Marquesan settlers in a human chain of workers who transferred the smooth rocks from Pololu Valley, about 12 miles distant. Later portions of the temple were built by Polynesians from Tahiti, around 1200 AD. Moʻokini was designated as the state's first national historic site in 1935. Many forms of worship took place here, but the heiau is best known for human sacrifices. Resting on the lawn on the ocean side are large stones, called **Pohaku, Holehole**, and **Kanaka**, which were used for stripping flesh from bone as part of the ceremony. The heiau has been presided over continuously by family kahunas (like priests), in modern times by Nui Leimomi Moʻokini Lum.

More Stuff: A marginal dirt road goes all the way to the heiau and birthplace. Go north on Highway 270 and turn makai at mm20 on **Upolu Road**. Continue almost 2 miles, past a wind farm, to the airport and turn left for 1.5 mile on a dirt road. Mud puddles and ruts often make driving passenger vehicles chancy.

From the primary parking spot, you can also hike south to **Honoipu Landing Park**. Look for the Puerto Rican memorial rock and a step-through on the fence to your left. An unimproved 'cow trail' leads above the shore (passing submerged pilings of the old landing) and then up, reaching the 13.5-acre private park after a ten-minute walk. Enjoy seaward views and artifacts of the small gauge railroad that served the landing in the sugar cane days.

6.   MAHUKONA BEACH PARK   HIKE, SNORKEL

WHAT'S BEST: Big fish and sunken relics await offshore North Kohala's best snorkeling site. A little-used, scenic coastal trail will attract whale-watching hikers.

PARKING: Take Hwy. 19 north from Kailua and veer left toward Kawaihae on Hwy. 270. Before mm15, turn makai on Mahukona Beach Park Rd. Continue for about .4-mi. *For hiking:* Keep left at the Shoreline Public Access sign and continue a short distance to the beach park. *For snorkeling:* Go right at the old railway building, toward another Shoreline Public Access parking area on the wharf.

HIKE: Coastal trail to Lapakahi Historical Park (2.25 mi.)

For the **Coastal trail to Lapakahi Historical Park**, walk by the camping area on the lawn and the metal-roofed pavilion. Behind the pavilion close to the shore you'll find and unsigned gate and the trail. Within the first .25-mile are a Coast Guard light and a sign marking the northern boundary of a marine conservation district that extends to Lapakahi. During the winter, you're apt to see whales.

MAHUKONA WHARF

More Stuff: Nearby **Kapa'a Beach Park** is nicely sited on a rugged cove—its seaside pavilion is an ideal spot for whale watching. *Driving:* Access is via Kapa'a Park Road, about a mile north of the road to Mahukona.

SNORKEL: Submerged relics, clear water, and unusual marine life combine to make **Mahukona Wharf** one of the better snorkeling spots on the Big Island—if conditions are safe. Walk to the end of the wharf and you'll find a ladder leading to the water. Not far offshore, water gets deep, 30- to 60-feet, amid rocks and a few coral heads. Manta rays and octopi have been spotted here, as well as turtles and reef fish. The propeller and boilers of a 1913 shipwreck lie in about 50 feet of water, while an anchor chain and railroad wheels are closer to shore. At the base of the pier is the 1930 **Hawaii Railway Co.** building, North Kohala's sugar shipped out from this harbor for many decades until the 1950s. *Be Aware:* High surf can make Mahukona treacherous. Water on the wharf's surface indicates a high-surf day. If you encounter high swells when in the water, wait for the set to subside and make your way to the ladder during a lull.

7.   LAPAKAHI HISTORICAL PARK   HIKE, SNORKEL

WHAT'S BEST: Anthropological detectives can roam this village and piece together all elements that were needed to sustain life. Dreamers can sit in the shade of a coco palm and get a feeling for it all before taking a swim.

PARKING: Take Hwy. 19 north from Kailua and veer left toward Kawaihae on Hwy. 270. Just before mm14, turn makai at the signed and gated park entrance. *Note:* Normal hours are 8 to 4, except for state holidays. If the gate is locked, park at the top and walk down.

HIKE: **Koai'e Village (1.25 mi., 150 ft.)**

SHORELINE TRAIL AT LAPAKAHI

A trail brochure should be available at the visitors center. A rocky path circles **Koai'e Village**—you may want to go left, or clockwise. Whatever; this hike is about wandering around. At the shore to the left (south) is **Koai'e Cove**, the park's most scenic spot. Far-off Maui provides a backdrop. Then continue along the coral- and black-rock shore, passing several hollowed-out flat stones that were used to extract salt from ocean water. At the far end of the cove is the former fire pit, where generations of villagers played konane, or Hawaiian checkers, on a board carved into a rock—all the while keeping an eye on offshore waters for passing fish that would send them rushing to their canoes.

Talk Story: Now within the 262-acres of the state park, the village in the 1400s was within the 10 square miles of the ahupua'a (division of land) of **Lapakahi**, which included about 4 miles of coastline and extended inland to an elevation of 2,000 feet. Hawaiians flourished here until the late 1800s, when maverick cattle and horses destroyed the arid farming lands. Aside from the prickly kiawe trees, the dozen or so species of trees here are among those brought centuries ago by Polynesians to sustain their fiber-and-stone culture. Originally, the rock platforms were topped by pole structures with grass roofing, and the interiors were carpeted with layers of soft matting.

SNORKEL: Within the Lapakahi Marine Conservation District, **Koai'e Cove** offers excellent snorkeling, when the conditions are tame. Huge boulders and ample coral support lots of fish, and the water is clear and strikingly blue. Near shore are depths of about 30 feet. Park people ask that you not enter at the left side of the cove below the historic house, the site of ancient graves. For an entry point, go to the right of the little rocky point in the middle of the bay, at the pebble "beach." *Be Aware:* The park people also ask that no towels or clothing be left on the beach. Feeding fish, normally a bad idea, is prohibited. High surf, common in the winter, can create treacherous currents.

8.   PU'UKOHOLA HEIAU-SPENCER PARK   HIKE, SNORKEL, SURF

WHAT'S BEST: This massive Hawaiian temple is where Kamehameha the Great—by trickery and happenstance—achieved final control of the Big Island. Close by, a garden path leads down the coast to a hidden, fine-sand beach with excellent swimming.

PARKING: Take Hwy. 19 north from Kailua and turn left toward Kawaihae on Hwy. 270. After mm2, turn makai at a sign for Spencer Beach Park and Pu'ukohola Heiau. *For heiau hike:* Go down the hill and turn right into the information center lot. *For Spencer Park and Mau'umae Beach hike:* Go left, and then to the far left of the beach park lot.

HIKE: Pu'ukohola Heiau (.75-mi., 150 feet); Spencer Beach Park to Mau'umae Beach (1.25 mi.)

Talk Story: The curving roof of the lava-rock visitors center at **Pu'ukohola Heiau National Historic Site** echoes the shape of the heiau, which sits above it. The heiau is Hawaii's most recent, built in 1790 as a tribute to the war god Ku at the behest of **Kamehameha.** The future monarch, then aged 32, had defeated Maui and Molokai,

PU'UKOHOLA HEIAU

ALA KAHAKAI TRAIL

but in his absence had lost some turf on the Big Island to his cousin, Keoua Kuahuʻula. This branch of the family from Hilo was Kamehameha's lifelong nemesis. At a dedication ceremony in 1791, cousin Keoua was the life of the party, or rather death, since he and his retinue were killed in a scuffle. Whether Kamehameha planned the attack, or it transpired by unforeseen events, is open to historical interpretation.

For the **Puʻukohola Heiau hike**, take the asphalt shoreline path from the information center (sadly, visitors are not allowed on trails at the top of the heiau). You'll pass **Mailekini Heiau**, an older site that sits below Puʻukohola. Then, off the path is a **Stone Leaning Post**, offshore of which the shark temple, **Hale o Kapuni Heiau**, lies submerged. Silt has all but buried the shrine, which was last seen at low tide in the 1950s. But the black-tipped reef sharks, the heiau's honorees, still frequent this bay, and on cloudy days you may see fins slicing the surface. For the prime Kodak moment, continue across the palm grove that was once the site of the royal courtyard. Then go left on the unpaved road and look back at king's temple of war, somehow looming larger from this more-distant view.

The trail from **Spencer Beach Park to Mauʻumae Beach** begins behind the beautiful stone pavilion that sits on the bluff at the south end of the park. The soft-dirt route penetrates beach trees alongside crashing surf. A wildfire in 2004 took out much of the greenery on this part of the state's **Ala Kahakai Trail**, which covers about 20 miles of coastline in disjointed segments. About halfway into the short hike you'll cross a stream bed, from where you'll be able to see the white sand cove, across the water beneath a bluff. Once at the beach, continue on the trail to its south end, which normally has the best sand and swimming. *More Stuff:* The **Ala Kahakai Trail** continues south toward **Mauna Kea Resort**. At the far end of the beach, walk up stairs and pass a few homes before the trail pops out to **Wai'ulaula Point**, a whale-watcher's perch less than .5-mile away. Mau'umae Beach also is reachable via a different route with a shoreline access permit from the Mauna Kea Resort; see TH9, page 51.

SNORKEL: In spite of the fire, **Mau'umae Beach** is a Big Island keeper, with sloping white sands for easy entry and excellent swimming along the rocks at the south end out to **Keawehala Point**. Coco palms and kiawes, and other tropical trees, shade the shore. Although the beach is not a secret, it is seldom crowded. *Be Aware:* Heavy surf can bring stronger current to this normally safe beach, and no services are available.

Spencer Beach Park normally is only fair-to-good for snorkeling, since the waters become murky due to stream runoff. But during dry periods, the stone-stairway entry at the pavilion is downright inviting. Spencer is best known for children's wave play, and for beach camping.

For confident snorkelers, a deep-water snorkeling spot nearby is **Kohala Waterfront**. *Driving:* Go north from Spencer past Kawaihae on Highway 270 and look left for a shoreline access and an improved lot at mm5.5. You walk a few hundred yards along a chain-link fence and scramble down to the right to a nook in the coast with entry of smooth lava. Boat tour companies take their paying customers offshore. *Be Aware:* High surf means hazardous snorkeling—not for novices.

SURF: Long boarders ride the rolling tiers off the most-westerly breakwater at the **Pua Kailima o Kawaihae Cultural Surf Park**. *Driving:* From Spencer, go north Highway 270. Just past two small bridges and mm3, turn left Port of Kawaihae. A friendly security guard will ask for some ID. (On Fridays, turn left after the first small bridge, just before mm3.) This industrial entrance leads to the surf park, which is off the breakwater at the end of the dirt wharf. A shower pipe sticks up in the middle of tables and small shade trees. You can make a loop by continuing to circle left around the peninsula, passing a smaller harbor, a longhouse with viewing decks set among palms, and coming to the **viewing area for Pu'ukohola Heiau** that is described above. Additionally, if you drive past the port on the highway and keep left, you'll reach the park where the **Kawaihae Canoe Club** puts in—often the scene for community happenings.

KAWAIHAE CANOE CLUB PRACTICE

South Kohala

GREEN SEA TURTLE, WAINANALI'I LAGOON AT KIHILO BAY

At first blush, the 25-mile South Kohala coast would seem most appealing as viewed from a speeding car in the dead of a moonless night. String-straight Highway 11 passes through vast fields of a'a lava, like piles of broken glass and razor blades, that have poured from several eruptions over the last 200 years, coming from both Mauna Loa and Hualalai volcanoes. But look again. Every mile or so is an oasis and beach, the best on the Big Island. Some beaches are wild and reachable by hikes, and others are on the grounds of posh resorts. Beach seekers will be as happy as seals in sand.

Farthest north, Kaunaoa Bay is home to the Mauna Kea Resort, a jewel that normally heads the list among word travelers desirous of tropical comfort. Surfing and snorkeling are excellent, and so is the coastal walk to Hapuna Beach State Park, the most-popular beach on the island. The perpetual sunshine, surfing waves, and snorkeling waters of Hapuna draw locals from the rainy climes to the north and east. A hike-to snorkeling beach and turtle tidepools of Puako extend for several miles south of Hapuna.

Just south of Puako, the Mauna Lani Resort boasts a triple-play that may keep you there all day—historic sites, snorkeling and surfing beaches, and coastal walks. An aspect of Hawaii few know about is revealed at the Puako Petroglyphs near Holoholokai Beach Park, and at the fishponds and village near the Eva Parker Woods Cottage Museum.

These ancient sites are melded with surrounding gardens of the resorts. Beach Club Beach and Pauoa Bay, are right off the cover of travel magazines, blue crescents fringed by white sand and coconut palms. The walk from the Mauna Lani to the Fairmont Orchid is from the lap of luxury to the bosom of opulence.

After a day at Mauna Lani, do it all over again at Anaeho'omalu. The beach park at big A-Bay is a winner for surfing and wind sports, and the beach trees of two large ponds that front the bay provide tranquil shade. Going south from Anaeho'omalu is a coast walk to untouched Kapalaoa Beach, a sunbather's haunt. Going north is a coastal hike by anchialine ponds to the resort-theme park of the Hilton—one of Hawaii's splashiest hotels.

Resorts take a holiday south of A-Bay, where miles of rugged coast and several beaches will swallow up day-trippers. The more obscure is the old Brown's Resort at Keawaiki Bay, a half-mile from the highway, a ghost-town retreat that was party-central for the celebrities of the 1920s. A salt-and-pepper beach entices snorkelers, while the rugged hammerhead of Weliweli Point dares anyone to get near the water. Just south of Ke-awaiki is better-known Kihilo Bay, with a frock of coco palms and turquoise lagoon—swimmers, start drooling. The remains of Kamehameha's huge fishpond contribute to an intriguing backshore at Kihilo and west Hawaii's best black sand beach is to be found at the southern end of the two-mile bay.

MAHAIULA BAY, KEHAHA KAI STATE PARK

After Kihilo, you have an opportunity to take a bird's eye view on the coast at Pu'u Wa'a Wa'a, the rippled butte that lies inland below Hualalai. Aside from its panorama, the old volcanic vent is a rich bird habitat, in one of the state's few remaining native dry forests. Then, ho hum, it's back to the coast for more beach hopping between two world-class resorts, the Four Seasons Hualalai and the Kona Village—although these high-end little grass shacks may still be closed due to tsunami damage. Expect a variety pack at this site of the former Kaupulehu Village. A boardwalk winds through a large petroglyph field at the Kona Village, and sitting below the tasteful lobby of the

FOUR SEASONS HUALALAI,
KEAWAIKI (FRANCIS BROWN BEACH)

Four Seasons is the Kaupulehu Cultural Center, quietly one of the better museums on the Big Island. You can walk a few miles of groomed coastal trail, beside both smashing surf and white-sand beaches. At the north end of the coast is Kahuwai Bay, a snorkeler's delight fronting the Kona Village. The south end of the coast features pretty Kikaua Park on Kukio Bay.

South of the resorts at Hualalai are miles of (mostly) open coast, where white-sand beaches await surfers and snorkelers who like to walk, but not *too* far. Kua Bay, known for its clear waters and white sand cove, is a short drive in from the highway. Pu'u Kuili is the landmark south of the bay, a destination view hike. South of the pu'u is Kekaha Kai State Park with its hike-to beaches, Mahaiula Bay and Makalawena. Bring water, pack a lunch, and set out on a snorkeling safari.

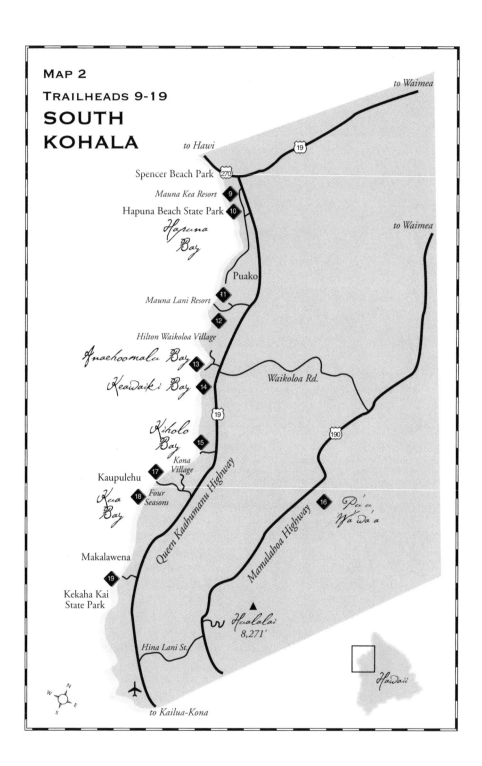

MAP 2

TRAILHEADS 9-19

SOUTH
KOHALA

to Waimea

to Hawi

19

Spencer Beach Park 270

Mauna Kea Resort 9

Hapuna Beach State Park 10

Hapuna Bay

to Waimea

Puako

Mauna Lani Resort 11

12

Hilton Waikoloa Village

Anaehoomalu Bay 13

Keawaiki Bay 14

Waikoloa Rd.

19

190

Kiholo Bay 15

Kona Village

Kaupulehu 17

Queen Kaahumanu Highway

18 Four Seasons

Kua Bay

16 *Pu'u Wa'awa'a*

Mamalahoa Highway

Makalawena

19

Kekaha Kai
State Park

Hualalai 8,271'

Hina Lani St.

N
W E
S

Hawaii

to Kailua-Kona

TRAILHEADS

9-19

TH :   TRAILHEAD
HIKE :   HIKES AND STROLLS
SNORKEL :   SNORKELING, SWIMMING
SURF :   BOARD, BODYBOARD, BODYSURF
MM :   MILE MARKER; CORRESPONDS TO HIGHWAY SIGNS
MAKAI :   TOWARD THE OCEAN
MAUKA :   INLAND, TOWARD THE MOUNTAINS

ALL HIKING DISTANCES IN PARENTHESES ARE ROUND TRIP. ELEVATION GAINS OF 100 FEET OR MORE ARE NOTED. SEE RESOURCE LINKS FOR CONTACTS AND TELEPHONE NUMBERS.

9.   KAUNAOA BAY-MAUNA KEA HOTEL   HIKE, SNORKEL, SURF

WHAT'S BEST: The Mauna Kea Beach Hotel is world-renowned for its white crescent beach and spacious grounds. Snorkel, surf, stroll, or just chill.

PARKING: Take Hwy. 19 north from Kailua-Kona. Pass the Hapuna Beach turnoff. Turn left before mm68 toward the Mauna Kea. Stop at entrance station and ask for public beach access; the road swings left in front of the resort to parking, and short paved path winds down to the beach. *Note:* If no beach passes remain, ask to visit the resort for a meal. In this case, you can park in the lot to the right of the resort. Or get a permit for Mau'umae Beach: Take the third right past the entrance (across from the Villas at Mauna Kea) cross two wooden bridges, and park after .5-mi. at pole #22; a signed trail leads down through scorched kiawe trees.

HIKE: Mauna Kea Beach Hotel (.75-mi.)

Talk Story: Prompted by Hawaii's post-war effort to bring tourism to the Big Island, Laurance Rockefeller and a big bag of money arrived at Kaunaoa Bay in 1960. He leased land from the Parker Ranch and opened the Mauna Kea Beach Hotel in 1965. Westin Hotels took over in 1978, followed by other owners. Previously, Kaunaoa Bay was a fishing haven for locals, some of whom had to sue in 1973 to retain public access. The hotel is often rated by luxury travelers as one of the world's best beach resorts.

For the **Mauna Kea Beach Hotel,** from the beach access, make your way up the beach, or wander inland through the spacious lawn area with its towering trees. Stairs lead up from the pool area up to breezeways replete with Asian art and tropical plants. From the open lobby, go left through the luau terrace to the snapshot view from **Ka'aha Point** at the north end of the bay. Continue north around the lava-reef seascape. You'll reach a golf cart path. Immediately left, is an elevated tee where Palmer, Nicklaus, and

MAUNA KEA BEACH

Player opened the course in 1964. If no golfers are around, the tee works as a serene viewpoint. *More Stuff:* A nature trail (Ala Kahakai) leads from the south end of Kaunaoa Beach near restrooms to **Hapuna Beach State Park**, described in TH10; see below.

SNORKEL: With a sand entry and adequate fish, **Kaunaoa Beach** is among the better beaches on the Big Island. Posh facilities and an idyllic setting don't hurt. **Kaunaoa Point**, on the south end, maybe has better coral, but the northern end toward **Ka'aha Point** is also good. *Be Aware:* High surf indicates rip current, often going out from the center of the beach to the southern point. Agitated sand will also lessen water quality on higher surf days.

SURF: **Kaunaoa Beach** attracts bodyboarders as well as board surfers. Bodysurfing novices can ride the foam closest to the beach. Board surfers like the right-break at **Ka'aha Point**, at the north mouth of the bay. When conditions are right, you can watch these dudes and dudettes do their thing from the luau terrace. *Be Aware:* Hotel beach attendants may post warnings when surf conditions are adverse. Impact injuries are common. Sand being drawn from the base of waves indicates a shallow-water hazard.

10.   HAPUNA BEACH STATE PARK   HIKE, SNORKEL, SURF

> **WHAT'S BEST:** The long swath of white sand at always-sunny Hapuna draws beach lovers from all over the Big Island. You'll find prime snorkeling and surfing spots, as well as a coastal trail leading to the cover-girl beach at the Mauna Kea Beach Hotel.

> **PARKING:** Take Highway 19 north from Kailua-Kona. Pass Puako Beach Dr. and mm70. Turn makai toward Hapuna Beach State Park on Kaunaoa Dr., continue .25-mi., and turn right into a very large parking area. Do not leave valuables in your car.

HIKE: Hapuna Beach to Kaunaoa Beach (2.75 mi., 150 ft.)

HAPUNA BEACH

Talk Story: The huge parking lot at Hapuna Beach is a clue. Only 10 inches of rain falls here yearly, compared to 100 inches or more on the Hilo side, only a hour's drive away. On weekends, the place is jumpin'. A half-mile of white sand gets scorched by sun and soothed by an almost continual shore break. A lawn and treed hillside rises from the shore, with shaded picnic pavilions.

To hike from **Hapuna Beach to Kaunaoa Beach** (and the posh Mauna Kea Beach Hotel) take any of the paths from the parking area and head to your right at the sand. On calm-sea days, wear your swimsuit and haul snorkeling gear. A few hundred yards from the lifeguard stations, a low bluff protrudes into the sand—which the ancients called **Ihumoku**, or Prow of the Ship. At low tide, go around at water's edge. At high tide, go not far inland and take a footpath under the sprawling branches of a large tree. In two minutes you'll be below the **Hapuna Beach Prince Hotel**, a modernistic vision with grand columns, glass balconies, and huge skylights. After a visit, skirt the edge of the hotel's lawn. At the far end of the lawn begins the **Ala Kahakai Trail**. Before rounding the point on the trail, you'll see **Hapuna Prince Stairs beach**, where a flight of stone steps drops to a patch of sand. Along the path amid trimmed kiawe trees are the remains of the **Ouli Ahupua'a** (village). Continue through a forest of 'danger' signs as the trail undulates and rounds Kaunaoa Point at the edge of a golf course, and then drops to the beach at **Mauna Kea**.

SNORKEL: Though known mainly for surfing, **Hapuna Beach** is also fairly good for snorkeling. Conditions are good offshore **Ihumoku**, the bluff that protrudes to the north. At the south end, rocky Kanekanaka Point is also where the fishes live. A fun swim in the immediate area is **Hapuna Prince Stairs**, reachable at the far north of Hapuna, as described above. Even on wavy days you can at least take a dunk. *Be Aware*: High surf can create dangerous currents.

The best snorkeling is nearby **Waialea Bay**, a.k.a. **Beach 69**. Big Island vets may lament the new paved road, picnic tables, and restrooms completed in 2006, but the word was already out on this once-secret locals' haunt. (Quit thinking dirty: the beach nickname comes from nearby telephone pole #69, formerly a key marker.) *Driving:* Go south .75-mile from Hapuna on bumpy **Old Puako Road**. to a large lot with a pipe gate. Some of the best snorkeling is in the middle of Beach 69, around a little "island" near shore that can be high and dry during low tides. But the coral shelves at the far south (left) of the beach are also excellent. A variety of beach trees provide shade and are playsets for kids. (Yes, that *might* be rocker Neil Young, who has a home nearby.)

SURF: You'll see bodyboarders almost all the time in the middle of **Hapuna Beach**. These guys race down from Waimea and up from Kona. Hapuna can be a great beach for novice wave riders. *Be Aware:* Seek advice a lifeguard; neck injuries are definitely possible. For board surfing, check out **Beach 69**. You can watch them ride the right-break from the point to the north (where some people spend their day).

11. HOLOHOLOKAI BEACH PARK   HIKE, SNORKEL, SURF

WHAT'S BEST: A large petroglyph field, and an obscure small one, will entice hikers and wow would-be athropologists. Two other short coastal walks lead to the swank Fairmont Orchid, and to the tide-pool coast of folksy Puako.

PARKING: Take Hwy. 19 north from Kailua-Kona. About .5-mi past mm74, turn makai on Mauna Lani Dr. Pass the entrance station. At the roundabout, go right on North Kaniku Dr. toward the Fairmont Orchid and Holoholokai Beach Park. Just before the hotel entrance, turn right toward the beach park. A paved lot is at the end of the road.

HIKE: Malama Trail to Puako Petroglyphs (1.25 mi., 100 ft.); Holoholokai to: Fairmont Orchid (.5-mi.) or to Puako (.5-mi.); 29 Marching Lonos (.25-mi.)

At **Holoholokai Beach Park** are leafy beach trees, palms, and picnic tables set beside a foaming turquoise seascape—let's do lunch. The **Malama Trail to Puako Petroglyphs** is on the right at the beginning of the paved lot. The rock carvings at the beginning are re-creations for people to make rubbings. The paved trail quickly ends, and you'll be weaving under a canopy of kiawes on a surface of dirt, roots, and smooth lava. After about .5-mile the trail crosses a gravel road, over a rise from which is the several-acre field of pahoehoe lava. Some 3,000 carvings, dating from 1000 AD to 1800 AD, are scattered about, most inside of an oval enclosed by a wood railing and low rock wall. *Be Aware:* Protect the etchings; admire them from behind the railing.

You can also walk from **Holoholokai to the Fairmont Orchid**, with its artful interiors and cute aquamarine cove. Go to the left as you face the ocean at the park. A rocky footpath leads out of the palm grove and soon reaches a concrete path on the lawn of the resort. Continue on the path to the pool area set back from little **Pauoa Bay**. You'll want to weave inland to admire the elegant décor of the Orchid. *More Stuff:* The path continues south about .5-mile to the Mauna Lani.

29 MARCHING LONOS, PANIAU

Going to the right from Holoholokai Beach Park, on the **Ala Kahakai Trail to Puako**, takes you away from resort world to a miles-long, near-shore reef that is bordered by 1950s beach cottages (some being scraped and replaced by big-money dream homes) frequented by surfers, fishermen, and tide-pooling turtles. You'll see the palm grove of **Paniau Bay** soon after setting out on the trail, in front of the huge estate. The reef-and-sand-patch is the last of several Shoreline Access turnouts off Puako Beach Drive.

The hidden **29 Marching Lonos** are perhaps the most fascinating petroglyphs in Hawaii. The stacked stick figures with a larger figure nearby are *thought* to represent 29 generations of ali'i (royalty) that ended with the death of Kamehameha's cousin, Keoua Kuahu'ula (see page 43). *Driving:* From Holoholkai, drive north on Highway 19, pass mm71 and, .5-mile later, turn left on **Puako Beach Drive**. (You could also continue walking another .5-mile from **Paniau Bay**.) Drive about two miles, until reaching the last house on the left, where a dirt fire escape road meets the paved road. Walk in to behind the fifth house and then jog inland 150 feet through an opening in a snarl of kiawes. Look for a white arrow painted on the smooth, pinkish rock. In a 100-foot oval clearing, a white arrow points right (south). The 29 Lonos are near the far end of the clearing. *More Stuff:* Some half-dozen Shoreline Public Access spots to tide pools are along a 3-mile stretch of sleepy Puako Beach Drive. Sea turtles hang out here.

SNORKEL: Man-enhanced **Pauoa Bay** at the **Fairmont Orchid** is an ideal cove, with a sandy entry and palms gracing the shore. But water clarity is not great. For the coral and fish, swim out the lava opening of the pool and explore the reef to the right. *Driving:* Head toward the beach park, but then veer left toward the Fairmont. Take a ticket at the automated gate; the front desk validates tickets for free. A path is hidden behind a tall hedge on the south end of the parking lot.

The best spot—for experienced snorkelers—is **Paniau Bay**, where a rare limestone reef angles to near the shore. You can swim out a channel and go right up the outside of the reef. Walk a short distance from Holoholokai and enter near the trailhead sign in front of the estate. Whales come close to shore; you may hear one while underwater. *Be Aware:* Surf creates current outside the reef, so be very cautious.

SURF: **Paniau** is known locally as **Ruddles**, the name of a nearby real estate office. Surfers don't waste time thinking up names when they can be out risking their necks on an offshore reef break. Drive 3 miles in on Puako Beach Drive.

12. MAUNA LANI   HIKE, SNORKEL

> **WHAT'S BEST:** Guests of this fabulous resort have a hard time leaving. Blue scoops along a white-sand beach are just right for swimming. Palm-lined coastal paths invite strollers and inland are lake-sized ponds, fringed by a tropical arboretum and a history park.
>
> **PARKING:** Take Hwy. 19 north from Kailua-Kona. About .5-mi past mm74, turn makai on Mauna Lani Dr. A roundabout is past the entrance station. Stay on Mauna Lani Dr., the middle of three options, going toward the resort and historic park. Park in the large lot to the left before reaching the resort.

HIKE: **Mauna Lani Fishponds and beaches (up to 3.5 mi.); Kalahuipua'a Village Historic Park (.75-mi.); Coast trail to Fairmont Orchid (1 mi.)**

Mauna Lani Resort's mile-long seacoast with white-sand coves, a unique 30-acre history park, and tranquil fishponds make it one of the best places to spend a day. For the hike to the **Mauna Lani Fishponds and beaches**, head from the parking lot toward the security building that is to the left of the hotel. You pass the resort's backside and reach small **Waipuhi Iki Pond** on your left. At the shore is the **Nanuku Inlet**, a protected swimming area. Go left at the shoreline. You'll pass a canoe shed and reach a green carpet of lawn that leads to **Eva Parker Woods Cottage Museum**. Inside the charming bungalow are local artifacts, such as bone fishhooks, wooden calabashes, and stone tools. On full moon evenings, the cottage is the site for a Talk Story—a medley of dance, chant, and music, hosted by the inspiring Daniel Kaniela Akaka, Jr. (catch it if you can). Just behind the cottage is the largest of the six fishponds; **Kalahuipua'a**, which covers five acres. The path continues past the cottage on a low wall. Here a narrow footbridge and stone wall protrude a 100 feet into the pond, reaching a little hut that is one of the most serene spots on the planet earth.

Next on the path is **Beach Club Beach**, a cove at the southern end of Makaiwa Bay. Hook inland around the shore of Kalahuipua'a Pond. Large native and Polynesian trees line the path, and benches beckon. Breadfruit, kukui, and palms create habitat, and birders will want to sit a spell. At the backshore of Kalahuipua'a are two other good-sized fishponds on your right, **Manoku** and then **Hopeaia**. Sturgeon, milkfish,

EVA PARKER WOODS COTTAGE MUSEUM, DANIEL KANIELA AKAKA, JR., MAUNA LANI RESORT, FISHPONDS AT MAUNA LANI

shrimp, and mullet—the "pig of the sea"— live in these waters. In ancient times they were raised only for royalty. (Runners would wrap fish in seaweed and sprint for miles, praying that the fish would still be quivering upon delivery.) After Hopeaia, the trail reaches a T-intersection. To the left is back to the beach. To the right crosses a road and enters the lower part of Kalahuipua'a Village History Park.

The **Kalahuipua'a Village Historic Park** trail undulates through a pahoehoe lava field that was home to hundreds of people for centuries, beginning around 1200 AD. *Note:* Upper trailhead parking is at a signed Shoreline Public Access on Puaoa Road, between the resort and the roundabout. Caves made from collapsed lava tubes are former homes, now missing the layers of woven matting and thatched structures. Many artifacts, such as canoe paddles and stone tools, were recovered in this site after Frances I'i Brown sold the property to the Mauna Lani Resort in 1972. At the lower end of the park are the **Kulia Petroglyphs**, including a helmeted warrior with upraised spear that is located 15 feet off the paved path to the right just before the fishponds.

MAUNA LANI QUEEN'S BATH

With all there is to do at the Mauna Lani, you may miss the **Coast trail to Fairmont Orchid** and Pauoa Bay. Grab your snorkeling gear and take the coral- and black-rock path that weaves north through coco palms and an occasional heliotrope. Inland are new luxury homes, but they are buffered by a greenbelt of small ponds where you can also find a petroglyph or two. *More Stuff:* A trail continues south on the coast from Beach Club Beach along a golf course for 1.25 miles to **49 Black Sand Beach**.

SNORKEL: Popular **Beach Club Beach** at the south end Mana Lani's coastline is the top South Kohala snorkeling venue. A nice sand beach with easy entry leads to luscious coral heads not far offshore, including a large one called **Turtle Mound**. Wave action outside the bay can stimulate a southerly current, but conditions are relatively safe inside. Showers, fine sand, and a shaded lawn are also pluses. For an exhilarating dip sans snorkel, try the small **Mauna Lani Queen's Bath**. From Beach Club Beach, go inland among the fishponds. The paved path swerves left and then right. Then go right on a cinder path toward the cliffs; the pretty anchialine oval is hidden in a lava-rock nook directly below the high-end tiled bungalows lofted incongruously right above it. Rock-and-mortar steps lead into clear water. Right in front of the Mauna Lani, the **Nanuku Inlet** is a nice big swimming pool, less than chest deep. Water quality is not excellent and fish are not abundant, but swimming is superb. Large milo trees shade the shore. Snorkeling improves outside the inlet, but watch for current.

Honokaope Bay-49 Black Sand Beach has good snorkeling from its sloping, gritty shores—ringed by tennis courts and swank condos. Restrooms are ultra. *Driving:* Go three-quarters around the roundabout and turn right on South Kaniku Drive. Then go left on Honokaope Place and ask for public access parking at the entrance station.

13. ANAEHO‘OMALU   HIKE, SNORKEL, SURF

WHAT'S BEST: Quietly observe centuries-old rock etchings and village ponds and then moments later revel in the Disneyesque opulence of a resort hotel (getting face time with dolphins). Between these extremes are white-sand swimming beaches.

PARKING: Take Hwy. 19 north from Kailua-Kona. Just before mm76, turn makai on Waikoloa Beach Dr. toward Anaeho‘omalu. *For the petroglyph preserve:* Drive in .5-mi., pass Queen's Marketplace on the left, and turn right into the Kings Shops. Keep right and park at the back near the gas station. *For Anaeho‘omalu Beach Park:* Across from the Kings Shops, turn left on Ku‘uali‘i Pl. toward Lava Lava Club and Shoreline Public Access.

For direct access to the anchialine ponds: Continue around Waikoloa Beach Dr., past the Kings Shops, and take the left-hand turn lane toward Shoreline Public Access. This is also free parking at the outer Hilton lot. *For direct Access to the Hilton:* Circle around Waikoloa Beach Dr., pass the above access, and turn left at an entrance station; a fee of about $20 is charged for this lot. A free Shoreline Public Access lot is directly across the road from the Hilton lot entrance.

WAIKOLOA PETROGLYPH PRESERVE

HIKE: Waikoloa Petroglyph Preserve (.5-mi.); Anaeho'omalu Beach Park to: Kapalaoa Beach and petroglyphs (1 to 2 mi.), or Anchialine Pond Preservation Area (1 mi.) and Hilton Resort (1.75 mi.); Hilton Resort stroll (up to .75-mi.)

Waylaid travelers recorded major events and the passage of their lives on the smooth, huge lava field that is the **Waikoloa Petroglyph Preserve**—now bordered by a golf course and massive beach villas. From the parking lot, follow the path around the pond to the street and walk left on the **Kings Trail**. The preserve is within the first .25-mile. The earliest carvings are from 700 AD, while the most recent, like a cowboy on horseback, date from the mid-1800s. The circles with dots in the center are thought to mark the birth of boys, and the semi-circles note girls.

Talk Story: **Anaeho'omalu Beach Park**— known as A-Bay—is privately owned, previously part of Parker Ranch until the 31,000 acres were sold for resort development in the late 1970s. Historical sites, ponds, and hiking trails have been preserved. Above large Anaeho'omalu Bay now sits the Waikoloa Mariott, and the grandiose Hilton.

To hike to secluded **Kapalaoa Beach and petroglyphs** head to the left as you face the water at the park, past the Lava Lava Beach Club. (At the beginning, look down the coast and spot a low lava point; the rock carvings are just inland at this point.) After a few minutes the coastal trail may peter out where surf washes into a mangrove thicket, but you can find a passageway cut through the sprawling trees. Sand dunes await on the other side of the tree-tunnel. The sand continues for .25-mile, to **Kapalaoa Beach**. A cove is fringed by palms and kiawe. The huge, unmarked **pertroglyph field** is less than .5-mile farther down the coast. One rough patch requires walking over coral-and-lava cobbles. Walk up the low lava point to find many dozens of etchings, including one that depicts a mother giving birth. *Be Aware:* Take care not to step on the carvings and don't pile or move stones.

Going north from the beach park are the **Anchialine Pond Preservation Area** and then the fabulous **Hilton Resort**. The ponds are about midway, where a spur trail connects the coast to the anchialine pond parking area. *Note:* You can use the *pond parking* to skip the beach walk: Walk by the ponds, go right on the coast to enter the Hilton the back way. Starting from the beach park, either walk the sand of the bay or, if Waikoloa's winds are sandblasting, cut behind the beach dune and walk the shores of two large fishponds. The first and larger is called **Kuʻualiʻi**, and the second, **Kahapapa**. *Anae* means "mullet," and *hoʻomalu* means "protected." Stick close to shore after rounding the bay. The rock-lined trail continues in front of fancy homes through leafy kamani trees and passes mounds of white coral. *Talk Story:* **Anchialine ponds** are brackish pools near the coast where underground fresh water and seawater percolate to the surface. The ancients used the ponds for agriculture, drinking, and raising fish and shrimp. Head inland on the paved trail to see the ponds, and then backtrack to continue along the coast to the Hilton. Climb stairs that take you to the resort's pool area, with its swinging bridge and artificial falls. Stay on the paved seaside path to reach the dolphin pool.

ANAEHOʻOMALU, THE HILTON

HILTON'S DOLPHIN LEARNING CENTER

The **Hilton Resort stroll,** a rainy day winner, is where luxury hotel meets museum-theme park—definitely the wow-factor for the family. A voluminous foyer leads to the hotel's **free monorail and boat rides**. On both you wind through building canyons and gardens. Beyond these platforms, is the **Grand Staircase**, an expansive portico with 100-foot columns leading toward the water. Or go left at the stairs behind a waterfall to the dolphin lagoon (near the "back entrance"). The **Hilton's Palace Tower** has 20-foot high vases and art galore. A man-made lagoon and beach is separated by a grassy spit from the lava shores of **Waiulua Bay**.

For most visitors, the show-stopper at the Hilton is the resort's **Dolphin Learning Center**, home to a dozen of our brothers and sisters of the sea. Grassy slopes provide a spot to sit down and go eyeball-to-eyeball with these creatures. But the real treat, usually in the afternoon, is when the well-trained staff of **Dolphin Quest** introduces small teams of lucky kids. It's a five-ring circus as kids, trainers, and dolphins charge about the lagoon timing out a splash-filled interplay. Feeding time is also good to take a gander. The nonprofit center sponsors research and oversees dolphin births.

SNORKEL: Although surf and sand create murky waters near shore, **Anaeho'omalu Bay** has some very good snorkeling. You need to swim a long way out, which may deter beginners. Snorkeling tour boats moor offshore in the middle of the bay. Beginners may prefer the south end, by the beach park. While not ideal, secluded **Kapalaoa Beach** is the pick at A-Bay. If you angle out from the little cove, keeping close to shore, clarity increases. A better bet is to find a shade warren in the kiawes just after the mangrove thicket and take dips alongside turtles in blue pockets of the reef. *Be Aware:* Rip currents accompany high surf. Also watch out for submerged rocks.

SURF: **A-Bay** is the top windsurfing and kite-boarding spot on the Big Island. Wind-surfers put in at the beach park, while kite-boarders fly high at **Kapalaoa Beach**. Surfers (including longboarders) like the area north of the bay, **Kaʻauau Point**—between the park and the Hilton. Due to shallow lava reefs, this is not a learner's locale.

14. KEAWAIKI BAY-BROWN'S RETREAT   HIKE, SNORKEL

WHAT'S BEST: In the early 1900s, celebrities and Hawaii's gentry used to gather at this now forlorn estate. You'll feel delightfully in the middle of nowhere on a rugged coast with excellent snorkeling pools.

PARKING: Take Hwy. 19 north from Kailua-Kona to mm78.5. Pull off to the ocean side at a patch of asphalt and pile of lava, which are inland from a large coastal palm grove.

HIKE: Keawaiki Bay (1.5 mi.) and Weliweli Point (3.25 mi.)

Talk Story: Francis Iʻi Brown, the Great Gatsby of the Big Island, was the grandson of the distinguished John Papa Iʻi, who was counsel to Hawaii's first three kings and in his later years recorded his experiences in seminal history books. His grandson, Francis, owned what later became the Mauna Lani Resort. He also purchased this 15-acre retreat at Keawaiki Bay in 1920 and over the next decades partied with the likes of Babe Ruth, Mae West, and Bob Hope. Recently the retreat is where author Paul Theroux kayak-camped and wrote about it in *The Happy Isles of Oceania*. In 1956, Francis Brown sold the estate to his grandson, and subsequent generations have installed a now-rusted 10-strand barbed-wire fence around the modest grounds.

To get from the parking area to **Keawaiki Bay**, go over a berm and past a metal gate toward the ocean on a crushed aʻa lava road, keeping a coco palm grove in your sights. (After a few minutes you cross the **King's Trail**, which, taken to the left, is the back way to the beach.) In less than .5-mile, you reach the over-strung fence, where a well-tramped trail leads to the right over rough aʻa lava and follows the fence line to the beach. At the coast, go left. A palm grove and other beach trees accent the retreat's squat stone cottages with metal roofs. At the far end of this stretch, the stones are worn down to salt-and-pepper pebbles and coarse sand, backed by kiawes and a few palms—the place to do beach time at Keawaiki. *More Stuff:* A scenic and recommended side trip is to go south around the pahoehoe lava reef to **Kawai Point**, which will add up to 1.75 miles round trip to your hike. You pass lava tide pools and a coral-sand camping beach. Kawai Point is about 200 feet seaward over smooth lava, before fearsome aʻa lava intrudes on the coastline.

To dramatic **Weliweli Point**, backtrack northward up the beach past the Brown retreat. You cross a low lava point and reach small **Pueo Bay**, where in 1859 the molten stampede of jagged lava that is just inland met its match in the relentless Pacific. Stay high on the black-pebble dune as it curls around toward a lone coconut palm, unless some misfortune has since befallen our noble botanical friend. Pause here to gaze inland at Mauna Kea, Hualalai Volcano, and the long slope of Mauna Loa. The lava you see at arm's length crawled 35 miles from Mauna Loa. On the north side of Pueo Bay, footing gets more difficult on chunks of coral and lava, but you'll soon reach the mound of stone at Weliweli Point. You're not in Kansas anymore, Toto. You're on a hammerhead of coral that is being smashed to sand by waves on the Big Island of Hawaii.

SNORKEL: The south cove at **Keawaiki Bay** is protected by a reef that angles north from Kaiwi Point. Snorkeling can be excellent here, provided wave action is not extreme. Coral heads lie scattered about in clear water close to shore. Beach aesthetics get high marks. You can also dip the fins farther up the shore toward the main house at the **Brown retreat**. You'll see a lava wall segment at water's edge. Entry is easy here.

Snorkeling is also good at **Pueo Bay**, although the water is normally rougher and you'll find no shade. Of underwater interest at Pueo is the freshwater intrusion that can be seen as ripples during periods of calmer surf. You're seeing anchialine ponds in action, as this water is flowing from ponds just inland. *Be Aware:* Observe the seas carefully, and test the current upon entry by floating face down to see if you stay in one spot.

BLUE (WAINANALIʻI) LAGOON

15. KIHILO BAY-BLUE LAGOON   HIKE, SNORKEL

> **WHAT'S BEST:** An enticing view from a scenic point lures visitors to this not-so-secret turquoise lagoon. Awaiting are a long black sand beach and Hawaii's best spot to commune with turtles.

Thurston Lava Tube, Kawaihae paddling club, Hawaii Volcanoes National Park, Hapuna Beach State Park

Hilton Resort Waikoloa, Hawaii Tropical Botanical Garden, Kailua-Kona Town, Hilo Farmers Market

Lapakahi Historical Park, Akaka Falls, Waipio Valley

Pololu Valley Lookout, Kehena-Pohoiki Scenic Coast, Hula halau Na Pua O Uluhaimalama, Wailuku River State Park

PARKING: **PARKING:** Take Hwy. 19 north from Kailua-Kona to mm82.5 and turn makai on a an un-paved road. A Kihilo State Park Reserve sign notes the gate closure at 6. *Be Aware:* Traffic can make this turn dangerous when driving north. You may wish to continue to a scenic view parking lot at mm82 and hang a U-turn.

For the Blue Lagoon hike: Continue .75-mi. down the unpaved road and park at a gated road on the right. *For Kihilo Black Sand Beach:* Continue another .1-mi, to where the road makes a right-angle left (and another road continues straight toward the ocean). Go left a short distance to a Shoreline Public Access turnout on the right, near an octagonal house on poles. *Note:* North of the scenic view parking lot on the highway is another trail down to the bay. Park .1-mi. south of mm81, where the highway cuts through a low hill. Though popular, this option is slightly longer, requires 200 feet of elevation change, and provides a better chance of getting lost.

BLUE (WAINANALI'I) LAGOON

HIKE: Blue Lagoon (2.25 mi.); Kihilo Black Sand Beach (.75-mi.)

At the north end of 2-mile-wide **Kihilo Bay, Blue (Wainanali'i) Lagoon** is a lu-minescent streak of turquoise that is difficult to resist. To walk there, get around the formidable gate and start down a private-residence road. *Fastest option:* Continue almost .5-mile, passing all trails and driveways on the left. The road narrows at an orange metal gate, after which are beach and shoreline access signs. A short trail leads through a thicket and reaches the beach north of the resort-sized mansion. Pay attention, since this trail is easy to miss on the way back. (Just south is the architecturally elaborate home of cosmetic magnate Paul Mitchell, who had the place shipped in pieces from Indonesia.) *Other options:* On the left from the wide road are **Kihilo-Huehue Trails,** which reach the beach south of the fastest option. Go right along the rocky shore. *For all options:* At the beach, circle around to the right to a coco-palm lined embayment, inshore of which are a few cottages and a tranquil fishpond. Staying close to the shore, cross two footbridges over narrow channels and continue over a pahoehoe section that leads to the open end of the lagoon. You can wade the channel to the spit on the other side. Or, try going right over the sprawling dollops of lava past some brilliant blue inlets. You'll circle the lagoon, passing salt-encrusted sunbathing turtles, and others gliding along under water. *Talk Story:* The lagoon was actually part of a massive fishpond built by **Kamehameha the Great** in 1810, which was considered an engineering marvel by early Western visitors. Walls 8-feet high and 20-feet wide formed a deep-sea fishpond that was nearly two miles around. An 1859 Mauna Loa eruption, which created Lae Hou Point that you can see to the north, destroyed much of the pond.

Kihilo Black Sand Beach, popular among weekend campers, begins at the south end of **Kihilo Bay**. From the parking at the octagonal house (built by folksinger Loretta Lynn), first head to your left. Look inland to see the spring-fed **Luahinewai Pond** set below a lava wall and bordered by palms and other beach trees. In ancient times coastal canoeists would stop in here for fresh water and to maintain the good hygiene for which the Hawaiians were noted. Then head up the beach. Black sand at Kihilo ranges from fairly fine to basketball-sized. You'll find three separate beaches over the southern shore, nuances in a rugged shoreline. You can beachcomb the 2 miles to reach **Blue Lagoon**, although high surf may bully you inland at times. In the 1890s, this end of the bay was where cattle from Pu'u Wa'a Wa'a Ranch were shuttled to ships offshore.

SNORKEL: Kihilo Black Sand Beach has water clarity, easy entry, and pleasant beach trees. The water gets deep fast. *Be Aware*: Wave action creates strong currents, especially during winter months. For a shallow-water dip with plenty of fish, head to the **small embayment** with cottages, but before Blue Lagoon; enter at the south end, left as you face the water, off a small tip of land. You need to navigate rocks, but snorkeling is good.

A few months after visiting the Big Island you may find yourself staring through a wall and thinking about snorkeling in **Blue Lagoon**. You can enter where the trail meets the lagoon, wade across to the spit, or—best bet—go right and find an entry from the lava. Green sea turtles feed and sleep in the lagoon. Encrusted salt turns their bodies white after they haul out into the sun on the shores the 5-acre inlet. *Be Aware*: Federal law and common decency require giving the turtles a wide berth. Although startlingly blue, the water is milky due to silt. You will also notice a chill, since volumes of freshwater enter the lagoon. Also, you'll be glad to have shoes on when wading across the channel.

---

16. PU'U WA'A WA'A AHUPUA'A   **HIKE**

WHAT'S BEST: Surrounding this rippled butte (a large cinder cone) above the South Kohala coast is one of the state's few remaining native dryland forests.

PARKING: From Hwy. 19 in Kailua-Kona, take Hwy. 190, or Palani Rd., up the mountain. North of mm22, look for the Pu'u Wa'a Wa'a Ranch gate on the mauka side, normally unlocked weekdays from 6 to 6. Drive in and veer left immediately. Continue to trailhead parking and the checking station. Call 808-333-0084 to volunteer.

HIKE: Pu'u Wa'a Wa'a trails (up to 12 mi., up to 1,000 ft.)

In 2006, state and federal foresters developed **Pu'u Wa'a Wa'a Ahupua'a** (really fun to say out loud) as a Hawaii Experimental Tropical Forest. Trails, which mainly follow old ranch bulldozer tracks, include the **Cinder Cone Trail, Ohia Trail**, and **Halapepe Trail**. A botanical trail brochure should be available on site. The Cinder Cone Trail, about 3.25 miles with a 1,000 feet of climb, scales the crater; go up to the back of the gully and curve around to your right. You won't get lost in these wide open spaces with blue water views.

Birders and botanists will particularly enjoy taking a look at an example of native low-land dry forest, which used to be common on the leeward slopes of all the islands—not the vine-laden, leafy jungle most people associate with Hawaii. The gray-barked ohia is the dominant tree, with its red bottlebrush flowers and burnt-coffee scent. The squiggly limbed wiliwili, its bark often orange with lichen, will lose its leaves during dry summers. Wiliwili flowers are a peachy-orange, and its berries are coral pink. A common shrub, with little yellow football-shaped fruits, is the ala'a. Among the exotic trees that grow here are the lavender-flowered jacaranda, and the pepper tree, with poisonous red berries. Birdsong is a constant backdrop to these visual delights. Pu'u Wa'a Wa'a is nearly 4,000 feet in elevation, less than half the height of green Hualalai Volcano at 8,271, which rises a few miles southward.

17. HUALALAI-FOUR SEASONS RESORT HIKE, SNORKEL

WHAT'S BEST: Miles of coastal paths around the 900 acres of Hualalai lead to snorkeling coves and pass the tranquil Four Seasons Resort. Petroglyphs and interpretive markers convey the history of this striking seascape.

PARKING: Take Hwy. 19 north from Kailua. Pass mm87 and, .6-mi. later, turn makai on Kaupulehu toward Hualalai Resorts. Keep left and stop at the entrance station for the Four Seasons Resort. You have parking options: *For Four Seasons and petroglyphs hikes:* Ask for North Beach access; this primary option is most central to activities, a 10-space lot within a larger lot to the right of the resort. *For Kukio Bay hikes:* Ask for public access permit for Kukio Bay, which is the south parking area. You turn left at the entrance station and wind down about a mile to a 40-space parking lot.

Notes: If the lot you request is full, ask to visit the Kaupulehu Cultural Center at the Four Seasons—a memorable stop by itself. In addition, if the Kona Village Resort has opened in 2014 as planned, you can veer right after turning in from the highway. The Kona Village parking is nearly .5-mile from the beach, coming out at the north end of the Four Seasons. *Last note:* To directly access pretty Kikaua Park at the south end of Kukio Bay, see *Snorkel* below.

KAUPULEHU PETROGLYPHS

HIKE: Four Seasons North Beach parking to: Kahuwai Bay (Kona Village) and Kaupulehu Petroglyphs (1.25 mi.); Kaupulehu Cultural Center (.25-mi.) Kukio Bay parking to: Kikaua Park (1 mi.) or Kumukehu Trail to Four Seasons (1.25 mi.)

To walk from the **Four Seasons North Beach to Kahuwai Bay and Kaupulehu Petroglyphs at the Kona Village,** weave through the resort's gardens, passing the **Kings Pond,** a large anchialine pool that is home to many colorful fish and manta rays. Go right at the beach. (If you parked at Kukio Beach, walk right for about .5-mile on Kumukehu Trail to reach the Four Seasons.) Either way, just north of the Four Seasons is the entranceway for the Kona Village's public parking; look for the chain-link fence. Continue along the beach, passing thatched-roofed cottages. *Notes:* Kona Village, closed due to damage from the 2011 tsunami, was scheduled to reopen in 2014. Free petroglyph tours previously were given daily at 11. The site is on private property, inland beyond a central lagoon, at the outer edge of the bungalows.

A railed boardwalk was built in 1998 to preserve the 400-plus **Kaupulehu rock carvings**—called ki'i pohaku in Hawaiian. *Talk Story:* The earliest petroglyphs date from about 1,000 years ago, the most recent from the early 1800s. The origin of some of the etchings is a mystery. Some of the pictures in rock, like the "surfing fisherman" and the ornately drawn sails, are unique to this field and the number of sails here far exceeds any other site.

The **Kaupulehu Cultural Center** is kitty-corner the mauka side of the Four Seasons main lobby, about 100 feet away underneath the golf store. Inside are some of the island's experts on Hawaiian culture and crafts, as well as artifacts and replicas that give a hands-on appreciation of what life was like in the 25,000-acre ahupua'a of Kaupulehu.

KUA BAY, KIKAUA POINT PARK

Of particular interest are 11 original paintings that depict village life by the late Herb Kawinui Kane (KAH-nay). A former Chicago advertising executive, Kane returned to his Big Island home to perpetuate the knowledge of the Hawaiians through his painting and writing. The center normally is open weekdays from 8:30 to 4.

For both Kukio Bay parking hikes, start down the paved path and boardwalk, passing **Halau o Kaupulehu**, a traditional Polynesian sailing canoe. For the hike to **Kikaua Park**, which is a beauty at the far end of **Kukio Bay**, depart the path and go left on the beach. At the end of the beach, a trail crosses a short section of lava before reaching the park, which is part of the high-end private development at Kukio. Palms, ironwoods, and the leafy kamani trees are nicely spaced. *More Stuff:* A rocky, remote Shoreline Public Access trail hugs the coast south from the Kikaua parking lot to Kua Bay. The **Kumukehu Trail to the Four Seasons**—to the right, or north, from the Kukio parking lot—is a paved path that skirts a golf course and the jagged seascape left by 1801 a'a lava flow that tumbled down from **Hualalai Volcano**. Interpretive signs mark the way. Whale watchers will want to pause midway during winter months at **Kumukehu Point**, before continuing to the Four Seasons. A section of the lava-rock King's Trail leaves and then rejoins the paved path.

ANCHIALINE POND

SNORKEL: The best and most reliable snorkeling is in **Kahuwai Bay**, offshore **Kona Village**. Use the the North Beach at the Four Seasons. You'll find coral heads and lots of fish as you swim out toward the point. You can also swim closer to the **Four Seasons**, where a long reef creates a protected swimming oval, offshore the resort's swimming pool. *Be Aware:* Keep an eye out for boat traffic in the bay.

While its shallow water may put off reef divers, kids and mommies love **Kikaua Point Park**, at the south end of Kukio Bay. Either use Kukio Beach parking described above or drive there. *Driving:* Just south of the Hualalai Resorts' entrance on Highway 19, look for a makai turn lane at mm87.25. Ask for a public access permit to the popular, 30-space parking lot. A paved path winds several hundred feet to the beach. Directly off the point is a dreamy pool with statuesque lava spires. A formation with a two-legged base is what's left of a lava stack that in Hawaiian mythology represents the local chiefess frozen forever after a love-triangle went bad. A sandy entrance leads to the pool, an excellent place to flipper around. For deeper water from this park, try off the point, or take the trail across the lava to the sands of **South Kukio Bay**—a stone's throw away. Entry can be tricky, but you should spot a sand channel used by kayakers. Wave action and currents can be a problem here. Dolphins at times join turtles swimming around **Kikaua Point**.

18.　KUA BAY　　　　　　　　　　　HIKE, SNORKEL, SURF

WHAT'S BEST: Surfers, sunbathers, and snorkelers love the aqua blue water at this cove. Hikers can scale landmark Pu'u Kuili or sample a wild section of the King's Trail.

PARKING: Take Hwy 19 north of the airport from Kailua-Kona to mm88.5. Use a left-turn lane across from Hawaii Veterans Cemetery. *Note:* Kekahakai State park gate is open from 9 to 7; closed Wednesdays. It's a 1.25 mi. walk to the beach from the highway.

HIKE: Pu'u Kuili (.75mi., 300 ft.); Kua Bay and Papiha Point (about .5-mi.); King's Trail to Kakapa Bay (1 to 1.75 mi.)

KUA BAY

A paved road, fancy restrooms, and picnic tables added in 2005 have put this once-secret locals' hangout on the map, but **Kua Bay** still delivers a wild-and-scenic punch. **Puʻu Kuili** is a **Kohala Coast** landmark rising above a sea of aʻa lava. For the unmarked trail, park about .6-mile in from the gate, where the road curves right near a 15 m.p.h. sign and between the second and third speed bumps. A rough, rock-lined trail traverses upward to the right, or seaward, on a gentle slope on the side of the puʻu. Once you reach the ocean side of Puʻu Kuili, it's an easy scamper to the top. An upright pipe marks the superlative view—a place to scope coastal hiking options, north and south.

To stroll **Kua Bay and Papiha Point** wind your way down from the picnic area and head right across the beach. The north side of the little bay is formed by low-lying Papiha Point, a good place to take in the views. From just inland the point, you can head up a sandy draw and go right on a road back to the parking lot. The **King's Trail to Kakapa Bay** is an authentic mini-adventure along the rugged backshore, site of the ancient village of **Manini Owali**. From the parking lot, walk down the road just left of the restrooms. At the anchialine pond and copse of kiawe and palms (where the road hooks left to the beach) go right toward signs that are above and behind the pond. The trail becomes obvious as it snakes up and then turns left, or north. Flat stones laid in the sharp lava are typical of historic coastal trails. Once at Kakapa Bay, energetic hikers can continue around to **Kikaua Point Park**.

SNORKEL: Kua Bay is known for its turquoise waters and snorkeling can be superb. Get in at the beach and swim out among the rocks that are just off of **Papiha Point** to the north. *Be Aware:* High surf can make for treacherous swimming. The winter surf at times washes away the sand at water's edge, leaving only boulders. Also, bring along a beach umbrella since shade is scarce.

SURF: The shore break at **Kua Bay** draws bodyboarding buffs. During higher surf, experienced boarders ride the wild right-break off Papiha Point, a sight to behold.

19. KEKAHA KAI STATE PARK   HIKE, SNORKEL, SURF

WHAT'S BEST: Long sandy beaches with snorkeling coves are set along three miles of wild parkland. Live the tropical fantasy, dude.

PARKING: Take Hwy. 19 north of the airport. About .5-mi. north of mm91, turn makai toward Kekaha Kai State Park. A gate is open from 9 to 7, but is locked on Wednesdays. *Be Aware:* The road can be hellishly rutted and bumpy, but normally it is okay driving for slow moving rental cars. *For Mahaiula and Makalawena beaches:* Park at a gate on the right that is 1.5 miles from the highway. *For Kekaha Kai Beach Park,* continue to road's end at 1.65 mi.

HIKE: Kekaha Kai Beach (.25-mi.); Kekaha Kai Trail to: Mahaiula Bay (.75-mi.), and Makalawena Beaches-Makalawai Oasis (1.75 mi. to 2.75 mi.)

MAKALAWENA BEACH

Kekaha Kai State Park, formerly Kona Coast State Park, covers 1,600 coastal acres. The state plans to improve the access road and put in showers, restrooms, and picnic facilities at Mahaiula Bay. An education center, canoe hale, and botanical gardens are also in the works. For now, the waterless restrooms and barbecue grills under picture-perfect palms at **Kekaha Kai Beach** are the extent of man's handiwork. This beach was called Second Beach by its former owners, and in ancient times it was known as **Kaelehuluhulu**, which is fun to say. A semi-circle of sand-and-rubble beach curves outward to form the south mouth of **Mahaiula Bay**, which you'll see around to the right.

For the hikes to **Mahaiula Bay** and **Makalawena Beaches**, beat tracks across the black cinder road beyond the locked gate. Bring a hat, lace-up shoes, and plenty of water. A green buffer of kiawes and coco palms hide the bay. Stay on the road and you'll wind up in the center of the half-mile wide crescent of sand. Though closer, this bay often sees fewer visitors. *Talk Story:* In the 1930s, this bay was part of the Alfred Magoon estate and the scene of days-long parties. Mahaiula was a fishing village in the older days, and the lava tubes surrounding the grounds were burial grounds after so many Hawaiians died from Western diseases in the early 1800s.

To **continue to Makalawena-Makalawai Oasis**, go right on the coarse sand, cutting in front of an open-air bunkhouse. Skirt the shore and then make sure to go right at a low wall and palm trees. A wide, crunchy trail dotted with stepping stones goes string straight across the hot a'a for a little more than .25-mile before reaching the fine white sand and shade at the backshore of Makalawena. Continue on the sand trail atop a long sand dune which is carpeted green with pohuehue (seaside morning glory). Midway on the dune, look right to see **Makalawai Oasis**, a teardrop shaped pool in the lava, buffered by a restful grove of palms. A sandy path leads to a contemplation spot within. Goats like it, too, part of the reason for algae growth. At the beach is a lava point, and the south side of Makalwena is technically **Pu'u Ali'i Beach**.

At the far end of the beach are parklike grounds, with a picnic table or two set in a stand of ironwoods. Cut inland to find **Opae Ula Pond**, a 12-acre shorebird sanctuary that is home to the endangered Hawaiian stilt, golden plover, as well as waterfowl and many wild goats (access may be limited). Over the next little rise from the parklike ironwood grove, is a five-star **keiki pond** next to a small sand cove. The trail continues north, reaching **Kaiwikohola Point** and the gate of a 4WD road that comes in from Kua Bay. A proposed wilderness campground is just north, at **Awake'e Bay**. *Be Aware:* **Kamehameha Schools** owns Makalawena, and this cove is normally the campsite of a beach host. Please: no camping, nudity, or venturing inland on private property.

SNORKEL: At quiet **Kekaha Kai Beach** (the best picnic spot) the snorkeling is just okay, due to an exposed near-shore reef. On calm days, however, go right to the sloping sands and you'll see a pretty good swimming spot. **Mahaiula Bay** is the best snorkeling choice—safe and protected, fine sloping sand, shaded by lovely palms and a spreading heliotrope. Entry is gradual, although sand is coarse and you do have to pick your way though small rocks on the north side. Decent coral heads await off-shore, but water clarity is not the best. Off-shore, clarity improves near a scuba divers' spot called **Arches**.

The south end of **Makalawena** has rocks at the shore break, but you can snorkel at a small opening, just as you top the dune. Or, better yet, cross the first stretch of fine-sand beach and try the next section be-yond the lava point. *Be Aware:* Stinging sea urchins can be a problem at the first part of the beach and a rip current channel goes out the center of this embayment. Go to the far end of the beach and enter near

MAKALAWAI OASIS

the rocky point. To be totally safe, try the **keiki beach** that is beyond the ironwood stand, continuing north. When the tide is up, this is one of Hawaii's best soaking pools.

SURF: Boardheads beat up their car's shock absorber driving in and then come run-ning to catch the right-break at **Kawili Point**, which is the north side of **Mahaiula Bay**. Big surf breaks across the entire mouth of the bay on certain days. You'll find bodyboarders at the north end of **Makalawena**, catching an offshore right-slide. Body surfers will be tempted at this beach, but be very careful of near-shore rocks, as well as rip current. Neck and head injuries aren't hard to come by.

Kona

KAILUA-KONA

TRAILHEAD PREVIEWS

Where's the beach?

Arriving at the airport, especially on days when the vog (volcanic smog) is creeping down the barren lava fields, Kona newcomers may be disappointed with the absence of a glitzy run of white sand that is normally associated with a resort area of such high repute. Don't despair. Remember that the big guy, Kamehameha the Great, could have lived anywhere in the Hawaiian Islands and he chose to spend his final decade on the shores of Kailua-Kona. Like much of the Big Island, Kona may not deliver the stereotype, but it offers much more after you've taken the time let the magic work.

Just north of town are three beaches, each with its own personality, that provide a quick getaway. Wawaloli Beach Park is a sandy nook with a chilly dipping pond. From the park is a beachcomber's hike to Kohanaiki Park (Pinetrees) Beach, a surfer's hangout. Just south of Wawaloli, at Honokohau Bay, is a pleasant snorkeling spot at Alula Beach, where you can also sit on a palm point at the mouth of the harbor to watch the deep sea fishermen return with their bounty. But the treasure at Honokohau is the Kaloko-Honokohau National Historic Park, featuring a picturesque swimming lagoon and a coast walk of nearly two miles, leading to a surfer's beach and royal pond. Anthropological sleuths will rejoice.

Closest to Kona is Old Airport Beach State Park, a place to take a stroll with a morning latte or a sunset cocktail, or vice versa, what the heck. A continuous coral-and-sand strip fronts an onshore lava reef, where you can also find some very good snorkeling. You'll have room to roam and a whole runway to park on, a getaway that is nearly walking distance from the hubbub of Kailua.

ROYAL FISHPOND, SUPER J'S, IRONMAN TRIATHALON FINISH

KONA PREVIEWS |77

PUʻUHONUA BEACH PARK, NET FISHERMAN, HULIHEʻE PALACE

Kailua, or Kailua-Kona, while a tad cheesy, still retains the tropical-seaport charm that you expect in the islands. Cruising sailboats anchor offshore, along with occasional luxury liners and the evening dinner-cruise barges. Sure, the place has it's tacky shops, but some are downright kitsch, and the historical layers of Old Hawaii are all here— the Ahuena Heiau of ancient times, the governor's Hulihe'e Palace, and Mokuaikaue Church, the first built by missionaries in the islands. You'll also find excellent snorkeling get-ins, right there in the buzz of Kailua Pier. Just down Ali'i Drive is where bodyboarding was born, at Hale Halawai. Bring your camera and get a front-row seat for this flipped-out sport.

Not far down the drive from Kailua is the ancient surfing site at Holualoa Bay, where today's wave riders carry on. What makes the bay doubly interesting is the Keolonahihi State Historical Park that is hiding in plain sight. Unsigned and overgrown, the place is aching for trailblazers with a true sense of adventure and long pants. Most of the action is farther yet down Ali'i, where snorkelers, surfers, and beach hogs can choose from three parks. The two northerly parks, White Sands and Pahoehoe, are better choices for the summer, since winter's epic surf can wash the sand away. But snorkelers can head to Kahalu'u Beach Park all year long. A reef-protected shore and copious knobs of coral have created a huge fish-lover's pool. This is the place to test the gear.

AHUENA HEIAU, KONA HULA DANCERS

A little farther south is Keauhou Bay, where King Kamehameha III was born. The bay is overlooked by many snorkelers, in spite of several good options. You'll also find coast walks north and south. North goes by hidden He'eia Bay, a place to check out if you're staying in the area. To the south is the wave-crashing hike to the Kuamo'o Battlefield, where in 1819 the old guard was defeated by King Kamehameha II, who had instituted reforms that, among other things, brought women to an equal footing with men in Hawaiian social structure. Keauhou serves up a guaranteed one-two punch for those looking for a swim and history hike.

The grandame of this trailhead section is Kealakekua Bay. Site of a major ancient village and Hikiau Heiau, the bay is known mainly as the place where British Captain James Cook ran out of luck in 1779. The bay, particularly at the Cook Monument, offers some of the best snorkeling in the Hawaiian Islands. It also has hidden treats, like exquisite Manini Beach Park and Ke'ei Village, where you get vistas of the Kealakekua's famous cliffs and a chance to see some non-tourist coastal hangouts. In the same area is Pu'uhonua o Honaunau National Historic Park, which preserves an ancient place of refuge, where

PUʻUHONUA O HONAUNAU

vanquished warriors and social miscreants could be safe. A coast hike south from the park is the bell-ringer, so check it out. Two Step, which is close by, is an excellent snorkeling spot, again, one of the best in Hawaii.

The Kona coast gets cliffy as you head south from Honaunau through coffee-and-macadamia country, but you can find two roads winding down to out-of-the-way coves. Hoʻokena Beach Park is a camper's beach, where both snorkeling and bodysurfing

can be good. Trails wind along a wild
coast. Farther south, the fishing village of
Miloliʻi is one of the few that has survived
from ancient times, although dugouts
have given way to aluminum boats, and
thatched huts have been replaced by
wood-frames. Still, the village will be
high on the list for seekers of true Hawaii,
and the short hike south from Miloliʻi to
Honomalino Beach is a fantasy experience, where coconut palms line a sandy
crescent, and dolphins swirl offshore.

South of Miloliʻi, the temperate zone
continues as you encounter large macadamia groves and native ohia forests. About
midway between Kona and Volcano is
Manuka State Park, perfectly situated
for a picnic or extended hike into native forests. Birders take note. You can
choose from a nature trail or longer trek
into the forest reserve that surrounds the
park. Just south of Manuka, the terrain
changes dramatically, becoming a desert
of aʻa lava.

MILOLIʻI, HONOKOHAU HARBOR

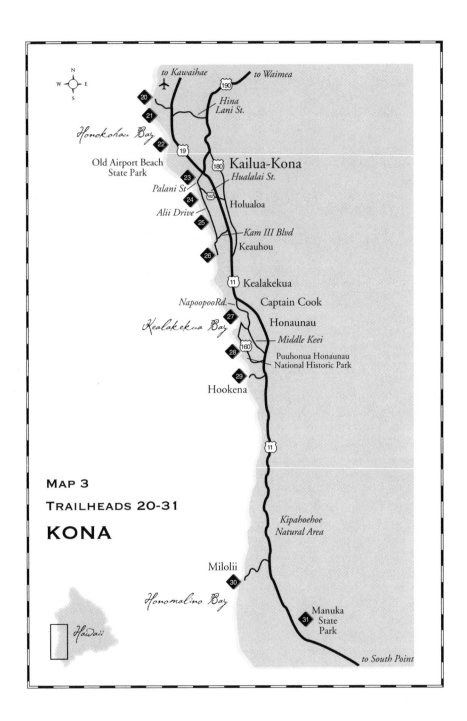

to Kawaihae   to Waimea

190

Hina
Lani St.

20

21

Honokohau Bay

22

19

Old Airport Beach
State Park

180   Kailua-Kona

Hualalai St.

23

Palani St

24   Holualoa

Alii Drive

25

Kam III Blvd

Keauhou

26

11   Kealakekua

Napoopoo Rd.   Captain Cook

27   Honaunau

Kealakekua Bay

160   Middle Keei

28   Puuhonua Honaunau
National Historic Park

29

Hookena

11

MAP 3

TRAILHEADS 20-31

KONA

Kipahoehoe
Natural Area

Milolii

30

Honomalino Bay

Manuka
State
Park

31

to South Point

Hawaii

TRAILHEADS

20-31

TH :	TRAILHEAD
HIKE :	HIKES AND STROLLS
SNORKEL :	SNORKELING, SWIMMING
SURF :	BOARD, BODYBOARD, BODYSURF
MM :	MILE MARKER; CORRESPONDS TO HIGHWAY SIGNS
MAKAI :	TOWARD THE OCEAN
MAUKA :	INLAND, TOWARD THE MOUNTAINS

ALL HIKING DISTANCES IN PARENTHESES ARE ROUND TRIP. ELEVATION GAINS OF 100 FEET OR MORE ARE NOTED. SEE RESOURCE LINKS FOR CONTACTS AND TELEPHONE NUMBERS.

20. WAWAIOLI & KOHANAIKI BEACHES   HIKE, SNORKEL, SURF

WHAT'S BEST: Beachcombers and shell-seekers will like this coastal path to a surfer's beach—a once out-of-the-way spot that has been transformed into a coastal park.

PARKING: *For Kohanaiki Beach:* Go north from Kailua-Kona on Hwy. 19 to mm95.2, and turn makai toward Kohanaiki Shores. *Notes:* You may have to pass the road, hang a U-turn, and then turn right. This access point may change as development progresses. *For Wawaioli Beach:* Pass Kohanaiki and turn at mm94 toward the Natural Energy Laboratory of Hawaii on OTEC Rd. Continue .75-mi. to where the road makes a right-angle.

HIKE: Wawaioli Beach Park to Kohanaiki (Pinetrees) Beach (2.25 mi.)

Wawaioli Beach Park is here courtesy of the energy lab, which studies how the temperature differential between warm surface water and cold deep water can create a current flow to generate electricity. The Big Island's most westerly land, **Keahole Point**, is just to the north (walk to the right); winds and currents here are so fierce that even the Hawaiian canoeists of yore would come ashore and paddle a 3-mile fishpond rather than brave the point. At Wawaioli, storm surf can wash over the road. But it is nonetheless a pleasant curve of sand, featuring a protected, chilly keiki pool—a channel in the lava shelf between the beach and the restrooms.

For the walk to **Pinetrees Beach (Kohanaiki Coastal Community Park)**, take the unpaved road that is to the left where the paved road turns right. You can shorten the round-trip hike by .75-mile by driving to a gate (open 7 to 7), where the road demands high-clearance vehicles. Or, you can drive directly to the park (see *Parking*). After the gate, the trail reaches a coarse coral-sand and rocky beach skirted by false kamani trees, the **O'oma Open Space**, which will appeal to tide-poolers and beachcombers looking for seashells. About .25-mile later is the north end of the new 38-acre Kohanaiki Coastal

Community Park. Just inland is the golf course and homes of the 470-acre **Kohaniki Shores** development. The park has restrooms, showers, and a campground, with parking pocketed along about .5-mile. The place jumps on weekends. A massive mangrove that used to mark the beach—misnamed by bonged-up surfers as pine trees—has been removed as part of a program to restore natural habitat and anchialine ponds. *More Stuff:* You can keep on truckin' south of the park, along coarse sand and a broad lava reef. Also, at the Kona Airport (use the main road in) is the **Onizuka Space Center**. Named for Hawaii's favorite son, Astronaut Ellison Onizuka, the center features a gravity well, moon rock, theater, and model of the Space Shuttle.

SNORKEL: Moms with folding chairs take toddlers to the **Wawaioli keiki pond**. At the lowest tides, Wawaioli Park can be without swimmable water. Experienced snorkelers can swim the reef offshore **O'oma Open Space**, where diving tour boats moor. *Be Aware:* Deep water current and wave action are hazards. Attempt only on calm days.

SURF: The main break at **Pinetrees** is about 200 yards directly offshore. Shallow water and a rocky bottom make this a spot novices should avoid. Observe the local boys before taking a ride on these waves. This is north Kona's primary surf scene.

21. KALOKO-HONOKOHAU HISTORIC PARK   HIKE, SNORKEL, SURF

WHAT'S BEST: An underrated, intriguing national historic park, locals' beach, and sports-fishing harbor combine for a variety show at this close-to-Kailua getaway.

PARKING: Take Hwy. 19 north from Kailua-Kona. *Primary (south) parking:* After passing mm98, turn makai toward Honokohau Harbor on Kealakehe Pwy. Continue until the road forks. *For the Alula Beach and harbor stroll:* Veer left at the fork and continue to the unimproved parking at the south mouth of the bay. *For Kaloko-Honokohau National Historic Park:* Turn right at the fork and continue along the harbor until the road right-angles left; a gate for the park is on your right.

Visitors center (midway) access: Use a turn lane at mm97 and park at the center, visible from the highway. *Kaloko Fishpond (north) access:* Continue .6-mile north of mm97, and turn left where the highway's double-yellow line broadens to a yellow-striped island. A .75-mile-long unpaved road (closed sunset to sunrise) leads to the fishpond. *Be Aware:* In traffic, this can be a dangerous left. For safety's sake, approach from the north.

HIKE: Alula Beach and Honokohau Harbor (up to .75-mi.); Honokohau Harbor to Kaloko Pond (3.5 to 4.5 mi.) *Note:* Longer hike includes petroglyphs and Queen's Bath.

You'll see **Alula Beach** to the left from the rocky bench at the primary harbor parking area. It's a decent-sized crescent of white sand backed by kiawe trees and protected by the lava finger that is **Noio Point**. Pick a tricky route over the humpback of lava at

AIOPIO FISHTRAP AT HONOKOHAU BAY

the shore, or cut left a little and come down the other side of it. At the beach, a tiny walk takes you across the sand to the point. For an added bonus, jog inland to see the sites of **Makaopio Heiau**, with its two upright stones, and **Hale o Lono**.

Honokohau Harbor was developed as a sportsfishing port 1970. Its sublime spot is the miniature park to the right from the parking area. From this patch of lawn, you watch fishing boats enter the harbor. Historically, black marlin and other game fish were hung and weighed at the marina store—these magnificent creatures photographed in the netherworld between being masters of the deep blue sea and becoming 1,000 grilled filets with lemon wedges on the side. These days, most are catch-and-release.

Talk Story: **Kaloko-Honokohau National Historic Park** was made a landmark in 1962 and upgraded to a park in 1978. The development of the 1,170 acres continues, with a new **visitors center** (see *parking*), called **Hale Ho'okipa**. Stop by for good advice and a free map. **Honokohau Village** ruins date from 1,200 years ago. In the early 1800s, the village gardens were a horn o' plenty for Kamehameha, who spent the remaining years of his life in Kailua—a respite that was spoiled by a wicked a'a lava flow from Hualalai, which added the jagged piles you see today. Though Costco, today's horn o' plenty, is in view inland, the park imparts a faraway feel, with petroglyphs, fishponds, ruins, and a mysterious Queen's Bath. *Be Aware:* When Western diseases depleted the Hawaiian population in the later 1800s, Kaloko's backshore was used for burial caves; take care not to disturb these or any other ancient site.

To walk the length of the park from **Honokohau Harbor to Kaloko Pond**, follow the cable along a short trail, alongside which keen eyes will spot a few petroglyphs. The trail soon reaches a canoe hale sitting beside a little cove that will be to your left. The pretty cove is actually a man-made **Aiopio Fishtrap**. A heiau and anchialine ponds

QUEEN'S BATH AND MYSTERIOUS MOUNDS AT KALOKO HISTORIC PARK

are on its southern shore. For the hike, head to your right on a tree-shaded road. *To see heiau ruins and petroglyphs:* Take a right-forking road near restrooms, which also goes toward the visitors center. The **Kaloko Petroglyph** field is on your right after less than .25-mile; look for a boardwalk with benches. The prize etchings are of rifles—a bad sign for the ancients. Heiau ruins, a rectangle 100 feet on a side with 3- to 6-foot walls, will be on the left, around the next curve from the petroglyphs.

After checking these sights, double back and continue north. You'll skirt the sandy shores of **Honokohau Beach** and pass **Aimakapa Pond**, a natural 20-acre lake that is home to Hawaiian stilts, coots, and also migrating shorebirds. *For the Queen's Bath:* After passing the pond, just under .5-mile from the trailhead, look inland several hundred feet for about a half-dozen rock mounds about 12 feet high. Then look for an unsigned trail that angles toward the mounds—the trail is before the main trail enters a sandy wash under a low canopy of beach trees. Once you reach the mounds, take a path between them to the **Queen's Bath**, hidden in a 10-foot depression only steps away. Teensy fish and a few stranded ocean fish live in the 25-foot oval in the lava. The mounds—intricately stacked and placed in an amorphous circle—are a mystery to archeologists. After spacing out for a while, return to the main trail and keep following the coast, as footing varies among lava, sand, and dirt, through kiawe and the leafy kamani trees. You'll come upon a palm grove and, extending from it, the 750-foot-long seawall that is the magnificently restored **Kaloko Pond**. This man-made 11-acre lake was the fish store of ancient times. Restoration of the pond's seawall is a years-long project that began in 2006. The wall is 20 feet wide and hundreds long.

More Stuff: The ahupua'a of Honokohau is included the lowlands of **Hualalai Volcano**, with native ohia and koa rain forest. *Driving:* Go north from Honokohau Harbor and turn inland on Hina Lani Street. At the top, jog left on Highway 190 and then turn right on **Kaloko Drive**. Kaloko switchbacks up for about 6 miles. Just before the top, go left at a water tank on Huehue; a gated road leads left from here to **Hinaka Crater**. To the right are **Kaupulehu Crater** and far above it at 8,721 feet the overgrown crater of Hualalai. *Be Aware:* Permission from Kamehameha Schools to access these trails is required. Hiking off trail around here is dangerous, due to hidden lava tubes and earth cracks. To get a deluxe look, take a trip with Hawaii Forest & Trail; see *Resource Links*.

SNORKEL: **Alula Beach** offers near-shore pool that is protected by a reef. The snorkeling is good. At the historic park, **Aiopio Fishtrap** is a harsh name for an attractive swimming area—a circle of sand with plenty of palms. Great for the keikis, but the water can be shallow and clarity is not the best. Snorkeling is also good at **Honokohau Beach**, a few minutes up the trail. Sit up on the dune that separates the beach from the pond. A beach of salt-and-pepper sand leads to the oval swimming area in the middle of the wide bay. An offshore reef protects the shore, but surf can be rough.

SURF: The waves **offshore Kaloko Pond** beckon the board surfers from Kailua-Kona. Use the north access to reach this spot directly. A shallow reef break and long paddle make this spot dangerous for beginners. You can watch from near the base of the seawall. Shade trees and picnic tables accent his peaceful place.

22. OLD AIRPORT BEACH STATE PARK HIKE, SNORKEL, SURF

WHAT'S BEST: You won't spend your entire vacation here, but this long sand-and-tide-pool coast is a stone's throw from Kailua and an ideal place for a sunset or sunrise stroll. There's room to roam, and an excellent reef-pool for kids.

PARKING: From Hwy. 19 just north of Kailua, turn makai on either Kawai or Makala. Then turn right on Kuakini Rd. Follow past Kailua Park. Enter a state park and drive to the end of the former runaway. Man, there's plenty of parking.

HIKE: Old Airport Beach to: Kukailimoku Pt. (2 mi.) or Keahuolu Pt. (1.25 mi.)

Old Airport State Beach owes its being to big jets: since there's not enough flat space for adequate extension, the airport was closed in 1970. **Kukailimoku Point**, lies to the south, or left as you face the water. Sand is not scarce, but a storm-washed reef runs along near shore. Rocks encroach farther south, as does the private land. *Talk Story:* In the 1980s, locals who were booted from this historic camping beach set up a tent city in protest. Camping was never reinstated, but a Shoreline Public Access was established. Kukailimoku, the site of this conflict, is named after Kamehameha's war god.

Keahuolu Point lies north from the parking area; pahoehoe lava hills curve seaward. A trail from the end of the runway soon enters the lands of the **Liliuokalani Trust**. Veer left and watch your step, as you follow the rolling lava along the shoreline between gnarly kiawes. (Queen Liliuokalani was Hawaii's last monarch, in office until 1893.) From Keahuolu Point you look over the waters of **Papawai Bay**. Continue on this rough route farther north to **Kaiwi Point**, where dive boats commonly anchor. *More Stuff:* Need a jogging fix? To the right of the runway is a mile-long oval, the **Makaeo Path**, with gardens and exercise stations. You're sure to meet fitness-minded locals.

SNORKEL: **Papawai Bay** has excellent snorkeling for experienced flipper fiends. Access the bay using the Keahuolu hike described above. Though coral is scarce, plenty of fish swim in this marine conservation district. Entry is over smooth lava near shore, not easy but not bad. Advanced snorkelers will want to swim out a narrow channel near the point and head north toward **Kaiwi Point**, the dive spot. *Be Aware:* There is usually current in the bay, stronger near the point. Wave action increases this hazard.

Locals head to the south end of **Old Airport** to a **keiki beach**. A flat reef near Kukailimoku Point has a protected swimming pond with a sandy bottom. You may spot sea horses swimming with tiny fish. *Driving:* Park behind the swim center at the south end of the runway. Walk left across the playing field toward goal posts. Go through an opening in the wall, cross a private road, and look for a Shoreline Public Access walkway.

SURF: The reef break offshore of the middle of the park is called **Old Airport** by local surfers. Conditions have to be right for this break to attract much of a crowd. Reef rash and worse await the novice in these shallow and rocky waters.

23. KAILUA-KONA   HIKE, SNORKEL, SURF

WHAT'S BEST: Kamehameha the Great, who could have lived anywhere he wanted, spent his final years at this little bay. Yes, Kailua has its cheesy and shabby accents, but you'll also find the romantic charm of a tropical Pacific port.

PARKING: From Hwy. 19, turn seaward on Palani Rd. Continue past a big shopping center and turn left on Kuakini Hwy. Pass the Kona Seaside and turn right into a free public lot on Likana. *If the Likana lot is full,* go back out to Kuakini, turn right, and continue to Hualalai Rd., where you turn right again. A free public lot will be on the left past the library. There are also a number of cheap you-pay lots between Ali'i and Kuakini.

HIKE: Kailua Town Stroll (1.75 mi.)

Begin the **Kailua Town Stroll** by walking down Likana and going right on Ali'i Drive. At the corner is the **King Kamehameha Hotel** (now Courtyard by Marriott), built in the '70s and featuring museum-quality paintings and ancient memorabilia, such as

a full feather cape and headdress. Artwork includes dozens of works by Herb Kane, and a display holds sportfishing trophies from the boozy 1950s that attracted actors like Lee Marvin and Richard Boone. Then duck out the back to see **Ahuena Heiau** sitting on the placid waters of **Kamakahonu Beach**. Ahuena (a re-creation) was Kamehameha's post-conquest place of worship, where he retired the war god and dedicated the temple to Lono, the god of peace and fertility. Kamehameha II, or Liholiho, was educated here, which was the capital of the Hawaiian Islands, from 1812 to 1819.

Jog left from the heiau grounds to **Kailua Pier**, home to cocktail sunset cruises, and also where the swim portion of the **Ironman Triathlon** draws a huge crowd every October. Continue down the seawall to the far end of the bay to **Hulihe'e Palace**, built in 1838 as a home for the Big Island's second governor, John Adams Kuakini. From the garden path along the seaside wall is an attractive look at the coral-and-lava rock structure. Banyans and other large trees provide atmosphere. Native hardwoods gleam in the interior, which is chockablock with the personal effects of post-missionary royal families. Across the street from the palace is **Mokuaikaue Church**, built a year earlier than the governor's house. The stone edifice, with a 112-foot steeple, is an upgrade of the thatched-roof model built in 1820 by the first missionaries to arrive in the Hawaiian Islands. Go inside to feel the sea-breeze air conditioning, an innovation of Reverend Asa Thurston.

MOKUAIKAUE CHURCH, HULIHE'E PALACE

Continuing along the ocean side of Ali'i, you can jog into the boardwalks of the **Kona Inn Shopping Village**, where budget-priced tourist stuff is piled in a series of cozy storefronts. In back of the **Kona Inn Restaurant**, which dates from 1928, is a spacious lawn and seawall where you can take a break. Just down the street from the shopping village is **Hale Halawai Park**. Behind this drab community center is a palm-lined path that is the grandstand for some of the world's best bodyboarding. Surfers peel into **Oneo Bay**—where the sport was invented in the 1960s. A few shops have closed on this southern end of Kailua: too far for cruise ship people to walk.

SNORKEL: Parade through Kailua in your swimsuit to try three, pretty good swimming beaches. The best is **Kamakahonu Beach**, behind the King Kam Hotel. A sandy beach with gradual entry leads to the protected inlet between the pier and the Ahuena Heiau. During calmer periods, experienced snorkelers can flipper beyond the pier and angle right toward the deeper water and coral off **Kukailimoku Point**. *Be Aware:* Rougher water and stinging sea urchins (on rocks) require your attention at the point.

Locals like **Kailua Pier Beach**, a little nook to the left at the base of the pier. Stash your towel and slippers in the wooden shelving on the busy sidewalk made for this purpose. Coral heads are near shore in a large area roped from the bay's boat traffic. At the opposite side of the bay from the pier—the far end of the seawall—is tiny **Kanuha Beach**. This little nook has more privacy than its cousin across the bay.

SURF: As mentioned in the Kailua stroll, **Hale Halawai** is a well-known bodyboarding spot. Locals call the beach **Spinners**. A reef just offshore creates a long right-break that rolls into little **Oneo Bay**. In the afternoons, the sun back-lights the translucent barrels. Due to the reef and submerged rocks, Spinners is not for learners.

24. HOLUALOA BAY   HIKE, SNORKEL, SURF

WHAT'S BEST: Kings and dudes have been surfing here for centuries. And hiding in plain view next to the bay is an overgrown state historic park.

PARKING: From Kailua, go south on Ali'i Dr., past Royal Poinciana Dr. and mm3. Park on the shoulder where the road skirts the bayshore. *Notes:* You can also go south past Kailua on Hwy.11 and take Kamehameha III Rd. down to Ali'i. Activities take place along a mile-long stretch of Ali'i.

HIKE: Keolonahihi State Historic Park (up to .5-mi.)

The 12-acre **Keolonahihi State Historic Park** is overgrown and unsigned. As yet, no trails exist among the two-dozen sites, which include a surfing shrine. The state purchased the property in 1990, originally named Kamoa Point Historic Park. To get a cover-shot of the surfers riding into the bay, walk the road's shoulder to the south end of the bay. From there walk a seawall to a trail that curves toward the point. The going gets tougher when you pass the rocky inlet where the boarders put in. *Note*: An easier Shoreline Public Access path is at the south end of the park; drive to just before Ke Alohi Kai Place.

SNORKEL: Don't bring your fins to **Riviera Pool**, but do bring the mask and kids, if you have either with you. A short gravel path ends at a large man-made, seaside infinity pool. *Driving:* Look for a Shoreline Public Access sign about .25-mile south of mm2 on Ali'i Drive. Turn makai into a small parking lot in front of the Kona by the Sea condos. *Be Aware:* The pool loses its appeal at low tide.

SURF: Holualoa Bay's south point break is a long left slide, known locally as **Lymans**. Hawaiians have been surfing here since waves were invented. The north side of Holualoa Bay, which people call **Banyans**, also sees action, including Hawaii Surfing Association events. It's across from Banyan Mart, .25-mile north of mm3. Board surfers also scope the reef break from Riviera Pool, at a place called **Rivies**, which is just offshore of the Kona Riviera Villas. Shallow reef makes this less popular than the other two places.

HALE HALEWAI AT SPINNERS, BANYANS, RIVIERA POOL

WHAT'S BEST: At the south end of Ali'i Drive is the Big Island's most popular family snorkeling spot. And nearby sea geysers highlight a wave-watchers stroll.

PARKING: Take Hwy. 11 south from Kailua. After mm118, turn makai on Kamehameha III Rd. Continue to the bottom of the hill. Turn right on Ali'i Dr., and go left at the shopping center traffic light. *For Keahou Blowholes:* Look for Shoreline Public Access at Keahou Surf & Racquet Club, address 78-6800. Park outside the gate. *For Kahalu'u Beach Park*, continue on Ali'i to mm4.5. The large parking lot fills up early.

HIKE: Kahalu'u Bay stroll (up to 1.25-mi.); Keahou Surf Blowholes (.75-mi.)

Warm up between snorkeling dunks with a **Kahalu'u Bay stroll**. To the north, or right as you face the water, weave through bodies, sand, and lava wall until you have to hop up to the road. Sitting on the tip of lava is the doll house **St. Peters Catholic**

KAHALU'U BEACH PARK

Church. As a statement of virtue, the church was built atop the sacred site of the "pagan" **Kuemanu Heiau**, where the ancients prayed for good surfing. The brackish pool of **Waikui** is where the fabled board riders would cleanse themselves.

Heading south from the beach park takes you into the lovely gardens of the former **Keauhou Beach Hotel**, where sacred **Po'o Pool** and a replica of King David Kalakaua's beach cottage are a quiet break from the beach scene. Along the water at the hotel is the tidal lagoon of **Kealiaia** and the 4,000-foot semicircle of boulders, the **Menehune Breakwater** built by the earliest Polynesians.

To reach the **Keauhou Surf Blowholes**, walk into the condo complex. To the right next to the tennis courts —talk about juxtaposition—are the remains of a 15th century heiau, **Lonoikamakahiki**. To the left of the entrance, between buildings, is a paved coastal path. Go left. When the big waves are rolling, this is a front row seat. The asphalt ends and you'll need to take a short lava trail to the edge of the golf course. Follow the fringe of the fairway and you'll find two openings in the reef, where pressurized sea water spurts in explosive geysers. You may get wet. *More Stuff:* Continue south on a coastal path to reach **He'eia Bay**, which is described in the next trailhead.

SNORKEL: It's best to show up early at **Kahalu'u Beach Park**, both to find parking and for the best snorkeling. The half-mile wide bay has sandy entrance channels, often made cozy by the legs of fellow fish-seekers, near the lifeguard station. The bay is shallow, protected by a long reef, and filled with just about every colorful fish in Hawaii. Turtles usually join in the fun. *Be Aware:* A rip current empties the bay to the right, heading out in front of the little church. Don't be shy about getting tips from one of the lifeguards. Also, those mushroom rocks offshore are living coral, which have been dying off because of people. Don't step on the coral. One last thing: It's against state law to feed fish in the bay.

The snorkeling at **White Sands Beach Park** (just north on Ali'i near mm4) is only fair, due to a rocky entry and onshore surf. During epic winter surf the fine sand at this beach leaves overnight, like the gal in a country song. The sand, scrubbed white and clean, gradually returns—hence this park is also known as **Disappearing Sands** or **Magic Sands**. Another alias is **La'aloa Beach Park**. During low surf, the best snorkeling is at a rocky inlet south of the park. **Pahoehoe Beach Park** (just north of White Sands), with a lawn shaded by large trees, is a place to sit a spell.

SURF: In the shadow of the surfing heiau, experienced surfers ride the offshore reef break at the north side of **Kahalu'u Bay**. The strong rip current and jagged rocks should deter beginners. The heiau is a good place to be a spectator. When the sand is back in the summer, **White Sand Beach Park** is a training ground for bodysurfers who can try a mellow shore break. When surf's up, the point break attracts bodysurfers to championship competitions.

26. KEAUHOU BAY   HIKE, SNORKEL, SURF

WHAT'S BEST: King Kamehameha III was born at this deep inlet that today is the starting point for snorkeling and a coastal hike. Nearby is where the last battle among Big Island royalty took place, and also Kona's swankiest resort.

PARKING: *For all activities:* Take Hwy. 11 south from Kailua-Kona to Kamehameha III Rd., which is south of mm118. Turn makai and continue to the bottom of the hill. *For Keauhou Bay and Kuamo'o Battlefield* go left on Ali'i Dr. *Then, for Keauhou Bay,* pass mm6.5 and turn right on Kaleiopapa Rd., follow to the end, and park near the docks.

KEAUHOU BAY

For the Kuamoʻo Battlefield hike, pass the turnoff to the bay. Park at a signed trailhead, on the left—after the by-pass road goes straight and where Aliʻi makes a sweeping right.

For Heʻeia Bay: At the bottom of the hill on Kam III Rd., go straight across Aliʻi Dr. Turn right on Manukai and look for a Shoreline Public Access sign on your left, just past Heʻeia Way. *Note:* If you continue on Kamehameha III Rd. you reach a cul-de-sac on north side of Keauhou Bay across from the parking described above—recommended access for busy days.

HIKE: **Keauhou Bay (.5-mi.); Heʻeia Bay (1.25 mi.); Kuamoʻo Battlefield (1.5 mi.)**

Talk Story: In 1814, Kalani Kauikeaouli, or Kamehameha III, was still-born in the shade of this cliff, and massaged to life by a kahuna on the rock that now has a plaque that commemorates the event. By age 11, both the boy's father, Kamehameha the Great, and elder brother, Liholiho, or Kamehameha II, had died. Although Kauikeaouli was now king, the monarchy was ruled at first by matriarchal prime ministers—his mother Keopuolani, and Kam I's favorite wife, Queen Kaʻahumanu. Rebelling against the womens' abolishment of the old kapu system, the young king spent his youth gambling, boozing, surfing, and chasing girls. Some things never change. But after his beloved sister died in 1836, Kamehameha III embraced his responsibility and became Hawaii's longest ruling monarch—for 29 years until his death in 1854.

Begin the **Keauhou Bay** stroll on a lush path along the cliff near the modest dockside buildings. From the end of the short path, walk across the dock area (site for tour departures) to the seawall that protects **Keauhou Park**. Up a grassy hillside is the storage shed for the local canoe club. Picnic tables and large trees make this a good sitting spot. You can continue around the bay, walking a lava wall seaward from the park.

From the parking off Manukai Street, a short path leads less than .25-mile down to tiny and wild **Heʻeia Bay**. At the bottom veer right, past the chirps of a bird study station, to a lava-and-coral path near the water. Go right, toward the low point with a lone kiawe tree, and pick up a cinder path that runs alongside the seawall of **Kanaloa Resort**. If energetic, you can continue past the Keahou Surf Blowholes and **Makolea Beach** to reach **Kahaluʻu Beach Park**.

From the Aliʻi Drive trailhead, a wide gravel path leads toward the **Kuamoʻo Battlefield**. The jewel of this hike is near the beginning, where the path makes a 90-degree left turn. When the big surf arrives, take a short trail to the right to a nook on **Kualanui Point**, where the waves roll by and explode against the lava shore. The main path continues alongside the frothy waters of **Maihi Bay**. Inland, those rock stacks you see are the burial mounds of **Lekeleke**. As the trail climbs, you reach a cattle gate. Head to the right on a rugged trail to **Kuamoʻo Point** for a great view and a look at a 20-foot-square lava shrine with a kiawe growing in the center. *More Stuff:* The main trail continues over cobbles, passing new homes, to a divot on the coast called **Paʻaoao Bay**, which should delight vowel fans. *Talk Story:* In November of 1819, six months after the death of his father, young King Kamehameha II used muskets to defeat the forces of Chief Kekuaokalina. The conflict was over reforms brought on by the new king at the behest of his mother, Keopuolani, and Kam I's favorite wife, Queen Kaʻahumanu. The royal women simply ate beside the king at a formal feast, thus flaunting the age-old system of kapus that, among other prohibitions, limited the rights of women. All the kapus were thus questioned, and the battle was on.

KUALANUI POINT

SNORKEL: **Keauhou Bay** has good swimming and decent snorkeling. Entry is easy from rock steps that lead down from the seawall. Water clarity improves as you swim out, though the bay is not known for visibility. Stay to your right near the shore, and you'll swim over coral heads. *Be Aware:* Avoid boat traffic.

The **Keauhou Sundeck**, is a familiar name for teensy-weensy **Mukukanekaula Island** at the south mouth the bay. *Driving:* As you head down Kaleiopapa Road toward the Keahou Bay, turn left on Ehukai Street. Continue for less than .25-mile, and look for Shoreline Public Access on the right where a tall lava wall ends. Park on the left in the lot for the **Sheraton Keahou Resort**. A lovely garden path curves to a lava reef. The sundeck is to the right, just offshore—a rock platform sticking about eight feet above the water. Snorkeling is excellent around the rocks. *Be Aware*: Big surf and tidal surge can make entry iffy, or downright dangerous. Watch the water for at least 10 minutes before entering. The **Sheraton Keahou**, quietly one of the island's better resorts, features an inner courtyard with a waterfall, oceanside garden terraces with a chapel, and a large lanai area perched over the bay—where at night the spotlights shine on **Manta Ray Village**, a popular dive spot.

SURF: Board surfers try the offshore break at **He'eia Bay**, a.k.a., **Walker Bay**, after Reverend Shannon Walker who ran a youth camp here in the old days. The main hazard is the point-blank slam of the waves into a bouldered shore.

27. KEALAKEKUA BAY   HIKE, SNORKEL, SURF

WHAT'S BEST: The cliffs rising above Kealakekua Bay are the Big Island's signature seascape. This is where Captain James Cook took his last breath, and where you'll find some of the best snorkeling in the islands. A nearby village walk is a true getaway.

PARKING: Take Hwy. 11 south from Kailua-Kona. Veer right toward Kealakekua Bay, on Napo'opo'o Rd., which is at mm110.5. *For Captain Cook Monument:* Park at a turnout immediately on the left after veering from the highway. *For all other activities:* Continue on Napo'opo'o Rd. for about 5 mi. At the bottom, you'll come to a stop sign and T-intersection, directly across from which is Napo'opo'o Wharf. Directions continue below.

HIKE: Captain Cook Monument (4.25 mi., 1,325 ft.); Manini Beach Park (up to .5-mi.); Ke'ei Village to: Palemano Point (1.5 mi.) and Ke'ei Seapool (2.25 mi.)

The hike and snorkel to **Captain Cook Monument** is a two-punch knockout, which has become more popular among adventure seekers since kayakers can no longer reach the monument from Kealakekua Bay. From the parking spot, cross the road, walk down a hundred feet, and take a wide path that goes right through tall cane at telephone pole #4 (looks like a 1, across from address 81-6236). Once on the trail, pass a dirt drive that veers right. You'll descend through seed cane, under big mango

CAPTAIN COOK MONUMENT

trees, down a steady, straight grade for the first mile. The vegetation becomes scarce as you approach the trail's only switchback, an a'a lava perch that overlooks **Ka'awaloa Point**. Go left here and take another long ramp to the bottom. There, the wall-lined path heads under the shade of big kiawes straight to the water. Although the monument is a short distance to the left, go straight to see the plaque that marks Cook's last stand, on February 14, 1779. At low tide you'll see it on a rock, under the curling horizontal branches of a large tree. *Talk Story:* Monumental ironies surround Captain James Cook's death, not the least of which was that this man, among the greatest of all seafaring navigators, could not swim, and therefore not reach a rowboat that rescued other members of his party. Walk over to the monument itself. The 28-foot white spire was erected by some of Cook's countrymen in 1874 and is actually British sovereign soil. On the land behind the monument are the remains of **Ka'awaloa Village**, including several heiaus. **Puhina O Lono Heiau**, where the bones of the English faux lono were interred is off the trail on the way down just north of the switchback. (Cook arrived during the Makahiki Festival and the Hawaiians first thought him to be an incarnation of Lono, their God of peace and fertility.) *Be Aware:* Conditioned hikers will have no trouble with this walk, but bring plenty of water and sun protection.

Manini Beach Park is one of the most dramatically scenic spots on the island. It's easy to miss. *Driving:* Go left at the Napo'opo'o Wharf, continue for about .25-mile, and turn right on narrow Manini Beach Road. Park where the beach road turns left. You'll see a gate and short beach access trail leading to the little park with its row of palms and views across the bay to the cliffs. Continue to the storm-washed point and hook left for less than .25-mile to reach the tiny coral cove of **Kahauloa Bay**.

Ke'ei Village, with its lava walls surrounding weathered cottages, blue-tarp awnings, and eclectic outdoor furniture, is tucked away from touristville. It's jumpin' on nice weekends, but on Wednesdays you might not scare up a cat. *Driving:* Turn left at Napo'opo'o Wharf. Pass Kahauloa and, .2-mile farther, go right on unpaved, unsigned Keawaiki Road. (The main road continues 3 miles to Pu'uhonua o Honaunau.) Another bumpy road joins from the right after .25-mile. Continue as the road hooks left and reaches the first buildings. Be sure not to block driveways when you park.

To get to the portrait-quality bay view from **Palemano Point** and continue to the **Ke'ei Seapool**, walk down the village road. Lava walls and tropical trees line the route, and the detail of village life will be hard to take in on one pass. Walk along a mortared seawall that takes you to the run of sand and coral rubble that is **Ke'ei Beach**. Palemano Point is beyond the beach, on the low, pahoehoe lava fields, where a 4-foot-high upright pipe marks the spot of the south mouth of Kealakekua Bay. Across a mile of water is the Cook Monument, and the white Ka'awaloa Lighthouse sits seaward of the monument, looking like its twin. Continue south on the smooth lava to the large pavilion of **Maluhia Camp**, fringed by coco palms and a lawn. The partially man-made **Ke'ei Seapool** is set in the lava reef opposite the pavilion, at the shore of rough **Mokuhai Bay**.

Talk Story: Inland is where the Battle of Mokuohai took place in 1782. Hawaiian Chief Kalaniopu'u had just died, leaving lands to his son, Kiwalao, while the war god Ku was entrusted to Kamehameha, then a strapping 24-year-old. A power vacuum created a struggle for land. The Kamehameha's forces were greatly outnumbered by those of Kiwalao, but the Lonely One was joined by his older mentor, the famed warrior Kekuhaupio, who was born in Ke'ei. They were able to use the treacherous a'a fields to outmaneuver the enemy, and the victory established Kamehameha's reputation.

SNORKEL: Take the plunge off the concrete jetty at the **Captain Cook Monument** to find snorkeling unsurpassed in the state. By late morning, tour boats normally lay anchor and drop dozens of flipper fiends. A multi-species coral reef boils downward to blue water 50-feet deep offshore. If you swim out into the bay you may see some of the 100 or more spinner dolphin who make their home in this 315-acre state underwater park.

Snorkeling is also good-to-excellent at the **Kealakekua Bay State Historical Park**. *Driving:* To reach the park, turn right at the Napo'opo'o Wharf and drive a short distance to road's end. If you sense crowds, park at the wharf (when the gate is open). Walk to the right of the seawall in front of the heiau to the cove and get comfortable on the beach boulders deposited by Hurricane Dot in 1969. Swim out to the rocks and circle left to find the best coral and fish. *Be Aware*: Shore break can knock you down and create unwelcome current. Rocks make the entry tough on the tootsies.

Talk Story: At the park is **Hikiau Heiau**. Once adorned with thatched platforms and an array of akua ki (wooden carvings of gods), this 18-foot high fortress was the first thing the crew of the Cook's *Endeavour* saw when they sailed into Kealakekua in January of 1779. Also atop the 2,500-square-foot platform were the crossed poles with tapa cloth hanging from them, symbols of the god Lono and the Makahiki peace-and-harvest festival that took place over the winter months. These symbols of Lono mirrored the

KE'EI BEACH

white sails of the ship's mast. Thousands of Hawaiians took to their canoes and Cook was welcomed as an incarnation of Lono. Everything was hunky-dory when the British sailors left, but a broken spar forced their return. Makahiki was over. When one of the ship's dories was stolen for its iron nails, the local Chief Kalaniopu'u was taken hostage. The crisis ended with Cook's killing and the death of several Hawaiians on the shores of the bay where the monument now stands.

Snorkeling is good at **Manini Beach Park**, although better choices nearby make this a less-popular destination. Look for a narrow sand channel through the reef, to the right just as you enter the park grounds. The **Ke'ei Seapool** (see *Hike* above) is a fun place to take an adventure dunk. Easiest entry in the middle of the pool, on the side opposite your approach. Study your exit, since you have to climb out; surf shoes are recommended. On calm days, explore the sea caves just outside the pool. *Be Aware:* During high surf, watch out for surge under rocks on both ends of the pool.

SURF: Bodyboarding is a big draw at **Kealakekua Historical Park**. The action is usually at the section closest to the seawall, which is also a good grandstand. Board surfers like the triple-tiered left-break at **Manini Beach Park**. They paddle out via the sand channel to the right as you enter the park. For the ultimate view, walk to the coral-and-rubble lava on the point. **Ke'ei Beach** is a status surfing spot with a rich tradition—and a big offshore break onto a shallow reef. Broken boards and bones are not uncommon. Long rides are the lure. When visiting by canoe in the 1840s, Mark Twain told of a surfer who "would fling his board upon a foamy crest and come whizzing by like a bombshell." Those guys are still doing it. Bring binoculars to get a look.

KEALAKEKUA BAY FROM MANINI BEACH PARK

28. PU'UHONUA O HONAUNAU NATIONAL PARK   HIKE, SNORKEL

WHAT'S BEST: This well-designed place of refuge, a national historic park, attracts scads of visitors. And the coastal trail and excellent snorkeling keeps them coming back.

PARKING: Take Hwy. 11 south from Captain Cook. Just south of mm104, turn makai at Hwy. 160, a.k.a., Keala O Keawe Rd. Continue downhill for about 4 mi. and turn left into the Pu'uhonua o Honaunau National Historic Park. *Notes:* An admission is charged to enter the park. The visitors center is open daily from 8 to 5:30. The beach park is open until 11 on weekends and holidays. *Alternate access:* Take the 3-mi. paved, no-shoulder road along the jagged lava shore from Kealakekua Bay.

HIKE: Pu'uhonua o Honaunau National Historic Park (.25-mi.); Pu'uhonua Beach Park to Ki'ilae Village coastal trail (3 mi., more or less)

Accept your park map and wander at will in **Pu'uhonua o Honaunau.** *Talk Story:* Tourist tongues had it easier when this place was called by its anglicized misnomer, City of Refuge. (Since it never was a city, and for cultural reasons, the name was changed in 1978.) Like others in the islands, it was where defeated warriors and violators of the kapu system could go voluntarily to escape punishment. When justice was a swift club, people break into jail. For minor kapu violations, the stay was overnight. Confinement appeased the gods, who would otherwise punish everyone with earthquakes, tidal waves, and volcanic eruptions. The park's premier attraction is the **Great Wall**—10-feet high, 7-feet thick, 1,000-feet long—that was dry-stacked in 1550 to separate the

HALE O KEAWE, PU'UHONUA O HONAUNAU

royals of Honaunau from the dwellers of the puʻuhonua. Coco palms sway over the park's re-created structures, all set beside little **Keoneʻele Beach**, a canoe landing that is an inlet of Honaunau Bay. Thatched-roofed **Hale o Keawe**, where the bones of 23 chiefs were interred, is prominent on the grounds, as is **Alealea Heiau**, a platform for sports and games. On many days, canoe carvers, weavers, and other Hawaiian artisans ply their trade. In 1920, establishment of a county park halted a deterioration of the site, and in 1961 the 180 acres became National Historic Park.

Puʻuhonua Beach Park is a pretty strip of sand, shaded by false kamani and coconut palms. A broad pahoehoe reef buffers the coast, and whales cruise outside the surf line in winter. *Driving:* Go to the left at the far end of the parking lot and take an unpaved road. You'll cross a narrow lava section (and one access to the village trail) before the road curves left on its quarter-mile journey to the park's beachside tables. The **Kiʻilae Village coastal trail** is at the far end of the picnic area. After a few minutes of walking, walls and enclosures of the village will appear to the left as the route veers toward the greenery-topped **Keaneʻe Cliffs**. A coral-sand beach at **Alahaka Bay** offers wading opportunities. After hiking over wide-open lava, you reach a junction for the trail that loops back to the left, toward the visitors center. The more scenic choice is to continue down the coast. About .5-mile into the walk, the road meets the cliffs, climbing up 25 feet or so in a cobblestone ramp—a historic piece of roadwork. At the top of this rise, look left for a cave, gated closed, which turns out to be a 150-foot-long lava tube that extends to an opening in the cliffs over little **Kiʻilae Bay**. (For generations, locals have jumped from here, as well as from the cliffs to the right of the cave opening, but park people have been cracking down on this risky frivolity.) Just past the cliff, on the right,

is the rock enclosure for the **grave of John Kekuiwa**, the last native Hawaiian to live here, who died in 1927. The trail continues south on more of an 1871 road that goes for several miles to **Hoʻokena**. You walk beside big kiawe trees, veering inland from the ocean and **Loa Point**. Footing is not the greatest—on original cobblestones—but the path is wide and pleasant. About .8-mile from the trailhead is the south boundary of the national park, but the route continues. Turnaround whenever, or power-stride for another 45 minutes to get a look toward Hoʻokena. *Be Aware:* Kiawe shoots and young trees can be a hassle in places, depending greatly on recent prunings.

SNORKEL: Those in the know head for **Two Step** at **Honaunau Bay** for the best drive-up snorkeling on the Big Island of Hawaii. Don't expect sand, but you can spread your towel on tabletops of smooth lava. The place can be a zoo on weekends when conditions are good. *Driving:* Turn right on a one-way lane just before the national park entrance, and continue a short distance to the boat ramp area where the road makes a 90-degree right turn. If parking is jammed, use the reasonably priced private lot across the street run by local guys. Or, better yet, walk over from the national park.

The 'two steps,' which are actually three or four, are opposite the entrance to this locals' parking lot. Walk across the smooth lava reef. You come to a ledge that has another ledge beneath it that gets washed by waves, and beneath that is a third, submerged ledge. Sit on the top ledge, gear up, then drop the fanny to the step below and use the submerged step to slide into water that is at least six feet deep. Off you go. Very clear water and lots of fish and coral await in the big oval of Honaunau Bay. Hug the shore or swim over toward the reefs at Puʻuhonua o Honaunau. Waters near shore will be around 30-feet deep, but the coral gets closer to the surface farther out. Angle to the right about 200 feet, and you'll see an "ALOHA" written in cinder blocks on a sandy bottom. On rough water days, some people and kids enter at the **Kapuwai boat ramp nearby**, although a shallow reef makes it iffy to swim out to the deeper water. *Be Aware:* Swell surge can raise the water several feet at the Two Step entry. Relax and let the swells lift you up. If waves are crashing on the upper reef, however, only advanced snorkelers will want to get in.

TWO STEP

Although not a snorkeling spot, the **keiki ponds** at **Pu'uhonua Beach Park** are scenic places for picnicking families to take a dunk. About midway in the park, walk out to the reef about 200 hundred feet. You'll see an amorphous shaped pool or two. Pool depth changes with the tides, and high waves can sometimes breach the reef, creating a hazard. On the calmest of days, snorkeling is good at the outer edge of the reef.

29. HO'OKENA BEACH PARK   HIKE, SNORKEL, SURF

> **WHAT'S BEST:** While not on everyone's "A" list, this popular fine-sand cove offers big mana, a remote hiking coast, and, on the right day, good snorkeling.

> **PARKING:** Take Hwy. 11 south from Captain Cook and the Hwy. 160 jct. After the school at mm101.4, turn makai on Ho'okena Beach Rd. Go down for about 2.25 mi. and veer left along a low lava wall to an unpaved parking lot at the beach park.

HIKE: Ho'okena Beach Park to Kealia Beach (1.5 mi. or more)

Talk Story: Now popular among campers, **Ho'okena Beach Park** in the late 1800s was a bustling trading village, where island beef and other commodities would go by steamer to Honolulu. Author Robert Louis Stevenson got his trousers wet at **Kupa Landing**, the ruins of which are in front of the parking area. Cliffs and a shock of tropical trees lie behind a gray crescent beach that receives the shore break of **Kauhako Bay**. By 1930, automobiles had driven the steamers out of business. Today, the landing is memorialized by a local group, **Friends of Ho'okena Beach** (328-8430), which has been able to ward off a major development at **Kealia Beach**; buy those drinks at their booth and help 'em out.

Begin the **Kealia Beach** hike along the coast in front of a picnic pavilion. You'll immediately come to where an unpaved lane joins the coast; you can drive to this point by turning right across from the entrance to the beach park. After a few minutes the road passes the crumbling walls of the old Catholic church that was abandoned after storm damage in the late 1800s and relocated to become the Painted Church above Kealakekua Bay. As you continue along the coast, coral chunks and lava rocks abound on the low onshore reef that extends for about 2 miles to **Loa Point**. After less than .5-mile on this coastal road, you reach houses and need to veer onto the lava, where you'll find the coarse white sand of **Kealia Beach**. *More Stuff:* Adventure hikers keep on trekking the historic route to Pu'uhonua o Honaunau.

SNORKEL: Most people snorkel **Kauhako Bay** at **Ho'okena Beach Park** on the south end, taking advantage of an easy shore access. But you'll see more coral and fish in the deeper waters of the **Kupa Landing** ruins, located by the parking area. Entry at the landing is more difficult, over rocks and some concrete. *Be Aware:* Surf can make water visibility poor. More experienced snorkelers can try their luck at remote **Kealia**

KEIKI POND AT PUʻUHONUA O HONAUNAU BEACH PARK

Beach. Palms and beach trees make for a cozy backshore. Snorkeling can be very good, but surf and current can cause problems.

CANOE BLESSING AT MILOLIʻI

SURF: Boogieboarders and bodysurfers like the left-slide into **Hoʻokena Beach**. The rollers are best in the summer, but winter storms also draw the short boarders.

30. MILOLIʻI   HIKE, SNORKEL, SURF

WHAT'S BEST: This authentic fishing village doesn't woo tourists and its links to ancient times may not be apparent at first, but seekers of Old Hawaii will want to pay a visit. On pretty days, the hike-to beach nearby is one of the island's eye-popping goodies.

PARKING: Take Hwy. 11 south of Captain Cook and Hoʻokena. Pass mm89 and turn makai on signed Miloliʻi Rd. Follow down for 5 mi., and pass homes and junk cars to the end of the narrow road. Park by the basketball court and picnic pavilion.

HIKE: Miloliʻi Beach Park to Honomalino Beach (1.25 mi.)

Talk Story: Outboards may have replaced canoe paddles, but the fishermen still net opelu, or mackerel, making Miloliʻi one of the few fishing villages that has survived to modern times. The rocky inlet just north of **Miloliʻi Beach Park** is where a cultural center is being developed to teach and preserve the old ways. This effort was furthered in 2003 with the launch and blessing of a traditional canoe, the first such ceremony in 85 years. A cultural event of a different nature took place at the shack that sits above the inlet, when Elvis filmed his 1962 bomb, *Girls, Girls, Girls!* And more recently, Hawaii's singing legend, the late Israel (Iz) Kamakawiwoʻole staged one of his last concerts in this hamlet. Near the picnic pavilion is yellow **Hauoli Kamanao**, the little church with big mana that hosts cultural events. In the 1980s, locals were able to convince backers of a resort complex to stay away from quiet Miloliʻi.

For the five-star walk to **Honomalino Beach**, take the road between the church and basketball court, threading your way to the right on a wall-lined shoreline public path. Lagoonlike **Ako Pond** will come up on your right. You'll cross a rock path at water's edge in front homes, on the other side of which is sandy **Omakaʻa Beach**. Then jog inland 50 feet, where a hand-drawn sign marks the trail—which continues to the right over rocks and branches. You drop into a gully and climb up a bit, passing a tree-shaded cemetery on the left and a sacred fishing shrine on the right. Shortly after the sacred site, the path pops out to an exposed section of aʻa lava and follows a utility line toward a good-sized palm grove. After this straight stretch, you'll come upon Honomalino, with its curving black-sand dune dotted with coconut palms. The snapshot view of the beach is from palm-covered **Kapulau Point**, the little tab that frames the north side of the bay. *More Stuff:* Trailblazers with happy feet can continue on a coastal trail south from Honomalino for 4 miles to **Niuou Point** and **Okoe Bay**, site of the Ahole Heiau and Holua, a slide. Additionally, if you want to see how vegetation fights its way through aʻa lava flows, pull off Highway 11 before Miloliʻi at mm90.5. A sign for **Kipahoehoe Natural Area Reserve** will be on the left, and on the right a crunchy road drops seaward. Ohia trees and ferns punch through the flows, dating from 1919.

SNORKEL: There can be no doubt of your genius if you have the good sense to be sitting in palm shade watching spinner dolphins circle the blue waters off **Honomalino Beach**, joined from time to time by a breaching whale farther out. Only occasional vog can take the some of the shine off the day. You can snorkel on either end of the beach, nearer the rocky points, but the north side by **Kapulau Point** may yield more

HONOMALINO BEACH

marine life. This beach has eroded some 75 feet in modern times and may not be here a century from now. Like all black sand beaches, the land giveth and the sea taketh away. *Be aware:* The water gets deep, right at the shore break.

Off the trail to Honomalino is a nice snorkeling nook, in tiny **Omaka'a Bay**. When you cross the gully below the cemetery, head 100 feet seaward and you will see a coarse-coral patch. You won't do much swimming in this small pool, but a fair few fish will be present near shore. Turbulence and rocks make swimming out from here not a good idea. At **Miloli'i Beach Park**, snorkeling can be good from the lava fingers that protrude from the ironwood grove at the shore—when surf cooperates.

SURF: Miloli'i Beach Park is a locals beach, since a shallow reef break and a long paddle out can get newcomers in trouble. The local guys gather south of the beach park, way offshore near **Moku o Kahailani** rock.

31. MANUKA STATE PARK   HIKE

WHAT'S BEST: Birders, botanists, and tree-huggers will make a special point to visit this native and exotic forest. Everyone else can appreciate the serene and expansive picnic spot, a refuge midway between Kona and Kilauea Volcano.

PARKING: Take Hwy. 11 south of Miloli'i. At mm83 enter the Manuka Natural Area Reserve. Before mm81, turn mauka at Manuka State Park.

HIKE: Manuka Nature Loop (2.5 mi., 400 ft.)

Enveloped by a 26,000-acre natural area reserve, **Manuka State Park** has an arboretum that surrounds a lawn and picnic area, plus comfort facilities. The 13-acre park section, established in 1952, sits just above the highway, an easy pull-off to take a break and short stroll amid the chirps of many birds. The **Manuka Nature Loop** starts at the back of the parking lot. *Be Aware:* It's advertised as 2 miles, but is actually longer, with some difficult footing in sections over a'a. Interpretive signs along the way label many of the 50 indigenous and 130 introduced trees and shrubs. Bring a plant book if you want lots of details. Keep your eyes peeled for Hawaii's state flower, the mao hauhele, a yellow hibiscus bush, as well as its cousin, the red-flowering hibiscus known as hau heleula—this trail is one of their few homes in the state.

The trail steps up a steady grade. A limb-and-leaf dome is high overhead, shading a healthy understory that includes lush ki and ferns. In about a mile you'll reach the **Pit Crater**. This overgrown, volcanic maw is an example of why you want to stay on trail. From the crater, the path hooks left. More ruins mark the highest elevation of the loop, near trailside marker #13. From here the trail makes a downward chute through vines, before reaching the last, homeward run through a'a lava and ohia.

More Stuff: A popular 4WD trip is **Road to the Sea**, a 7-mile, swath of bumpy cinder. *Driving:* The road begins just north of mm79. It travels through a 1908 Mauna Loa flow and reaches **Humuhumu Point**, a cone that is being eroded by the sea to form a green sand beach. About .25-mile before reaching the coast, a road veers right from Road to the Sea and goes to **Awili Point**, which is the green-and-black sand beach north of Humuhumu.

Additionally, big-league wilderness hikers who really want to wander native forest can attempt the **Kaheawai Trail**, an ancient route that drops 1,900 feet over 6 miles, and reaches the coast, about 3.5 miles south of Manuka Bay. *Driving:* The trailhead is hard to spot: Go south of the state park and continue .25-mile south of the reserve boundary sign. The trailhead is on top of a 15-foot high bank on the makai side of the road (at mm79.6). If you continue a short distance to Aloha Boulevard (boulevard?) and hang a U-turn, you can more easily see the trailhead sign. Only experienced hikers should try this trail. Most hikers make it a car-shuttle by going south at the coast to get a ride up on the Road to the Sea.

A few miles from Road to the Sea, the **Pu'u Ki Petroglyphs** will attract gung-ho Indiana-Jones types. The hike is almost 5 miles round-trip, exposed to harsh weather on a lava road. *Driving:* Go south on Highway 11, pass mm78 in Ocean View and turn makai toward the post office—on Prince Kuhio Boulevard. Then make your first left on Maile Drive, continue a mile past four roads, and turn makai on Kohala. Go down to the end and park. Walk about 2 miles toward the ocean, and veer left before reaching the coast at **Pohue Bay**. The large field of rock carvings lies near the pu'u on the mauka side. This walk can be a scorcher, so bring water and sun protection.

MANUKA STATE PARK

Mauna Loa

KILAUEA IKI CRATER

Mauna Loa is not spectacular at first sight, looking from a distance like an oval soup tureen turned upside down, albeit a large one, 30 miles by 60 miles. As seen on the horizon, the shape looks like the profile of a shield, hence the term "shield volcano." Then you learn that the "Long Mountain," when measured from its base on the seafloor, is nearly twice as high as Everest and is easily the planet's most massive mountain, containing 100 times the volume of mainland volcanoes, like St. Helens and Rainier. All this size has come from lava squirting up from the Pacific's Hot Spot, piling up and spreading out like cake batter.

And the fat lady hasn't sung yet. The big mountain has begun to inflate, and in 2002, the neighboring volcano of Kilauea sent forth a renewed river of lava toward the sea. Both cones are part of the huge Hawaii Volcanoes National Park, but the event has caused scientists to believe that they may also be geophysically related, so that swelling of Mauna Loa means more lava at Kilauea. A vent explosion in 2008 in the Halemaumau Crater, within Kilauea, supports this theory. Or perhaps a new eruption is brewing at Mauna Loa, which in 1984 sent a stream of lava to within 4 miles of Hilo.

Nobody knows for sure what's in store, but all visitors to the world's most active volcanic zone will appreciate that geology is not the study of rocks, but rather of rocks in *motion*. This appreciation will be underscored if their visit coincides with the next stage of Mauna Loa, the Giant Landslide Stage, when scientists speculate that the entire 4,000-foot-high mass of Kilauea may break loose and slide into the sea.

STEAMING CLIFFS, VOLCANOES NATIONAL PARK

PETROGLYPHS, CHAIN OF CRATERS ROAD

One of the best views of Mauna Loa is from South Point, where the southwest rift zone tapers gently into the sea. Yes, this is the most-southerly land in the United States, but to the Polynesian trans-Pacific voyagers this land was the far north, the end of a 2,000-plus-mile journey in open sailing canoes. A heiau commemorates this feat, first accomplished around 100 AD.

As you round South Point and proceed through Na'alehu, you have two opportunities to visit the shore before the highway heads up the volcano. Whittington Beach Park has serene ponds where shorebirds are happy, along with dock ruins from when cane was king—a pleasing rest stop or picnic place. Punalu'u Beach Park is a lovely black sand crescent on the tour-bus circuit; you can take in a large heiau here and enjoy an unusual lava trail over imbedded smooth rocks.

Inland from these beach parks is the rain forest that doesn't get any respect, the Kau Forest Reserve. Old volcanic vents of Ninole have eroded into buttes and filled in with rain-forest greenery. You can get up close in Wood Valley, or at several other trailheads into the forest reserve (and the newest section of the national park). Just up the mountain from the Kau Forest is the Ainapo Trail, the backdoor to the summit of the long mountain. Although few will attempt the grueling crusade to the summit, the lower reaches of the trail are a birdland forest, home to the Hawaiian goose, the nene.

Kilauea Crater is the centerpiece for Hawaii Volcanoes National Park, delivering scenic delights unsurpassed by any of America's mainland wonders. An 11-mile drive around the crater, the former lake of lava, can be done as a day trip. At Volcano House you're in a fern forest with a view over the expanse of lava. On the other side of the crater, you're in a steaming moonscape, site of the Halemaumau Crater, which spewed red-hot as recently as 1974. In between are excellent short hikes, like one to the floor of the Kilauea Iki Crater and the tourist-trot through the dripping cave that is the Thurston Lava Tube. Circling the caldera are the park's visitors center, Volcano House Hotel, Jaggar Museum, and Volcano Art Center. The 2008 blast from Halemaumau Crater has closed portions of the park temporarily—in geologic terms.

Stealing the thunder from Kilauea Crater—at least during the last two decades it has been roiling lava—is Pu'u O'o, which is off Chain of Craters Road. The 20-mile road drops to the coast, passing a dozen inactive craters before reaching sea level. Where the lava meets the sea is a towering plume of sulfuric steam. Depending on the day's conditions, and that's a big 'depending,' you can walk to view the steam tower a little closer. (To see lava these days, you need to head to Kalapana Bay.) From Pu'u Huluhulu, which is a short hike from upper Chain of Craters Road, is a long view of the fuming volcano. Pu'u Loa Petroglyphs, one of the island's better sites, is also down this road.

Hilina Pali is a 2,000-foot cliff reachable by a fork off Chain of Craters Road. Give it top marks as a view drive, with the potential to add on hikes of varying lengths. The stone hut at road's end is dramatic, set above the pali with a commanding view of the seacoast to South Point. The coastline below the pali has several shelters with water that combine to make for an excellent backpacker's circuit. Day hikers who want an all-day sucker can strap on the pack and go.

THURSTON LAVA TUBE

The upper slopes of big mountain are also part of the national park. A 10-mile drive takes you to the Mauna Loa Lookout, at almost 7,000 feet, where the summit trail begins. The lookout is a prime viewpoint for Kilauea Caldera, and a place to start up the mountain and gain an appreciation for its massive, domelike shape. On the way to the lookout is a family hike through a native forest that was spared lava flows, one of the better native-bird-viewing trails.

The windward side of Mauna Loa is lush and green, and includes the Olaʻa Rain Forest that is also part of the national park. You can catch a glimpse of these botanical marvels on a memorable hike through a tree fern forest (these things are as high as

PART OF MAUNA LOA OBSERVATORY

giraffes) in the Makaʻala Forest, which shares a border with the rain forest. Just down the mountain from this fanciful trail, is the Big Island's best rain forest hike, a challenging jaunt into the dank and ferny recesses of the Kahaualea Natural Area. The kicker for this hike is a view of Puʻu Oʻo.

To see the north side of Mauna Loa, you need to head up to the middle of Saddle Road—from either Kona or Hilo, take your pick. The Puʻu Oʻo Horse Trail is part of the old paniolo route, when the cattle from Parker Ranch were driven through the saddle and down to ships in Hilo Bay. The trail takes you across pahoehoe lava fields at 6,000 feet, fringed by ohia and koa forests, with the two big mountains rising like twin Kilamanjaros, north and south.

HALEMAUMAU CRATER FROM JAGGAR MUSEUM

If you really want to hike to the summit, the Mauna Loa Observatory Road is a best-kept secret. Beginning near the road to Mauna Kea, this paved tract is a way for passenger cars to get to the weather observatory at 11,000 feet. North Pit is still a bit of a stroll—about 8 miles round-trip and 2,000 feet —but it's definitely doable. Regardless, the view of Mauna Kea, Maui, and Hualalai are fabulous from the observatory. If you want to thank someone for teaching the human race about global warming and harmful particulates in the atmosphere, this is the place to do it. These under-funded scientists are watching out for Mother Earth—and keeping an eye on Madam Pele, who occasionally sends streams of lava their way from lofty heights.

ACTIVE PU'U O'O, FRESH LAVA

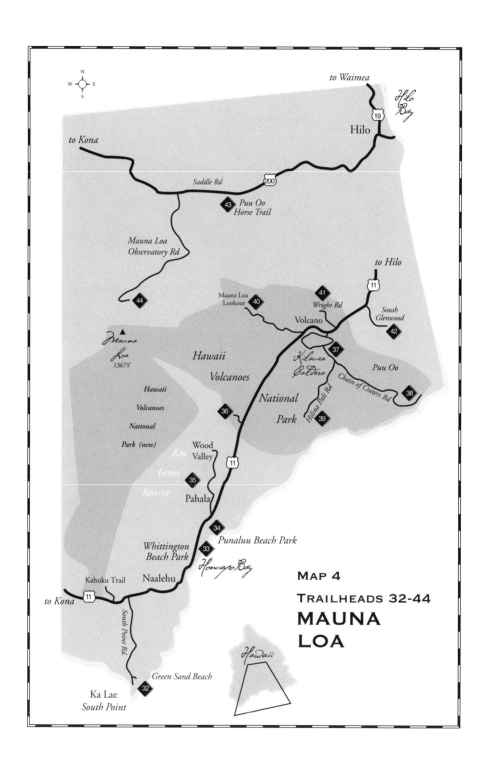

to Waimea

Hilo Bay

19

Hilo

to Kona

Saddle Rd

200

43 Puu Oo
Horse Trail

Mauna Loa
Observatory Rd

to Hilo

11

44

Mauna Loa
Lookout
40

41
Wright Rd

South
Glenwood

Volcano

42

Mauna
Loa
13679'

Hawaii

Volcanoes

Hawaii

Volcanoes

National

Park (new)

Kilauea
Caldera

37

Puu Oo

Chain of Craters Rd

38

National

Park

Hilina Pali Rd

39

36

Wood
Valley

Kau

Forest

35

11

Reserve

Pahala

34

Punaluu Beach Park

Whittington
Beach Park
33

Honuapo Bay

Kahuku Trail   Naalehu

to Kona
11

South Point Rd

MAP 4

TRAILHEADS 32-44

MAUNA
LOA

Hawaii

Green Sand Beach

32

Ka Lae
South Point

TRAILHEADS

32-44

TH :	TRAILHEAD
HIKE :	HIKES AND STROLLS
SNORKEL :	SNORKELING, SWIMMING
SURF :	BOARD, BODYBOARD, BODYSURF
MM :	MILE MARKER; CORRESPONDS TO HIGHWAY SIGNS
MAKAI :	TOWARD THE OCEAN
MAUKA :	INLAND, TOWARD THE MOUNTAINS

ALL HIKING DISTANCES IN PARENTHESES ARE ROUND TRIP. ELEVATION GAINS OF 100 FEET OR MORE ARE NOTED. SEE RESOURCE LINKS FOR CONTACTS AND TELEPHONE NUMBERS.

32. SOUTH POINT & KAHUKU/VOLCANOES N. P.   HIKE, SNORKEL

WHAT'S BEST: Stand at the most-southerly point in the Hawaiian Archipelago and hike to wild green sand beach. Or, trek a tropical pastures with views in the newest section of Hawaii Volcanoes National Park—but on weekends only.

PARKING: Take Hwy. 11 south of Miloli'i. *For South Point-Green Sand Beach:* Turn right (makai) at mm69.3 on signed South Point Rd. Continue on the one-lane paved road, past the wind farm generators. *For South Point,* veer right 10 mi. from the highway at a fork. Go another mile and park at an unpaved lot on the right. *For Green Sand Beach,* veer left at the fork and continue .75-mi. to a parking lot, or continue a little farther and park where the road loops. *Be Aware:* Leave your car free of valuables Bring water and prepare for wind and sun. *For Kahuku/Volcanoes National Park:* Turn left (mauka) before South Point at mm70.4. Hours are Saturday and Sunday, 9:30 to 3; closed first Saturday of the month.

HIKE: South Point-Canoe Ladders-Kalalea Heiau (1.5 mi., 150 ft.); Green Sand Beach (5 mi., 250 ft.); Kahuku/Volcanoes National Park (up to 11.5 mi., 675 ft.)

Ka Lae, "The Point," is where the first Polynesian voyagers are thought to have made landfall, and the entire southern tip of the Big Island is a national historic landmark. Fishermen still rely on the **canoe launch ladders** that descend a 30-foot cliff at the parking area. The deep seas are sometimes safe enough for swimming, but even the ancients were wary of the turbulent Halaea Current, named for a chief who was swept away in his canoe. To get to the **Kalalea Heiau** and the actual **South Point**, walk down the grassy road that parallels an old wall leading away from the canoe ladders. Within .25-mile you'll see the heiau (40-foot-square, low walls), which is dedicated to fishing gods and to the success of oceanic voyages. The two rocks nearby the heiau are symbols of Ku'ula, the fishing god, and his son, Aiai. Continue down the gradual slope to South Point, where the land gently tapers into the sea on the southwest rift zone of Mauna Loa. This taper continues down another five miles under the ocean's surface. Vegetation is scarce along this windswept shore, where currents from both sides of the island join. Since all the major Hawaiian Islands are well south of Florida, the more significant fact is that South Point is the tip of the 1,600-mile Hawaiian Archipelago.

For the popular, wind-blown hike to **Green Sand Beach**, walk down the rutted road to the boat launch

SOUTH POINT CANOE LADDERS

area at **Kaulana Bay**. Following a road, hang a left at the bay, passing through a pipe gate. Over the next mile or so the road undulates along low bluffs. At times, two or three routes interweave; it doesn't matter which you select. After about 1.5 miles you reach a grassy plain, from where **Pu'u Mahana** is visible—the cone sits above **Mahana Bay** and the beach. After crossing the grassy plain, you come upon the 80-foot cliff that forms the south shore of the bay and the olive-green beach. The trail down is over the lip of this cliff. Once you hop down, it's easy. A rock ledge and path traverses downward and inland, making a little switchback just above the beach. The beach owes its color to olivine, a gemstone that is eroded by wave action from the base of the pu'u.

The sloping, treed pastures of the **Kahuku Unit** are part of 116,000 acres of a historic ranch that were added to the national park in 2003, doubling its size. Too bad it's only open 7 days a month for 5.5 hours per day. **Kahuku Road** extends 5.6 miles in from the highway, passing five trailheads along the way. First up, after less than .5-mile, is the **Pu'u o Lokuana Trail**, a short stroll from a picnic area. The 2.6-mile **Palm Trail Loop** begins about 2 miles from the highway (and is also accessible via a second trailhead .8-mile farther). Volcanic fissures and a cinder cone contrast with green fields. Views are panoramic. About four miles from the highway is the **Lower Glover Trailhead**, starting point for the **Kona Trail**, which makes a 6-mile loop on either side of the road. The **Upper Glover Trailhead** is .75-mile farther, at road's end. From there, you can go right (on the Kona Trail again) for .6-mile and then keep left for another .75-mile to reach Kahuku's high point, at about two thousand feet.

More Stuff: The huge **Kau Forest Reserve** was formerly one of the best tropical forest hikes in all of Hawaii—before state planners erected a formidable fence to separate

KAU FOREST AT LORENZO ROAD

the reserve from the **Kahuku Unit** of the national park, which it borders. Previously, you could walk open pastures at the edge of the dense forest. But adventure hikers can still follow hunters' trails into a lush ohia-and-tree-fern forest, sprinkled with wild ginger. *Be Aware:* Getting lost is easy, so keep the fence in view. *Driving:* Turn mauka on **Lorenzo Road**, which is at mm69.5, on the Kona side of South Point Road. Drive up about a mile to where road narrows to a grassy lane; then walk or drive the grassy lane .35-mile to a forest reserve sign (passenger cars can usually navigate the lane).

SNORKEL: On rare calm days **Kaulana Bay** is the best spot around South Point, though not great. A boat landing provides easy entry, and the harbor offers protections from the swells. **Green Sand Beach** is better for wave play than snorkeling, and it's hardly worth the effort of dragging your gear along on the hike. The **canoe ladders**, believe it or not, can also have safe and excellent snorkeling, but to get in there requires a leap of faith. *Be Aware:* Waves, cliffs, and the current can make it risky.

33. WHITTINGTON BEACH PARK   HIKE, SNORKEL, SURF

WHAT'S BEST: A wild cove, serene tide pools, fishponds, and ruins from the sugar cane days—relax with the locals and shorebirds at a 500-acre coastal park.

PARKING: Take Hwy. 11 south, past South Point Rd. and Na'alehu. Descend a long grade, pass mm61 and, .5-mi. later, turn makai into Whittington Beach Park. Continue .25-mi. to an improved parking lot near restrooms.

WHITTINGTON BEACH PARK

HIKE: Whittington Park and Honuapo Tide Pools (up to .75-mi.)

Talk Story: At **Whittington Beach Park** is an interesting stroll along the shore of **Honuapo Bay**, which has twice been turned from thriving community to ghost town by raging tsunamis. The fishing village was wiped out in 1868. The sugar cane port, took the knockout in the big wave of 1946. In 2006, a wave of local citizens—Ka Ohana o Honuapo, see *Resource Links*, page 231—formed to halt commercial development of 225 acres of tide pools and fishponds next to the park.

You can see the pilings and other ruins off the lawn area of the **Whittington Beach Park**. Large mangos and a smattering of coco palms add to the scene, which is most dramatic as viewed from the base of the old wharf. To see the placid **Honuapo Tide Pools**, go left as you enter the park to decrepit concrete slabs associated with the sugar days, next to which are the fishponds. Shorebirds, including the white-tailed tropic birds that nest in nearby cliffs. The tide pools are offshore the fishpond.

SNORKEL: Under freakishly calm conditions, the base of the wharf ruins at **Whittington Beach Park** is an excellent place to snorkel. Fish like decaying pylons. But you are more likely to encounter rough seas unsuitable for dipping. Local kids and parents alike dip in the reef-protected **Honuapo Tide Pools**, a refuge on this rough coast.

SURF: If there are waves, then there will be surfers. At the south point of **Honuapo Bay** local boys ride a he-man left-break. Summer months are the best.

PUNALU'U (BLACK SAND) BEACH

34. PUNALU'U (BLACK SAND) BEACH   HIKE, SNORKEL, SURF

WHAT'S BEST: Pick a time when tour buses aren't lined up and you'll see why this is Hawaii's most popular black sand beach. At any time you can find solitude and ancient sites on intriguing coastal hikes.

PARKING: Take Hwy. 11 south from Kona, past Whittington Beach Park. At mm56.75, turn makai on Alanui Rd. *For Ninole Cove:* Turn right toward the Seamountain golf course; continue for 1.1 mi. and park below the clubhouse. *For Black Sand:* Continue nearly 1 mi. and park next to a picnic pavilion, or continue to the beach park. (You can also take Ninole Loop Rd. from the highway to the beach; turn at mm55.75.)

HIKE: Punalu'u (Black Sand) Beach to: Kane'ele'ele Heiau (.5-mi.), and Nahuluhulu Point (2.5 mi.); Ninole Cove (.5-mi., 100 ft.)

Talk Story: Punalu'u, known also as Black Sand Beach, has attracted tourists since the late 1800s, when it was a stopover for volcano-bound visitors. Its place name, "diving springs," derives from the sweet fresh water that issues from the middle of the bay. Villagers would dive with gourds to get to it. The Pahala sugar industry created a need for a port on rough Kuhua Bay, and a railway ran up the mountain to the fields. All these historical threads, including the most recent, defunct resort at the backshore of the beach, have been frayed by 50-foot tsunamis.

To hike from **Black Sand Beach to Kaneʻeleʻele Heiau and Nahuluhulu Point,** walk from the parking area, which is the county campground, to the curve of black sand that is backed by coco palms and a serene pond. Vendors offer trinkets and Kau coffee. Continue around the sand to old concrete slabs at the far end of the beach. (The slabs are part of a World War II military installation to prevent the Japanese from coming ashore.) At the inland side of the slabs, take an unmarked trail up about 15 feet to the aʻa lava bench. Go seaward atop the bench, toward **Kahiolo Point,** and you can't miss **Kaneʻeleʻele Heiau,** since it is more than 500-feet square. You should see a platform raised by poles, called a lele, where Hawaiians leave offerings to this day.

For the ancient trail to **Nahuluhulu Point,** cross over the crunchy lava along the inland wall of the heiau and walk toward the ocean along the north wall until you see the trail to your left. Flat, smooth stones embedded into the sharp aʻa continue intermittently for at least .25-mile—a building technique typical of ancient trails. Go through a green gully and come up where a Jeep trail enters from the left. Continue right around the black rock and coral rubble of **Keoneʻeleʻele,** a storm beach. You then hit more of a dirt trail through dwarf kiawe as you continue to the rounded Nahuluhulu Point.

For **Ninole Cove**—a short walk with a big payoff—take an unmarked, grassy trail from under the large kamani trees at the parking spot. In 5 minutes you'll be at the coral-cobble cove. From there, go right on a portion of the **King's Trail** and you'll come to several heiau and shrine ruins atop the nearest hill. *Talk Story:* The **Kaieie Heiau** ruins are associated with the nearby ponds that were the best swimming holes around until flash floods of the early 1980s brought tons on boulders upon them. Geology happens in real time on the Big Island of Hawaii. Speaking of which, if you stare at the ocean horizon due east from Ninole Cove for 10,000 years, you will see the emergence of Hawaii's next island, **Loihi,** now a 15,000-foot-high seamount that is boiling lava into water 3,000-feet deep above its summit.

SNORKEL: Kuhua Bay at **Punaluʻu Beach Park** is known more for its mean rip current than snorkeling, but on the right day intrepid snorkelers can give it a try. A lava reef fronts much of the beach, so you want to go left as you face the water and enter at a small boat ramp. The bay offers lots of turtles and decent water clarity. *Be Aware*: Unfortunately, the best entry point is also the mainline for the rip-current express. Use caution at all times and stay out when the surf is up. The better chance for snorkeling is **Ninole Cove.** Sand channels provide decent entry and lava pools at the shoreline are good keiki pools. *Be Aware:* Stay within the cove and exercise caution.

SURF: Submerged rocks and swift current at **Punaluʻu Beach Park** limit surfers. When conditions are right, you'll find board riders attempting the right-break at the south end of the beach, which is **Puʻumoa Point.** The rocks off the point that are obstacles for surfers also serve to slow down the erosion of the black sand beach.

WHAT'S BEST: Tucked below the dry slopes of Mauna Loa and above the Kau Desert is a lush rain forest. Adventure seekers will be lured into this exotic habitat, home to a Buddhist temple.

PARKING: From Kona, take Hwy. 11 south. Pass South Point and continue to mm52. Turn mauka toward Pahala. Follow Kamani Rd. a few blocks, turn mauka on Pikake Rd., and continue uphill. Pikake becomes Wood Valley Rd.

HIKE: Kau Forest (about 3 mi., 300 ft.); Wood Valley Walkabout (2.5 mi., 100 ft.)

Talk Story: From the highway north of Whittington Beach Park heading is a Cinemascope view of the 50,000-acre **Kau Forest Reserve**. The green buttes, including the prominent **Pu'u Enuhe**, are the 100,000 year-old volcanic blocks of **Ninole**, a subformation of Mauna Loa. The whole zone is now a rain forest.

For the **Wood Valley-Kau Forest** hike, continue up Wood Valley Road, passing Norfolk pines and Macadamia trees, for about 4.5 miles. As the road makes a sharp left turn, the unpaved trailhead road is to the right. Then go left at the first fork (the right fork goes to Kapapala Ranch), and park anywhere. Indigenous koa as well as forestry-planted trees buffer the unpaved road, and woodland birdsong is pronounced. After about .5-mile, keep left where another road goes right. You'll pass to the right of the Buddhist center. From there you will find many forestry roads that interconnect two gulches, heading up to your right. Pick your own route, and backtrack on your return.

WOOD VALLEY TEMPLE

The **Wood Valley Walkabout** takes in rural backroads. Go left a short distance at the ninety-degree turn and park at the **Wood Valley Temple** (a $5 donation is requested). The 25-acre Buddhist retreat was dedicated in 1980 by the Dali Lama. Terraced gardens surround the colorful buildings. Then walk up the paved lane, now called **Wood Valley Loop**, a sleepy road enveloped in flowering gardens and exotic trees that add a healthy dose of tranquility to your Big Island vacation. Pass the first street (South Road, the return route) and then keep making lefts to wind up where you started. How Zen.

36. AINAPO TRAIL   HIKE

> **WHAT'S BEST:** Day hikers won't make the 20-plus miles and 10,700 feet to the top of Mauna Loa. Fair enough, but consider checking out the forested birdlands that lie at the start of the trail. The catch: You're supposed to call the night before to get permission.
>
> **PARKING:** Driving north on Hwy. 11 from South Point, pass mm41. At mm40.5, turn mauka on Ainapo Rd. and proceed to a gate and sign noting the Kapapala Forest Reserve. For access: Call Kapapala Ranch the evening before your hike between 7:30 and 8:30 (928-8403). Then call the next morning between 4:30 and 7 to get the combination to the gate lock. Or just walk in. You'd think they could make it easier.

HIKE: Ainapo Trail sampler (4.5 mi., 1,100 ft., more or less)

For the **Ainapo Trail** sampler, pass through the gate and park near a hunter check-ing station in the open field. Cross the meadow and begin the gradual ascent on the ranch road. *Note:* **Ainapo Road** continues for 8 miles, climbing several thousand feet through Kapapala Ranchlands to the Ainapo Trailhead. The suggested hike is on the lower portion of this road.

You may well see nene soon into the hike, as they often waddle and flutter in the lowlands of the sparse native for-est. The walk begins at 2,500 feet. Ohia trees, with red bottlebrush flowers are quite large at this elevation, and you'll also see some koa, which have pointed leaves similar to some eucalyptus. About 1.5 miles into the hike—after ascending 650 feet—stay to the right at a fork in the road. A half-mile and 300-plus feet after the fork, you'll pass the scattered ruins of the ancient village of Ainapo. In the late 1700s, during the Battle of Bitter Rain, an army of Kamehameha's

AINAPO

men led by Chief Kaiana retreated to this point until reinforcements from Kona came to bail them out. Another .5-mile and 300 feet above Ainapo village, the road crosses another contouring Jeep trail in **Keakapulu Flat**. Pick your own turnaround spot.

37. KILAUEA CALDERA   HIKE

WHAT'S BEST: This former lava lake, four miles across, is the centerpiece of Hawaii Volcanoes National Park, one of America's greatest monuments. Take the drive on the rim and sample a variety of landscapes, from the bizarre to the sublime.

PARKING: From either Hilo or Kona, head to mm28.5 on Hwy. 11 and turn into Hawaii Volcanoes National Park. Stop at the entrance station, pay the admission fee, and pick up a map. *Note:* Hikes are described from the entrance station, going right (counterclockwise), and then left (clockwise), both directions on Crater Rim Drive. A four-mile section of the rim drive (from Jaggar Museum to Chain of Craters Road) will probably be *closed* due to hazards from Halemaumau's eruption of 2008. *Be Aware*: Bring warm clothes and drinking water. For the lava viewing hike, see TH50, page 156.

HIKE: *Going right, or counterclockwise:* Kilauea Visitors Center-Volcano House-Volcano Art Center (.75-mi.); Volcano House to Kilauea Caldera floor (3.25 mi., 425 ft.); Steaming Bluff (.25-mi.); Kilauea Overlook to Jaggar Museum car-shuttle (.5-mi.); Halemaumau Crater Overlook (.5-mi.); *Going left or clockwise:* Devastation Trail to Puʻu Puai car-shuttle (.5-mi.); Iki Crater loop (4 mi., 400 ft.); Thurston Lava Tube (.25-mi.)

Going right (counterclockwise) from the entrance station: The **Kilauea Visitors Center**, renovated in 2005, is on the right .25-mile from the entrance station. It has excellent films and displays, and a number of enthusiastic and informed staff. When the lava is flowing, the center has the energy of a newsroom on deadline. Many visitors miss the **Volcano Art Center**. As you face the visitors center, go left to the ranch-style building sitting by itself—which is the original Volcano House, built in 1877. The nonprofit art center is the site of periodic cultural events and one of the best places to buy or view art in the state. Upon leaving the center, jog right across the trees and lawn to see an authentic hula platform and thatched building.

The **Volcano House Hotel** is across the street from the visitors center. Hawaii's oldest operating resort has gone through many incarnations (moved, rebuilt, burned down) since its beginnings in the mid-1800s—including a major spruce-up and rate hike in 2013. Walk through the hotel to the observation area for your first look at of **Kilauea Caldera**, a view that is at once panoramic and detailed. For the five-star hike from **Volcano House to Kilauea Caldera floor**, go right on the walkway at the observation area and you'll soon find the pillar that held the first view-scope for the Hawaii Volcanoes Observatory, put there by founder Thomas A. Jaggar in 1912. After a few minutes, stay left on the **Crater Rim Trail**, and a few minutes after that, go left again on the well-constructed **Halemaumau Trail**. Serenaded by native birds, you make a switchbacking descent under a canopy of tree ferns and native ohia and over a carpet of mosses, smaller ferns, and native shrubs. Earth cracks here and there add mystery. It's fantastic. After about .75-mile, the greenery becomes sparser as you make the final drop onto the barren, rolling floor of the caldera. Following 3-foot-high rock cairns, you'll want to walk out a ways to get a sense of scale and contrast with the fecund greenery of the descent. *Note:* The trail across the caldera floor may be closed.

After exploring Volcano House area, jump back in the car and proceed .75-mile to the **Steaming Bluff**. A short walk out a path joins the **Crater Rim Trail** at the sulphur-misted bluffs, an ethereal stroll. The **Kilauea Overlook**, featuring a nice picnic spot, is next on the drive, about 2.25 miles from the entrance station. In 1823, Missionary William Ellis became the first Westerner to see the caldera from this spot, although at the time it was 500-feet deeper. Currently the magma is about 2 miles beneath the caldera floor. For the **car-shuttle hike to the Jaggar Museum**, go the overlook, which is on the Crater Rim Trail, and head to your right. Fast runners may beat the driver, who must turn in at 2.75 miles to get to the museum parking lot. A towering plume of volcanic gas creates a striking view of Halemaumau, the crater within the Kilauea Caldera, a mile from the museum's eye-popping observation area. Science-heads will enjoy displays and everyone will get a chill from Herb Kane's red-hot portrait of Pele. *More Stuff:* The **Kau Desert Trail** crosses the highway at mm4, a 9-mile, arid trek to a trailhead on Highway 11 that is at mm38.25. About .5-mile after this trail is the Southwest Rift, where you can stroll over a moonscape created by a 1971 lava flow. *Note:* Crater Rim Drive may be closed after Jaggar Museum due to the 2008 eruption.

The **Halemaumau Crater Overlook**, 5.5 miles from the entrance station, was blown to smithereens at 3 a.m. on March 9, 2008. Entrance to this post-apocalyptic landscape 250 feet above the crater floor may yet be closed. *Talk Story:* Halemaumau is the home of **Goddess Pele**, who traveled here from the northern islands of Kaua'i and Ni'ihau. Pele had a duplex at Halemaumau until 1790, when an explosion turned two craters into one. Since then some 21 eruptions have taken place, including one in 1974 that sent a curtain of fire skyward. For two decades, ending in 1924, the crater was a dazzling lake of lava. On one occasion, the crater floor collapsed 400 feet. The 2008 blast widened a vent from 90 feet wide to 300 feet, and covered 65 acres with debris. *More Stuff:* Other trails (probably closed) from here: The Halemaumau 3.5 miles across the caldera floor to Volcano House. The Byron Ledge Trail follows a vegetated ledge above the caldera floor and reaches to the Devastation Trailhead, after nearly 3 miles.

Going left or clockwise on Crater Rim Drive: Parking for **both** the **Iki Crater Trail loop** and **Thurston Lava Tube** hikes is 1.5 miles if you turn left after entering the park. *Note:* When this parking is full, use Kilauea Iki Overlook parking, located .5-mile closer to the park exit. **For the Iki Crater**—an over publicized yet excellent hike—head

HALAU NA PUA ʻO ULUHAIMALAMA, HALEMAUMAU CRATER
THE HULA IS THE PURITY OF SPIRIT WITHIN EACH INDIVIDUAL, KUMU AND DANCER. THE
HULA MUST ALWAYS HAVE ITS "PIKO", THE CENTER OF BALANCE.
IT IS THE LIVING ENERGY AND BECKONING FORCE.—KUMU EMERY ACERET

down the stairs across the street from the lava tube. You switchback through a rain forest before spilling onto the fractured floor of Iki Crater. Iki, more properly called **Kilauea Iki**, erupted in 1959. Steam rises in cracks all around, as you follow a cinder path straight across the tilted pahoehoe tabletops, encircled by 400-feet high walls.

The trail heads toward the open end of the crater. Snake up a jumble of lava and veer to the right. At the green edge of the crater, you'll reach a railed stairway section. Up you go, in trees now, keeping right at two trail junctions over the next .5-mile. At the **Crater Rim Trail**, keep right again, over a pleasant ascent of .75-mile to the **Kilauea Iki Overlook** (alternate parking). Then gobble up the last .5-mile on a splashy view section of rim trail.

Arrive early to avoid the big tour buses at the **Thurston Lava Tube**, a.k.a. **Nahuku**. This memorable short hike is a family pleaser. You begin curving down through a spectacular ohia-and-tree fern forest, serenaded by native and exotic birds. The 600-foot lava tube, lit by dim lights, has a dripping ceiling about 15-feet high. Lava tubes are formed when the surface of fast-moving pahoehoe lava cools and hardens. The hot lava continues to flow underneath until the source ceases, and the tube drains. The tube continues for another 1,000 feet, but this section was closed in recent years.

The **Devastation Trail to Puʻu Puai Overlook** is actually lush compared to the southwest zone. You'll find the trailhead at 3.5 miles going left from the park entrance, opposite Chain of Craters Road. Take the right fork at the beginning of the easy-walking path. You'll skirt an ohia-fern forest, cluttered with birds. The big cinder hill that is **Puʻu Puai** will be to the left. Keep one eye to the ground and you may find Pele's tears, black droplets of lava, or Pele's hair, glassy black filaments, both a result of molten rock blowing skyward and cooling in the air. *Note:* You can also start at the Puʻu Puai Overlook (of Iki Crater) parking lot, which is .5-mile before Devastation Trail. *More Stuff:* Crater Rim Drive is open to pedestrians past Chain of Craters Road for about .5-mile to the **Keanakakoi Overlook**.

WHAT'S BEST: Flowing lava meets the sea near the bottom of this 20-mile drive from the visitors center. Along the way is a hike with a view of the fuming crater, and another to a petroglyph field that has survived centuries of lava flows.

PARKING: From either Hilo or Kona, head to mm28.5 on Hwy. 11 and turn into Hawaii Volcanoes National Park. Turn left after passing through the entrance station, continue on Crater Rim Dr. for 1.5 mi., then turn left on Chain of Craters Rd. *Notes:* Directions continue below. Of late, to view flowing lava, you need to drive to Kalapana Bay; see page 156. Check with rangers or call 961-8093 for current lava conditions.

HIKE: Pu'u Huluhulu (2.75 mi., 300 ft.); Pu'u Loa Petroglyphs (1.25 mi.); Pu'u O'o flows and steam plume (2 mi., more or less)

Talk Story: Extending eastward from Kilauea Caldera are a **Chain of Craters**, more than a dozen of them covering the first 12 miles of the east rift zone. Nearer Kilauea, the pu'us are overgrown and lush. Midway, the lava flows date from the late 1960s and early 1970s, and in the eastern section, the molten rock has been bubbling out of **Pu'u O'o** since 1983. The road follows the earliest craters and the middle zone, and then drops down the 1,000-foot **Holei Pali** to where present day flows sizzle into the ocean.

From the top of **Pu'u Huluhulu** you are about 6 miles from the action at **Pu'u O'o**, close enough to get a good look, but binoculars will help. *Driving:* Head down **Chain of Craters Road**, perhaps stopping at several of the jungly craters on the way—small **Lua Manu**, steaming **Puhimau**, forested **Ko'oko'olau**, and **Pauahi** with its com-

DEVASTATION TRAIL

PU'U O'O LAVA TOXIC STEAM

manding viewing platform. **For the hike**, look left for **Mauna Ulu**, and head to a large parking lot. Walk down the road and hang a left at the trailhead, where pahoehoe lava from 1970s flows covers the asphalt. The **Pu'u Huluhulu Trail** curves through a pahoehoe lava field, marked by rock cairns and yellow reflectors to aid night-time hikers. Vegetation is scarce, mostly dwarf ohia. The indirect route swings left around the lava field and then back right, along the base of the forested cone. Make sure to go left on the spur trail up the pu'u, rather than continuing on the Napau Trail. You ascend several switchbacks through trees before reaching viewing area at the top. Mauna Loa and Mauna Kea loom inland. Pu'u O'o has been gurgling lava since 1983, including 43 fountain bursts reaching as high as 1,500 feet. In 1997 the cone had grown to over 1,000 feet when a catastrophic collapse lowered it to its present 825 feet in less than 24 hours.

More Stuff: You'll need a free permit, available at the visitors center, to hike the 7.5 miles to **Napau Crater**, which is about 2 miles from Pu'u O'o. The walk is a heatstroke special, over the barren lava of **Mauna Ulu** and passing the **Makaopuhi Crater**. A day hike is feasible—wilderness camping is available—but leave early and don't skimp on water. Heed the warnings about staying away from the crumbling slopes of Pu'u O'o.

The **Pu'u Loa Petroglyphs** field hike takes you across old pahoehoe lava to a wooden-railed walkway from which you can view the rock carvings. *Driving:* Go 13 miles down the road, below the Holei Pali. A signed trailhead is on the left, before the road makes its big left turn and continues up the coast. (A highlight on the way down, near mm9, is **Kealakomo**, a picnic pavilion set at cliff's edge with a spectacular view.) The rock carvings (called ki'i pohaku) depicting circles and semicircles with dots, commemorate births. Sailing images are also present at this field, which is near the landing point of Polynesian migrations. *More Stuff:* The **Puna Coast Trail** is across the street from the petroglyph trailhead. The trail leads 6.5 miles to primitive coast campsite at **Apua Point**.

The **Puʻu Oʻo flows and steam plume** hike changes with Peleʼs moods. *Driving:* Continue about 20 miles to where barricades mark the end of Chain of Craters Road. After sunset is the busiest time, when red streaks of flowing lava can sometimes be seen on the far-off slopes. From the end of the road, rangers may mark a path with yellow reflectors as least partway to a viewing area of the steam plume at the ocean. (Lava walks most likely will begin at Kalapana Bay; see page 156.) *Talk Story:* Puʻu Oʻo has added some 750 acres to the coastline during its current outburst. In November of 2005, 44 acres crashed into the sea, including 10 acres of old land. In 2008, a new vent

MAUNA ULU ROAD

redirected flows toward Kalapana. At temperatures of 2,100 degrees, molten lava goes wherever it wants. Walking across the gleaming, crunchy new lava is not dangerous, but you need to heed precautions and be prepared. An average of one visitor a year has died viewing the volcano during the recent eruptions. Daily, yes daily, it sends 2,000 pounds of sulfur dioxide skyward. *Be Aware:* Burns, explosions, lethal vapors, heat exhaustion, and broken bones are some of the treats awaiting the oblivious hiker.

More Stuff: You can watch the **Holei Sea Arch** fight its losing battle with the surf by taking a short, signed trail toward the ocean before the end of Chain of Craters Road. On the return leg of this stroll, look mauka to the **Holei Pali** and notice the aʻa lava streaks dripping over the cliffs, frozen in time since the 1970s.

39. HILINA PALI   HIKE

WHAT'S BEST: This 2,000-foot sea cliff is the gateway to the Big Island's most appealing coastal wilderness.

PARKING: From the park entrance station turn left on Crater Rim Drive for 3.5 mi. and then turn left on Chain of Craters Road. After 2 mi., turn right on Hilina Pali Rd. and follow 8.5 mi. to road's end. *Note:* To protect endangered Nene, the state bird, the road *may* be closed some winter months 4 mi. in at Kulanaokuaiki campground. Drive slowly.

HIKE: Hilina Pali Overlook (.75-mi., 150 ft.); Ka'aha Shelter (7.75 mi.; 2,100 ft.)

Aside from being the nexus for excellent backcountry hiking, the **Hilina Pali Overlook** is one of the sublime view spots on the Big Island. The road down is paved, easily navigated by passenger vehicles. About 4 miles into the drive, you pass the improved **Kulanaokuaiki Campground**. The road continues through scrub grasslands and red pahoehoe fields until reaching a comparative oasis at the overlook, where an attractive stone hut is bordered by small koa trees. Walk down the face of the cliff on the **Hilina Pali Trail** to get a huge view of the coast.

To reach the **Ka'aha Shelter**, think like a goat and descend the cliff face, dropping 2,000-plus feet during the initial 2.25 miles. Then veer right at a junction where the Hilina Pali Trail goes left toward other primitive camps at Halape and Keauhou. From this junction, the downgrade is more gradual over the next 1.5 miles through lava grasslands. Then, at another junction with a connector trail that comes in from the left, you drop over a 200-foot lip and make the last .25-mile to the shelter. Water should be available at the Ka'aha Shelter, but check with park rangers beforehand, and bring a pump or water treatment tablets. *Be Aware*: Although highly unlikely, if you feel the earth shake when you're down here, head up the trail fast. Localized earthquakes can create tsunamis that arrive without warning.

More Stuff: This coastal wilderness trail system connects four shelters with catchment water supplies. The **Pepeiao Shelter** is a cabin with actual beds, while the **Ka'aha**, **Halape**, and **Keauhou** shelters are three-walled. All are in arid grasslands with big sea vistas. Permits are free, and so is the advice you should get from park rangers before embarking. Wind and sun exposure are the downside.

40.   MAUNA LOA LOOKOUT   HIKE

WHAT'S BEST: A bird park delivers with tweets galore amid a stroll through old growth native trees. Or keep driving to the high country of Hawaii Volcanoes National Park for a smash-bang view of Kilauea Caldera and the start of the long trail up 'Long Mountain.'

PARKING: From the entrance road to Hawaii Volcanoes National Park, head west (toward Kona) on Hwy. 11. Pass mm30 and Pi'i Mauna Dr. At mm30.6, turn mauka on Mauna Loa Rd. Directions continue below.

HIKE: Kipuka Puaulu loop (1.2 mi., 240 ft.); Mauna Loa sampler (4 mi., 700 ft.)

The **Kipuka Puaulu loop**, known as Bird Park, is a saunter through 50-foot koas and smaller ohia trees, some of which have died. *Driving:* Continue 1.5 miles on Mauna Loa Road to the large cul-de-sac and trailhead that is on the right. This bird habitat is surrounded by the **Keamoku lava flow**—an island of vegetation that is called a **kipuka**. At the hike's midway point, benches invite birders. Nearby, a ferny lava tube will attract the curious. Fearless black pheasants will be in plain sight along portions of the trail, more obvious than the native woodland birds. Look for the bright-red apapane, which has black wings and tail and loves to swill sweet nectar from the ohia blossoms. Another red one is the i'iwi, slightly bigger and with a curved bill, and the yellow ones are most likely amakihi, the Hawaiian honeycreeper. Cardinals, the crew-cut red guys, are not native. On the loop's homestretch, vines, ferns, and leafy ti buffer the path, and a bench beneath an enormous koa begs for a sitter.

For the **Mauna Loa Trail sampler**, continue through an open gate up the road, which becomes **Mauna Loa Scenic Strip** and climbs to an elevation of 6,662 feet over 10 miles of smooth pavement. On the drive up—half the fun for this trailhead— you get glimpses of Mauna Loa, but the big view from the lookout is of the Kilauea Caldera. After a half-mile on the scenic strip, you pass through **Kipuka Ki**, a mile-long ecological area surrounded by lava. Large trees form a tunnel at the lower portions of the drive, but flora dwarfs after you get above 5,000 feet. The stone kiosk of the **Mauna Loa Lookout** is in a grove of native trees.

Even with the head start from the lookout, you'll need to walk more than 18 miles one-way and climb 6,500 feet to reach the summit. But a shorter hike reveals the mountain's tremendous mass. You start on a contour over red, smooth lava, and then traverse up to your right for a half-mile, reaching the margins of the black a'a of the Keamoku flow. Here you head more directly up the slope, weaving through red rock. The trail becomes less distinct, following rock cairns. The temptation is to keep pushing upward hoping to catch a glimpse of the summit. But this is folly. The gently curving slopes of Mauna Loa translate to a horizon that keeps moving away as you climb. Pick your turnaround spot and keep a sharp eye on the trail that is easy to lose. *Talk Story:* Measured from base to summit, Mauna Loa is the second highest on the Big

MAUNA LOA LOOKOUT, NENE, THE HAWAIIAN STATE BIRD

Island, and the second highest on the planet earth—estimated at 56,000 feet from its submerged base. But the amazing statistic is its mass. At some 19,000 cubic miles, you could fit more than 100 mainland volcanoes, like Rainier and St. Helen's, inside of it. *More Stuff:* Known as the **Trail of Tears**, the **Mauna Loa Trail** is a challenge. All of it is exposed to wind, sun, and harsh temperatures. The **Red Hill Cabin** provides shelter 7.5 miles from the lookout, at just over 10,000 feet. The next cabin is near the summit, a long 11.5 miles and 3,000 vertical feet away. Obviously, check with park rangers to obtain permits and information on this hike. Also, see TH43, Mauna Loa Observatory, for more on the summit, and the "easiest" route there.

Are you thirsty and sober? No problem. Head for **Volcano Winery**, which is just up Pi'i Mauna Drive near mm30, on the Hilo side of Mauna Loa Road. Macadamia Nut Honey and Volcano Red (featuring jaboticaba berries) are just two taste-bud adventures that await at their always-open tasting room ($5) and gift shop. The place is friendly and fun, and the wines make intriguing gifts.

41. MAKA'ALA TREE FERN FOREST   HIKE

WHAT'S BEST: This enchanted rain forest of giant tree ferns may have you seeing elves—on the fringes of the Ola'a Forest Wilderness, part of the national park.

PARKING: Drive toward Hilo on Hwy. 11 from Hawaii Volcanoes National Park. Pass mm26.5 and turn mauka on Wright Rd. (Hwy. 148). After 2.5 mi. the road makes a 90-degree left and, .5-mile farther, turn right on Amaumau Rd. Follow for 1.6 mi. to a cul-de-sac. Drive (or walk) a grassy two-track road for .25-mi. to the trailhead.

HIKE: Maka'ala Tree Fern Forest (2.5 mi., 150 feet)

Begin the hike through the **Maka'ala Tree-Fern Forest** by heading up the trail opposite the road leading in, not by going left on a utility road. The trail's early portions are typical—soft dirt and muddy sections, inlaid with steps made of rust-colored tree-fern trunks. You will be enveloped by greenery as the trail curves and undulates. Close by to the right is the border for the 100,000-plus acres of the **Ola'a Wilderness**. Although companion ohia trees are present, you are essentially in a tunnel of the fronded trees, called hapu'u in Hawaii. Some are 25-feet high. After a wondrous mile-plus, near some large shaggy ohias, you reach a fence marking the boundary of the 12,000-acre natural area reserve. *Be Aware:* Hiking off-trail is dangerous and nearly impossible due to thick foliage and earth cracks. Backtrack immediately if you become entangled.

More Stuff: Trailblazers can continue by hopping the boudary fence and taking the public trail into the **Kulani** and **Upper Waiakea forest reserves**. Also, additional access to the **Ola'a Wilderness** is available at Old Volcano Road at mm 23.8 off Highway 11. But the real adventurer's access to these reserves is via **Stainback Highway**,

MAKAʻALA TREE FERN FOREST

which heads mauka from Highway 11 south of Hilo—take the same turn as the zoo at mm4.5. At mm11.5 on Stainback, look on the left for Road Q, the north end of the **Maka'ala Natural Area Reserve**. Just prior to that on the right is **Tree Planting Road** (Road P), a wide swath that continues for miles to Saddle Road. At mm8.6 on Stainback, on the left, is additional **Waiakea Forest Reserve** access. You'll see a number of roads in between these, labeled alphabetically and interconnected. *Be Aware:* Keep your bearings. It's easy to get lost.

42. KAHAUALEA RAIN FOREST   HIKE

WHAT'S BEST: Get beyond the beyond after only a short distance into a native Hawaiian rain forest. Then keep trekking to a view of Kilauea's east rift zone and see Pu'u O'o blowing its stack about a mile away.

PARKING: Take Hwy. 11 toward Hilo from Hawaii Volcanoes National Park, or head toward the park from Hilo. Turn makai on South Glenwood Dr., which is .25-mi. on the Hilo side of mm20. Continue 3.5 mi. as the road becomes Captains Dr. and then Ala Kapena Dr., and goes from paved to graded to a grassy two-track at the end. Park at signed trailhead. *Note:* The trail *should* be open after a several-year closure due volcanic hazards.

HIKE: Kahaualea Natural Area to Pu'u O'o viewpoint (8.25 mi., 350 ft.)

Be Aware: Pack rain gear, plenty of water, food, a rabbit's foot, and a hiking pole before entering the 17,000-acre **Kahaualea Natural Area**. The trail corkscrews through ferny muck, roots, and mossy upheavals of lava on its way to the **Pu'u O'o viewpoint**. And make sure to follow the trail, which should be marked by plastic ribbon at eye-level branches in critical places. If you encounter heavy rain or fog, turn back. No, it's not *that* bad, but you want to respect this hike. It starts out innocently enough on some grassy straight sections, over the roots of a towering canopy of ohia and koa, and beside an understory of several varieties of fern and shrubs. If you don't feel like an odyssey, just walk in a short distance from the trailhead and hang around. Branches twist ornately, decorated by moss. Birds circulate in all directions.

About a mile into the rain forest, you'll cross a shallow gully and step over one of several earth cracks. After this point, the trail becomes a drunken snake, slithering left and right, hiccuping up and down 6 to 12 feet. At 2 miles, you'll reach a clearing of sorts, mostly moss and ferns, and think you're nearly out of the woods. But, no. The trail continues toward daylight in the trees that seems to get close without arriving. Finally, after about 2 hours of diligent marching, and maybe 10 minutes after stepping over the third earth crack, you'll notice the forest trees dwarfing in size. Then you reach the last of them and you peer like a pagan at the fuming vent of **Pu'u O'o**. You won't find a better place to bust out the Tarzan yell. *Be Aware:* Don't be lured closer. Aside from lethal fumes (tons of sulfur dioxide are sent airborne each day) and collapsing lava tubes—you may not be able to find your way back to the Kahaualea Trail.

SADDLE ROAD TRAILS

43. PU'U O'O HORSE TRAIL   HIKE

WHAT'S BEST: An underrated trail on the open plateau between the two most massive mountains on earth imparts a large sense of place—and you'd never guess it was Hawaii. (This is a different Pu'u O'o than the lava-spitting one.)

PARKING: *From Kona,* take Hwy. 190 toward Waimea and near mm7, turn right on Saddle Rd. Continue past the Mauna Kea Rd. turnoff. Turn off to the right at mm22.5. Parking is clearly marked at a lava turnout. *From Hilo,* take Hwy. 200, Waianuenu Ave. west from town. Yellow highway signs are a clue that the trailhead is near.

HIKE: Pu'u O'o Horse Trail (up to 7.5 mi., 200 ft.)

Talk Story: Cattle and paniolos (cowboys) hoofed this trail in the 1800s, contouring around Mauna Kea from Parker Ranch, coming through the saddle on the way to Volcano town, and thence to awaiting ships in Hilo Bay. The Pu'u O'o Ranch and the old cone are on the Mauna Kea side of Saddle Road; see TH65. So get along little doggies, and don't forget to pack rain gear and equip your pack for a wilderness hike. The **Pu'u O'o Horse Trail** weaves through pahoehoe lava and native ohia, roughly on the boundary between the **Upper Waiakea Forest Reserve** and the **Ainahou Nene Sanctuary**. About .5-mile into the hike, you'll drop into a large grassy swale affording a big view of both Mauna Loa and Mauna Kea. You climb gradually from this swale, veering left over pahoehoe lava flows from 1855. Both right and left are islands of vegetation, kipukas, with old -growth koa providing rich bird habitat. The trail gets curvy and you have to keep your eyes peeled for worn areas and rock cairns. Still angling left, you cross over a more recent flow from 1881 before the horse trail joins

Powerline Road. You could return on this straight road, which joins Saddle Road about .5-mile east, toward Hilo, from the Pu'u O'o trailhead. *Be Aware:* Start early, since fog and rain are common later in the day.

More Stuff: Toward Hilo from the Pu'u O'o Horse Trail parking are several more public trails. The **Powerline Road** is at mm21.5, and takes off to the right, or south, over a hellish a'a lava field, and continues all the way to the Ainapo Trail. A couple of miles farther, on the right at mm18.6, is the **Kaumana Trail**. This promising Na Ala Hele state hiking trail never gets far from the highway; addtional access is at mm19.8. On the right at mm16.2, is the wide swath of the **Tree Planting Road**. Mountain bikers will be most interested in this forested pathway 10 miles long, running between Saddle Road and Stainback Highway. Beyond Tree Planting Road, about .25-mile but on the Mauna Kea side of the highway, is an access to the large **Hilo Forest Reserve**. Desolate slopes support wiliwili trees, a suitable place to wander off and have existential thoughts.

44. MAUNA LOA OBSERVATORY   HIKE

WHAT'S BEST: Though no cakewalk, this trailhead is by far the easiest way to get up Mauna Loa. You begin at 11,150 feet, where you can take a look around the installation that is keeping an eye on the world's atmosphere. The drive up is easy and unforgettable.

PARKING: Heading toward Hilo on Saddle Rd., Mauna Loa Observatory Rd. is at mm27.6, on the right—just past the road to Mauna Kea and the Pu'u Huluhulu trail-head. Passenger cars can make the 17.5-mi., 4,500-foot climb to the trailhead, but use caution. The road is newly paved—*except* for the first .25-mile. *Notes:* Saddle Road has been widened and paved. Gas up. Start early to avoid the marine cloud layer which sometimes rises in the afternoon. Bring warm clothing, water, and food.

HIKE: Mauna Loa Observatory (.5-mi., 100 ft.); North Pit (7.75 mi., 2,000 ft.)

Ascending the lower end of the road, you'll drive through a Marslike ocean of lava (smooth and jagged; rosy pink, chalky white, and devil's food brown; both dull and glistening) deposited by several eruptions in the late 1800s and in 1935. On the left is the **Ainahou Nene Sanctuary.** To acclimatize to the altitude, stop for 30 minutes or so, about 8.5 miles from the bottom, where the observatory road makes a sweeping right turn at a telecommunications installation. Then continue to public parking at the end of the paved road. The **Mauna Loa Observatory** is a short hike up the hill on a gated road to an assemblage of metal buildings and boardwalks looking like an Arctic outpost laid down on lava instead of ice. *Note:* MLO doesn't mind walk-up visitors, but be sure to respect the scientists' work spaces. To arrange a once-weekly tour, e-mail them or call 808-933-6965. Under the auspices of the **National Ocean and**

Atmospheric Administration and other agencies, the MLO has been keeping tabs of the air we breathe for 45 years. Gases, particulates, and aerosols are all measured, including carbon dioxide, which has increased 20 percent during the years of study. Yes, global warming, depletions of the ozone layer—the charts are on the walls of these faraway buildings. But don't forget to marvel at the view of Mauna Kea, Maui's Haleakala, the Kohala Mountains, and Hualalai Volcano.

For the hike to **North Pit**, start down the a'a lava road heading east from the parking area. After a little more than .25-mile, the **Observatory Trail** joins the road, and you want to go left. Thus begins a steady climb over mostly pahoehoe lava on a route marked by precious rock cairns, 2- to 3-feet high. Don't space out and lose these babies, especially coming down when they're harder to spot. The four-wheel drive road continues up the mountain, too, making five switchbacks on the way, crossing the trail a few times. A slow pace will ward off the effects of thin oxygen. You'll eventually reach the lip of the pit, elevation 13,120 feet, a little inlet off the larger crater of **Mokuaweoweo Caldera**, spreading out before you in a three-mile oval. It is not deep or precipitous, but the austere caldera is one of the world's most distinctive topographical features, the barren dimple upon the most massive mountain. *Be Aware:* If it's not obvious already: Only seasoned hikers should attempt this hike, prepared for severe weather.

More Stuff: Several trails intersect where Observatory Trail ends at North Pit. The **Mauna Loa Summit Trail** comes in from the left—see TH39—and also continues to the right for 2.5 miles and 500 higher feet to **Mauna Loa's peak**. If you go left from North Pit, the trail rims the other side of the caldera, passing small **Lua Poholo Crater** on the way to **Mauna Loa Cabin**, 2 miles away, and up another 150 feet.

MAUNA LOA OBSERVATORY AND SUMMIT TRAIL

FISHERMAN AT MOKU OLA

Hilo's rain is legendary. Proverbs lament the perpetual gloom that mercilessly brought hundreds of inches of rain each year down upon the people. When the King Kalaniopu'u died in the late 1700s, the young warrior Kamehameha earned his stripes by defending the sunny lands of Kona from the covetous grasp of Chief Keawemauhili of Hilo, who, when you peel away the political squabbling, seems simply to have been desirous of some of that dry west-side air.

Today, east-siders have laid down armaments and picked up big umbrellas, to them as much a part of Hawaii as sunglasses and swim fins. And don't knock it until you've tried it, since strolling through a warm downpour in a rain forest garden is among the unique memories to take home from the islands. To be fair, the rain comes in buckets, not drizzles, and it's interspersed with generous displays of tropical sunshine that make Hilo glisten like Eden. Unless you see Hilo and Puna, you will miss the mind-boggling greenery that says, "Hawaii." Most of the world's supply of exotic flowers is flown out daily from the east side.

Once the capital of the islands, Hilo has a sense of place that would otherwise be absent on the Big Island. Show up on a Saturday or Wednesday for the farmers market and crafts fair and you'll be wandering through a romantic bazaar of a faraway land. Roam the dilapidated-and-gentrified city blocks of historic Hilo, and you will be transported to the 1950s. This old section was spared two horrific tsunamis, in 1946 and 1960, which tragically wiped out communities that crowded the bay. Two parks—Bayfront and Waiola River—are expansive greenbelts that compliment the bustling funk of the historic section.

Hilo Bay is below the saddle between Mauna Loa and Mauna Kea. The waters running off these two great peaks join to form the Wailuku River that runs through the old town, spanned by several quaint bridges. A couple of miles up the hill is the Wailuku River State Park, home to Rainbow Falls and Boiling Pots, a series of turbulent pools that lie below Pe'epe'e Falls. Both of these attractions receive the big tour buses, but you need to visit these "destructive waters" to further appreciate Hilo's sense of place.

Then head to nearby Liliuokalani Gardens and Moku Ola, a.k.a. Coconut Island. The gardens are of formal Japanese design. The little island, reachable via footbridge, is protected by the post-tsunami breakwater across part of Hilo Bay. Excellent snorkeling and swimming are available. From the island is a stunning view across the bay to Hilo, with the world's highest mountains lofted above. Put Moku Ola high on the list of places to stand and take in the immense beauty of the Big Island.

The outer portions of Hilo Bay are home to a half-dozen beach parks that are locals playgrounds on weekends. Just north of town is Honoli'i Beach Park, a black-sand beach in a jungle gorge that is Surf City. When the larger waves roll in, spectators line

the cliff above the beach. Heading east of Hilo, for 5 miles outside the breakwater, are several beach parks buffeted by an arboretum of tropical flora. You won't find long runs of white sand, but you will discover several, man-enhanced lagoons, which are excellent for snorkeling. You can pick a favorite, but be sure to see Onekahakaha, Carlsmith, and Richardson Ocean Park. They're not far apart, and each has its own personality, proving once again that the unique is typical on the Big Island.

East and south of Hilo, Puna's Kehena-Pohoiki Scenic Coast drive plays second fiddle to none in the Hawaiian Islands when it comes to tropical scenery. Starting farthest south, Kalapana is a bay that was filled by lava in the 1990s, and now sports the newest black sand beach with access to lave flows. Just up the scenic drive is Kehena Black Sand Beach, tucked into a lush shore. A few delicious miles north of Kehena are the bluffs of Mackenzie State Park, set in the largest ironwood grove in the state. Isaac Hale Beach Park, where locals and fishermen hang out, is the next stop north of Mackenzie. Its stout wharf provides underrated waves for surfers. Only a mile or so farther up the coast is Ahalanui County Park, which alone makes the trip along the coast worthwhile. A man-made warm pool is set at ocean's edge, dappled with the shade of palms and other beach trees, a free spa that is rarely if ever crowded.

The Waiopae Pools, which are not far north of Ahalanui, can be nominated as Hawaii's best snorkeling venue. A dozen or more pools, from waders to Olympic-sized, adorn a broad reef at the south shore of Kapoho Bay. Colorful coral competes with sparkling fish for your attention. On the north side of Kapoho Bay is Cape Kumukahi, the eastern-most spot in the Hawaiian Archipelago, which boasts the purest air you can breath in the world at sea level. The lighthouse at the point escaped the lava of a 1960 eruption by a few feet. You can take a short hike to the dramatic cape, or a slightly longer one to the warm Kapoho Sea Pool, which lies off the north shore of the bay; or head inland to Green Lake, site of prehistoric markers.

Lava Trees State Monument lies inland from the Puna coast, in papaya-and-orchid country. A fast-moving lava flow in the late 1700s, about 12-feet deep, clung to tree trunks which later burned away, leaving these weirdly formed statues. A canopy of enormous monkeypod trees and a ground layer of ferns and leafy ti complete the scene, which is more like walking through museum grounds than on a park trail. Birds go wild in the native ohia forest that envelops the monument.

KEHENA BLACK SAND (19-MILE) BEACH

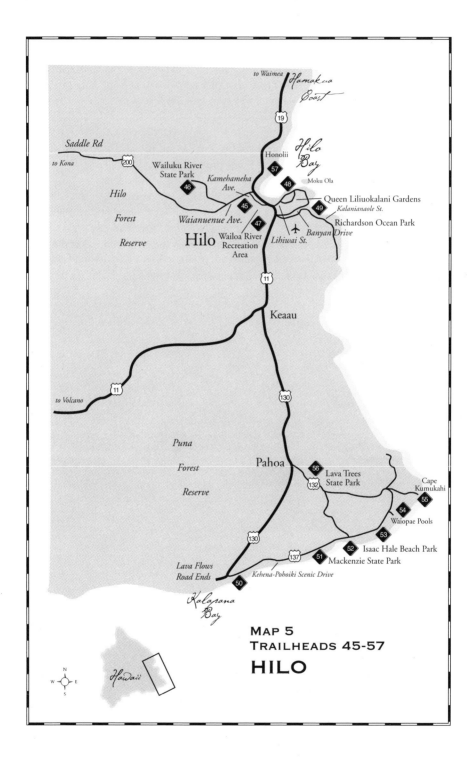

to Waimea *Hamakua Coast*

19

Saddle Rd

to Kona

200

Wailuku River
State Park

Hilo

Forest

Reserve

46

Kamehameha Ave.

Waianuenue Ave.

45

47

Hilo

Wailoa River
Recreation
Area

Honolii

Hilo Bay

57

48

Moku Ola

Queen Liliuokalani Gardens

Kalanianaole St.

49

Richardson Ocean Park

Banyan Drive

Lihiwai St.

11

Keaau

11

to Volcano

130

Puna

Forest

Reserve

Pahoa

56

Lava Trees
State Park

132

Cape
Kumukahi

55

54

Waiopae Pools

130

53

52

Isaac Hale Beach Park

137

51

Mackenzie State Park

Lava Flows
Road Ends

50

Kehena-Pohoiki Scenic Drive

Kalapana Bay

MAP 5
TRAILHEADS 45-57
HILO

N
W   E
S

Hawaii

TRAILHEADS

45-57

TH :	TRAILHEAD	
HIKE :	HIKES AND STROLLS	
SNORKEL :	SNORKELING, SWIMMING	
SURF :	BOARD, BODYBOARD, BODYSURF	
MM :	MILE MARKER; CORRESPONDS TO HIGHWAY SIGNS	
MAKAI :	TOWARD THE OCEAN	
MAUKA :	INLAND, TOWARD THE MOUNTAINS	

ALL HIKING DISTANCES IN PARENTHESES ARE **ROUND TRIP**. ELEVATION GAINS OF 100 FEET OR MORE ARE NOTED. SEE RESOURCE LINKS FOR CONTACTS AND TELEPHONE NUMBERS.

45. HILO TOWN   HIKE

WHAT'S BEST: Yes, it rains in Hilo, and that's why it's so beautiful. The pre-war old-town section has soul and charm, plus a greenbelt for a coastal stroll.

PARKING: From Kona, take Hwy. 190 to Waimea and continue on Hwy. 19, approaching from the north. After crossing the river on the steel (singing) bridge, turn right on Waianuenue St., and then immediately turn left on Kamehameha Ave. Pass Kalakaua St. and park in the public lot that extends for several blocks.

HIKE: Hilo Town (1.25 mi.); Bayfront Park (.5-mi., or more)

Time your visit to **Hilo Town** for a Saturday or Wednesday morning to take in the **Hilo Farmers Market** (although mini versions take place daily). From the parking, follow the old-fashioned storefronts on Kamehameha Avenue to Mamo Street. You'll find just about every fruit, flower, and vegetable you've ever seen, plus numerous tropical varieties only Dr. Seuss could dream up. Across the street from this organic orgy is a bonanza of hand-crafted potential souvenirs—sarongs, shell jewelry, blown glass, wood carvings, instruments—just go and ye shall find. The market is under awnings, providing welcome shelter, rain and shine.

Historic Hilo hangs as loose as hula hips, so loose some of it appears ready to topple. But sidewalk planter boxes and arty signs attest that the town is on the up-tick. You can see much of it by making a loop. Head up Mamo Street from the market and go right on Kilauea Avenue. Across to the left, is **Hawaiian Force**, the place to pick up locally designed clothing with a cultural flair. After a block, Kilauea becomes Keawe Street, where you can jog left on narrow Furneaux Lane to check out the 1925 **Foresters Building**. Continue on Keawe and cross Haili Street, featuring the Art Deco **Palace Theater**, also built in 1925 and still thriving. Farther down Keawe, jog left on

Kalakaua to see the **Old Police Station**, now a cultural center designed like an old Hawaiian hale. Next door is the **Hawaiian Telephone Company Building**, designed by C.W. Dickey, whose 20th century style fused Hawaiian with California Mission. Across the street take a soothing break at **Kalakaua Park** (named after King David), with century-old shade trees and a long fountain.

A block after Kalakaua Street, hang a right on Waianuenue Avenue. Look left as you do to see the **Burns** and **Pacific buildings**, vintage wood-frames. Down the block, where the avenue meets Kamehameha, is **Koehnen's Building**. Fine gifts may draw your eye, but take a look at the koa walls and ohia floors. To the left on Kamehameha

WAIOLA RIVER RECREATION AREA, PALACE THEATER, KALAKAUA PARK

MOKU OLA (COCONUT ISLAND)

is **Basically Books**, featuring a Hawaiiana collection that is among the state's best. Then turn right on Kamehameha and go one block back to Kalakaua and the **Pacific Tsunami Museum**. Inside are a variety of interactive displays and videos. The main videos take place in a vault, within a former bank building, designed in 1930 by Dickey. Finish up your loop by continuing down Kamehameha. On the way you'll pass the S.H. Kress Building, a 1932 Art Deco. At Furneaux, is Abundant Life, an organic hangout with lots more than health food. Then comes the S. Hata Building, built in 1912, a renaissance revival gem that houses the **Mokupapapa Discovery Center for Hawaii's Remote Coral Reefs**. Kids love this newer museum (with free admission) that reveals the 1,200-mile archipelago northwest of Kauai that is the nation's largest conservation area. Hands-on displays make the information accessible.

Bayfront Park is across the highway from Hilo Town, a 1.5-mile greenbelt from the Wailuku River to the Wailoa River. A large gazebo, **Mo'oheau Park**, is where community gatherings take place. Wharves and dock buildings used to crowd a bustling shoreline, but nature's cruel urban planning, 30-foot waves, wiped them out in 1946 and 1960. On weekends and evenings, local canoe teams add color to the scene.

More Stuff: To behold the power of **Kamehameha the Great**, head to the county library, which is a few blocks up Waianuenue Avenue. That big coffin-shaped stone in front is the **Pohaku Naha**, all 3.5 tons of it. As a test of royal blood, a young Kamehameha budged this stone and later was bestowed custody of the war god, Ku. To see the stately **Shipman House** (now a B&B), where Jack London sojourned in Hawaii, turn right past the library on Kaiulani Street and continue a short distance after crossing the river. For a more ancient history—and a scenic look at Hilo's river bridges —take a look at **Maui's Canoe** (Ka Wa'a O Maui): Go back down Waianuenue and turn left on Kino'ole. Cross the river on the **Wainaku Bridge**, built in 1919. That gouged-out

finger of bedrock downstream is the legendary site where the demigod Maui left his canoe when he rescued his mother at Rainbow Falls. Lastly, on rainy days, **Lyman Museum** gets foot traffic. Its bureaucratic curb-side appeal belies a fine collection of artifacts and cultural history that await inside. The Mission House on the grounds dates from 1839. From Kamehameha Avenue, go up Haili Street to the corner of Kapiolani.

46. WAILUKU RIVER STATE PARK   HIKE

WHAT'S BEST: Two scenic waterfalls are just a few miles from Hilo, up the river that joins the runoff of Mauna Loa and Mauna Kea. Bring a swimsuit on nice days.

PARKING: Coming from the north into Hilo on Hwy. 19, cross the steel (singing) bridge and turn mauka on Waianuenue Ave. Continue about 1.5 mi., and keep right on Waianuenue where Hwy. 200 veers left. Shortly thereafter, turn right on Rainbow Dr. and continue to the Rainbow Falls parking lot on the right.

HIKE: Rainbow Falls and pools (.5-mi.); Boiling Pots (up to 1 mi., 125 ft.)

Wailuku River State Park spreads its 16 acres along a roiling mile of the river, which creases the saddle from the island's mammoth twin peaks. Arrive in the morning to have a chance of seeing the misty spectrum of color for which **Rainbow Falls** is named—

and to avoid the big tour buses that hammer the place. The falls' twin (triplet at high water) falls drop about 80 feet. A cave behind the falls is where the demigod Maui rescued his mother, the goddess Hina, from Mo'o Kuna, the giant eel lizard. Hot tip: To reach the pools just above the falls, go up the stairs to the left and continue into a dip beneath a huge banyan. Look right for an opening through an 8-foot high rock bank, and a short, well-used trail. *Be Aware:* Swift waters can be dangerous.

To get to **Boiling Pots**, continue on Rainbow Drive, which loops back out to Waianuenue. Pass Waiau and turn right on Pe'epe'e Falls Street. A sidewalk leads to the overlook of "boiling pots," a succession of pools connected by both underground and surface flows. Basalt lava columns line the pools, and upstream you can see **Pe'epe'e Falls**. A steep, short trail leads down, beginning to the right, beyond the railing. You'll get far away in a jiffy, arriving at bedrock banks with a view of the falls. *Be Aware:* This is a fun swim, but when the pots are boiling to venture near them is suicidal. Wailuku means Destructive Waters. People die here. *More Stuff:* To see the top of the falls, drive up Waianuenue and turn right on on **Manaolana**, toward a radio station. The river, just above the falls, is at road's end. Use extreme caution, especially in high water.

More Stuff: Spelunkers and other people fond of dark, dank holes will want to know that **Kaumana Caves County Park** is not far away. Head back down Waianuenue and turn right on Highway 200, which is Kaumana Drive heading up the mountain. Pass Akala Road on the right and mm4, and look .25-mile later for the park on the right. Park on the shoulder across the highway, and grab your flashlight. Steep, railed stairs lead into a mossy cavern, created by a collapsed lava tube from an 1881 flow. To the right you can make your way about 200 feet over broken sheets of lava.

47. WAILOA RIVER STATE RECREATION AREA   HIKE

WHAT'S BEST: If staying in Hilo, don't overlook this huge, tranquil pond-side park. A Kamehameha statue and tsunami memorial are two highlights.

PARKING: Coming into Hilo from the north on Hwy. 19, cross the steel (singing) bridge, continue along the bay shore, and cross the bridge over the river. Turn mauka immediately on Manono, and turn right again on Pi'ilani. Pi'ilani ends at Park Rd. and the entrance to the large parking lot. (From Hwy. 11, go left on Hwy. 19 to Manono.)

HIKE: Waiakea Fishpond to Kamehameha statue (.75-mi.)

Huge trees—palms, mangoes, monkeypods—laze about the 150 acres of lawn, picnic tables and open water at the **Wailoa River State Recreation Area**. Scalloped footbridges invite you to head across sprawling **Waiakea Fishpond**. Fed by high-volume springs and a stream, the pond was the exclusive grey mullet fish tank for three generations of Kamehamehas, and hence is also known as the **Royal Pond**.

LILIUOKALANI GARDENS, TSUNAMI MEMORIAL CLOCK

To reach the **Kamehameha statue**, cross the first bridge and veer right at the shoreline, setting your course for a second scalloped footbridge that crosses an arm of the fishpond. You'll pass the modernistic **Tsunami Memorial**, there to honor the souls living in the settlement that was swept away by the big wave of 1960—killing 61 people and demolishing 300 structures. The Kamehameha statue will be to the left after crossing the footbridge. On the return leg, angle toward the ocean side of the pond to where it narrows and behold the **Wailoa River**. Then tell your friends you've seen the shortest river in the United States—about one-third mile. *Note:* You also can reach the statue by turning right before the river bridge, on little Bishop Street (one past Pauahi).

More Stuff: Two family attractions are nearby: One is of this earth, the **Hilo Forestry Arboretum**, where you can stroll rolling acres planted with exotic trees and get a free permit to pick fruit. *Driving:* Continue away from the bay on Manono until it veers right and becomes Kawili; the arboretum will be on the right at light at Kilauea Avenue.

The second attraction is out of this world, the **Imiloa Astronomy Center**, where both modern and ancient Hawaiian astronomy is presented in exhibits and planetarium shows. *Driving:* Continue on Manono, veer right on Kawili, and cross Kilauea to Puainako Street. Turn right on Puainako and then go right again on Komohana, and then right on Nowelo at the University of Hawaii. An admission is charged.

WHAT'S BEST: The ancients believed swimming at this tiny island would cure what ails you. Quite possibly, but for sure you'll get a five-star, romantic view of Hilo and a chance to stroll formal gardens that could be in Kyoto, Japan.

PARKING: Coming into Hilo from the north on Hwy. 19, cross the steel (singing) bridge, continue along the bay shore, and cross the wide highway bridge. Turn left immediately on Lihiwai and then go right on Banyan Dr. Continue .25-mile and turn left on Lihiwai, a one-way through Liliuokalani Gardens. Then turn right immediately on Keli'ipio toward Moku Ola. (From Hwy. 11, cross Hwy. 19 to Banyan Dr.)

HIKE: Moku Ola and Liliuokalani Gardens (.75-mi.)

A concrete footbridge spans a narrow channel to **Moku Ola**, also known as **Coconut Island**. A tiara of palms surround the island's several acres of lawn. This is the perfect place to take a midday rest, as in ancient times when ill people came to bathe in the island's curative waters; Moku Ola means 'island of healing.' From the bridge you get a view that makes you fall in love with Hilo, and anyone else nearby. The town sits across the waters of Hilo Bay, with the 13,000-foot-plus peaks of Mauna Loa and Mauna Kea rising to either side. If staying in Hilo, try catching a moonrise here.

Lovely **Liliuokalani Gardens**, built in honor of the queen who was the nation's last ruling monarch, are across the quiet street from the island's parking lot. Curving footbridges of stone and painted hardwoods connect little islands in **Waihonu Pond**. Sloping lawns around the shore are graced by large banyans, mangos, palms, and kukui. Small Asian statuary add accents. The serene landscape was designed by the University of Kyoto's Kinsaku Nakane. In ancient times, a sacrificial heiau stood on the peninsula. *More Stuff:* **Reeds Bay County Park** is a sailboat cove with a pool at the head of the bay, called **Ice Pond**. On a hot day, dip a toe and find out how the pool got its name.

MOKU OLA DIVING TOWER

CANOE PRACTICE BAYFRONT PARK

Driving: Continue around the peninsula on Banyan Drive. Also, across the narrow bay is one of those sublime spots, where under the shade of banyans and palms is an evocative view of sailboats anchored in the small harbor. *Driving:* Veer left at Banyan Way as you drive past the Reeds Bay and then keep left on Kalanianaole Avenue. Look immediately on the left for a Shoreline Public Access sign at the Reeds Bay Clinic.

A timeless attraction, the **Waiakea Tsunami Memorial Clock**, is forever stopped at 1:04, as a tribute to all who lost their lives when the tsunami struck in the dead of morning, May 23, 1960. *Driving:* It stands at the corner Lihiwai and Highway 19.

SNORKEL: Cute **Moku Ola** is also one of the east side's better and most convenient places to swim. Protected by the vast breakwater, surf is calm and water clarity is good (unless rains have filled the rivers). As you walk onto the island, head to the right, and you'll find the 15-foot **diving tower**, a two-tiered mortar-rock structure that has survived at least two tsunamis. High school kids do risky flips from the top. The inlet on the inside of the tower is a seapool, known as **Pua'akaheka**. If you're feeling a bit sick, take a swim around the rocks that lie opposite the tower in this inlet. Ailing Hawaiians, under the supervision of a kahuna, would do so for its healing properties.

49. HILO BEACH PARKS   HIKE, SNORKEL, SURF

WHAT'S BEST: Pick a sunny day and you'll understand why Hawaiians flock to this 5-mile strip of coast that boasts a half-dozen beach parks with protected seapools, sand patches, gardenscapes, and sections of wild reef—definitely underrated.

PARKING: Head to the junction of Hwys. 11 and 19 in Hilo, which is across from Banyan Dr. Then go east (straight) on Kalanianaole Ave., or Hwy. 137. Further directions follow.

HIKE: Onekahakaha Beach Park (1.25 mi.); Carlsmith Beach Park to Lokoaka Wilderness Park pandanus grove (.5-mi.); Leleiwi Beach Park to Richardson Ocean Park (1.5 mi.); Lehia Beach Park tide pools (1.5 mi.)

This coastal stroll is the back way to **Onekahakaha Beach Park**, which features a large seapool and picnic pavilions, and was one of the Big Island's first public parks—dedicated in the 1930s. *Driving:* Soon after **Keaukaha Park** and Apapane Street, turn left on Keokea Loop (opposite Andrews). Pass **Arnott's Lodge**, drive to end of the cul-de-sac, and park near a hidden beach access sign, on the left near address 87. (For the main beach parking lot, continue on the highway and turn left on Onekahakaha Road.) A short, shaded path along a lava wall leads to **Lihikai Beach**, a cove of white sand and coral rubble. Circle around this small beach to the blunt **Keokea Point**, where the boomers roll in. Ironwoods join palms at the shore. Continue from the point, picking your way through grassy ponds, and you'll get to the main park. Roam at will.

At lovely **Carlsmith Beach Park**, a path leads by an attractive pond and trees to the park's reef-protected shore and adjacent wilderness. *Driving:* Carlsmith just down the road at mm4. It shares a small bay with James Kealoha Beach Park, a local kids'

LELEIWI BEACH PARK

hangout. If crowded, park just past the six-story Mauna Loa Shores apartments at a fenced, 20-space Shoreline Public Access parking lot. You may decide to loll around the emmaculate gardens of Carlsmith, gazing offshore to tiny **Scout Island** that lies near the point. Across the street from the park is 30-acre **Lokoaka Fishpond**, into which some 100-million gallons of freshwater permeate daily from its porous lava bottom. For the instant getaway to the **Lokoaka Wilderness Park pandanus grove**, take a forest trail at the parking lot past the Mauna Loa. Keep right on a paved path, which then becomes dirt, over roots and through a tree tunnel of dense flora. At the shore you'll reach a thicket of pandanus trees, called hala in Hawaii, which are used in the weaving of baskets and hats. *More Stuff:* You can also reach the wilderness by taking a sketchy shoreline trail around **Pohakea Point** from Carlsmith Beach Park.

Leleiwi Beach Park is less than a mile down the highway from Carlsmith. On weekends the barbecue's are smokin'. Pick a path along the intricate, tree-lined shore which features tide pools and ponds, heading to your right as you face the water. Beyond Leleiwi's picnic pavilions walk the top of a low lava wall to reach **Richardson Ocean Park**, formerly part of the David Malo estate. In front of ocean center building is an inlet with a small black sand beach. Continue around the shore in front of the center and walk by the park's larger black sand beach, **Waiolena**, which sits at the end of the serene garden path that is the park's main entrance.

The wild-and-scenic **Lehia Beach Park tide pools** lie just beyond Richardson at road's end. Drive past the gate and park past the W.P.A.-era rock wall. The tide pools reside on the low lava point (Leleiwi) that is the farthest land you can see from the end of the seawall. Big ironwoods and heliotropes provide a green ceiling as you weave your way along the shore, around amorphous clear ponds and over boulders that make for

tricky footing. From the tide pools you can make your way for several miles down the coast. If you want 'out there,' here it is.

SNORKEL: Richardson Ocean Park offers very good snorkeling, under the right conditions, but it is not the best swimming along this coast. Try the inlet in front of the ocean center, or the Waiolena black sand beach, the park's easiest place to get in. Lots of rocks make for good fish habitat and interesting swimming, although chest clearance will be a problem in spots. You'll also get a chill from freshwater intrusion in places. *Be Aware*: Rip current can accompany even moderate surf at this park. The rock in the center on the bay is known as "suck rock" because of the powerful current.

Carlsmith Beach Park has an excellent swimming seapool, complete with stairs leading down from a small dock area. It's made cooler by fresh water intrusion. Turtles may join you near shore. Under lower surf conditions, check out **Scout Island** and the rocks off Pohakea Point. The big, sandy-bottomed seapool at **Onekahakaha Beach Park** is a parent's dream, and anyone can have fun swimming around, protected by a boulder reef. Lawns and even some precious white sand await in between dips. At the far end of the beach park, to the left past the ponds, is **Lihikai Beach**. Sand channels make for adequate entry. *Be Aware:* Be very mindful of rip currents caused by wave action.

Adventure seekers can try the **Lehia tide pools**, which are a perfect queen's bath under the right conditions. For a bracing freshwater swim, go native and try the **Akepa Pools**. Protected by a reef from the sea's direct blasts, several open ponds make for a swimming park frequented by teenagers. They're onto something. *Driving:* The pretty pools are between Carlsmith and Leleiwi beach parks. Look for Akepa Street on the mauka side of the road, across from which is Shoreline Public Access. It's a keepa'.

SURF: Board surfers ride the rocky break off **Keokea Point** at Onekahakaha Beach Park—not a good choice for beginners. The point, also known as **3-Miles**, is a good grandstand for watching. More popular is the offshore break at **4-Miles**, which is the bay shared by Kealoha and Carlsmith beach parks. Most popular of all is **Richardson Ocean Park**, where a consistent surf breaks at the reef extending from Leleiwi Point. Rocks and riptide make this a ride for experienced board heads only.

50.   KALAPANA LAVA BAY   HIKE, SNORKEL

WHAT'S BEST: Eruptions of the 1990s filled this bay with lava, but a new black sand beach has formed. Of late, this is the spot for adventure seekers to see hot lava. On the way are steam caverns in a rain forest, and down the road is another black sand beach.

PARKING: From Hilo on Hwy. 11, drive about 6 mi. toward Volcano and turn toward Pahoa on Hwy, 130. Bypass Pahoa and keep right on Hwy. 130. *For Pahoa steam caverns,* look for a scenic point turnout on the left at mm15. *For Kalapana Bay,* continue to mm21. Veer left on Ahia Rd. to reach Hwy. 137. Then go right to a cul-de-sac. *To see lava flows:* At mm21, stay right on Hwy.130, Kaimu-Chain of Craters Rd.; don't veer left on Ahia Rd. Conintue .5-mi. past the first road closed sign on a one-lane road.

HIKE: Pahoa steam caverns (.25-plus-mi.); Kalapana Lava Bay (1.5 mi.); Kehena Black Sand Beach (.25-mi., 100 ft.)

The **Pahoa steam caverns** are a weird little side trip. Take the unsigned trail etched through guava, ferns, and ohia, and you'll soon come upon steam escaping from rock jumbles. Scamper up the highest rock pile to see the first of two 12-foot diameter, 8-foot deep indents. Ladders and benches invite visitors. *More Stuff:* The **Star of the Sea Painted Catholic Church**, built in 1928, features frescoes depicting Father Damien and stained glass. *Driving:* Look left at mm19.8 just before the Highway 137 junction.

From the parking area, check out the aloha at **Uncle's Awa Club** and then head seaward toward **Kalapana Lava Bay** on a red-cinder path over black lava. Midway to the surf, look back to notice the curve of coco palms that once lined the black-sand beach and Harry K. Brown Beach Park, a bay now filled with lava. Some 200 homes were destroyed, along with Kaimu Beach Park. Also gone is the Wahaula Heiau, one of the oldest, having been built in 1250 AD. At the shore, a new, rough-water beach has formed, which took place when hot lava met cool water, sending silicates into the air which rained down as black sand. **The lava viewing site** is 'open' from 3 to 9 daily, although visitors arrive earlier. From the parking, get the skinny from locals and then walk about one-third mile to pavement's end. Lava flows are often less than a mile away over rolling pahoehoe, but the location varies. Bring water, hiking shoes, good judgment, and flashlight at night. Call 808-961-8093 for recorded information.

Kehena Black Sand Beach requires a hands-on descent to a big dollop of black sand, which is backed by a cliff dripping with tropical greenery. *Driving:* A few miles from Kalapana on Highway 137, just before mm19, pull in makai at a turnout. As you face the ocean, go left on a steep, short trail down a small promontory. *Talk Story:* Pele made this beach in a 1955 eruption, and thoughtfully added a new point of land that has inhibited the sea from reclaiming the beach. Kehena was jolted by a 1975 earthquake which dropped the shoreline five feet in a jiffy flat, as evidenced by a severed concrete stairway that is on the right side of the promontory as you walk down.

SNORKEL: **Kehena Black Sand Beach**, also known as **19-Mile Beach**, is the sandiest spot to take a dip on the coast. It's known for swimming, rather than snorkeling. People who want to be unlawfully naked also gather at this beach. *Be Aware*: Kehena's sand drops off steeply, creating undertow that can be a problem. Weekends can be crowded.

51. MACKENZIE STATE PARK   HIKE

WHAT'S BEST: The largest ironwood grove in Hawaii is along a spectacular coast.

PARKING: From the junction of Hwys. 130 and 137 in Kalapana, go left, heading north. See the previous trailhead for directions to Kalapana. Pass mm14 and, .25-mi. later, turn makai at sign for Mackenzie Park.

HIKE: **Mackenzie State Park (.75-mi.)**

Talk Story: For a dozen miles north of Kalapana, Highway 137 is the **Kehena-Pohoiki Scenic Coast**, penetrating a remarkable coastal gardenscape. And unlike most coastal drives, you don't wind in and out of stream valleys, since the slopes of young Hawaii haven't yet had time to erode. The scenic drive, a country lane beside sea-washed buffs, is a tree-tunnel of breadfruit, palms, pandanus, and other varieties right out of a tropical tree-finder manual. The road took a hit and was moderately realigned after the 2006 earthquake, but now old road sections provide some nice long turnouts.

The 13 acres of **Mackenzie State Park** are surrounded by hundreds of acres of the **Malama Ki Forest Reserve**. Unique lava tables and stools stand near a rock picnic pavilion, and a new (2013) lava-rock restroom adds to an inviting campground. Head right from the picnic pavilion. Within .25-mile you'll find a heiau ruin, enhanced by shrines of recent visitors. Nearby is a cave, opened by a collapsed lava tube. You can also walk the bluffs to the left, or north; the **Mahinaʻakaʻaka Heiau**, lies about .75-mile in that direction. *Talk Story:* The ironwoods were planted in the early 1900s by Ranger A.J.W. Mackenzie, a Scotsman who arrived on the Big Island in 1890. The tree's droppings are not needles and cones, and the ironwood is not related to a pine, according to those zany botanists. The salt-resistant plant is from the South Pacific. *Be Aware:* Earth cracks hide in the forest debris, and sleeper waves pound the bluffs.

What's Best: On weekends this spruced-up beach park is pumpin' with a Puna-style, surfer-and-fisherman scene. Pick an off-hour on a weekday to relax in a natural warm pool.

Parking: Best accessed as part of a trip up Hwy. 137, on the Pohoiki Scenic Coastal Drive. From south of Hilo, follow Hwy. 130 past Pahoa to the coast and go north on Hwy. 137. The beach park is north of mm12, where Pohoiki Rd. joins the coast. Park near the shore, or at the new lot, restrooms, and playing field that is inland.

Snorkel: The **Pohoiki Warm Spring**, a tepid pool, is a short walk away. Head in front of the cottage around the shore of the small bay, and look for a well-used path heading into the dense vegetation. Maybe 75 feet from the shoreline, the cozy pool is roughly 10-feet across and sunken into rock. Easy entry. Best seen while wet. *Talk Story:* Serviceman Isaac Hale (HAH-lay) was killed in 1951 during the Korean War. His family had received the coastal property as part of a land swap with the Puna Sugar Company in the early 1900s. The coast's only boat launch for miles was essential for local coffee and timber producers. These days, lava-viewing tours depart here.

Surf: Bodyboarders, including kids and learners, ride the left-break at the tip of the breakwater into little **Pohoiki Bay**. Walk to the end of the breakwater for the Kodak view. Brave boys and girls on boards head for the treacherous reef break that is to the left, or north, of the boat parking area. Aʻa lava and shallow break present hazards at this surf spot, called **Bowls**. New picnic tables are pocketed along this shoreline.

AHALANUI COUNTY PARK

PUNA COAST

53. AHALANUI WARM POND PARK   SNORKEL

WHAT'S BEST: How much would you have to pay to luxuriate in a warm pool set beside the blue Pacific in a coco palm grove? Zip. This county park is a notable freebie.

PARKING: Best accessed as part of a day trip up Hwy. 137, the Pohoiki Scenic Coastal Drive. From south of Hilo, follow Hwy. 130 past Pahoa to the coast and go north on Hwy. 137. Ahalanui County Park is at mm10.5, just north of Isaac Hale Park and the junction with Pohoiki Rd. A paved parking lot is secured by a chain-link fence.

SNORKEL: Ahalanui County Park is a man-enhanced seaside pool, about 200 feet by 50 feet, heated by geothermal energy just below body temperature. A underground channel from Kilauea's east rift zone warms the pool, which used to be chilly until the 1960 eruption altered the subterranean waterworks. High tide brings slightly cooler temps, but the core thermostat is set to Pele's mood swings. Surrounding the pool is a paved path-slash-sundeck. Entry is made easy by several rock stairs. Swimming with the humans in the chest deep water is a variety of fish and the occasional eel that washes over a spillway where the pool meets the ocean. Previously called **Puala'a Park** and shown on some maps as **Secrets Beach**, Ahalanui has been a county park since 1994.

A lifeguard is on duty from 9:30 to 4:45, but the park is open from 7 to 7. *Be Aware:* Signs warn of bacterial risk if using the pool with open skin sores, as is the case with all freshwater swimming in Hawaii.

54. WAIOPAE TIDE POOLS   SNORKEL

WHAT'S BEST: Some say these coral-rich tubs serve up the best snorkeling on the island—a broad reef of tide pools connected by channels. Adventure snorkelers ... go!

PARKING: Take Hwy. 11 from Hilo and go left on Hwy. 130 toward Pahoa. Use the Pahoa bypass, veer left on Hwy. 132, Kapoho-Pahoa Rd. and continue several miles to the stop sign at Hwy. 137. Turn right, or south. After mm9, turn left on Kapoho Kai Dr., toward Vacationland. After .7-mi., turn right on Ho'olai and then keep left at Waiopae St. Park at reef access, where a cable crosses an open area. Or (better yet) park 100 yards before the cable at an access trail through shaded greenery. Both spots are $3 self-pay.

SNORKEL: A broad pahoehoe reef extends several hundred yards at the south end of Kapoho Bay, in which there are a dozen or more swimmable depressions—the **Waiopae Tide Pools Marine Conservation District**. Pools rich in coral and other marine life extend about 200 yards from the road—curve to the right as you walk out. If using the pathway access (see above) you enter at a grass-banked pool. Some of the pools are more for wading, but farther out they are Olympic-sized, up to 10 feet deep and chockablock with multi-colored coral and smaller reef fish. At high tide you can swim channels that connect pools. Sometimes you need to instantly evolve and walk. Stay well inshore of the breakers, as currents drain the tide pools at the edge of the reef.

55. CAPE KUMUKAHI   HIKE, SNORKEL

WHAT'S BEST: Breathe the freshest air in the world at the most-easterly land in the Hawaiian Archipelago. Then take a dip in sparkling warm water. This spot has big mana.

PARKING: Take Hwy. 11 from Hilo and go toward Pahoa on Hwy. 130. Take the Pahoa bypass and then veer left on Hwy. 132, the Pahoa-Kapoho Rd. Continue for nearly 10 mi. to a stop sign at Hwy. 137. Go straight for 2 mi. to the end of the unpaved road.

HIKE: Kumukahi-Kings Pillars loop (1.25 mi.); Kapoho Bay Seapool (2.25 mi.)

Talk Story: Cape Kumukahi, or "First Beginnings," was given new life by an eruption in 1960, just 4 miles inland. Flowing lava broadened the coast a half-mile on either side of the cape, sparing the lighthouse by a few feet. A beacon has replaced the lighthouse, but you can still see where the fresh lava parted. The cape, with favorable winds and an expanse of ocean, has the purest air in the world according to scientists.

For the **Kumukahi-Kings Pillars loop**, head toward the ocean from the parking area near the light beacon. A road heads over the pahoehoe—not the crunchy a'a road that goes to the right, which is the return route. The path is defined as much by where you can't walk, i.e, the jumbled a'a that flanks the route. In a few minutes you'll hit the road that loops around from the parking lot. Go left on the packed lava chunks and you'll soon reach the east point, marked by a stack of stones. The rock pile on the point is one of the **Kings Pillars**, which are believed to have been erected by Chief Pi'ilani of Maui in the 1500s to help his canoes navigate the treacherous waters. Double back on the return leg and stay on the a'a road to loop around to the parking spot.

KAPOHO BAY SEAPOOL (CHAMPAGNE COVE)

The **Kapoho Bay Seapool** (also known as **Champagne Cove**) is south of the lighthouse. Start out on the four-wheel drive road to the right as you face the water. Keep right on the wider road and you'll pass rock ruins on your left and then come to upright steel posts. Not far ahead is the gravelly beach that gives way to the lovely seapool—a long curling inlet with a few houses on one side and beach flora on the other. *Alternate access:* The seapool is also reachable via a (same-distance) walk through the gated residence of Kahpoho Beach Lots, .4-mile in on KBC Road at mm8.25.

More Stuff: The **Kuki'i Heiau** is an older ruin, mostly overgrown. Seeking a place to make astronomical observations in the 1500s, Chief Umi is believed to have erected the edifice, which is roughly 40-feet square. *Driving:* Go left .25-mile in from the highway toward the Kumukahi Point. Park at a gate and walk the road up to the left, before the little cemetery. The top is about 250 feet and .75-mile away. Also, at bucolic **Green Lake** is a chance to walk lush lands and check out some pyramidal-type ruins that were noted in the 1800s and are thought to predate the earliest Hawaiians. *Driving:* The private road is mauka the highway near mm8, across from KBC Road. A $5 day permit is required; call 965-5500. Organic fruits and lots of aloha are also on hand.

LAVA TREE STATE MONUMENT

SNORKEL: A rocky beach, camper vans, and beach houses on the opposite bank may detract from instant appeal of the **Kapoho Bay Seapool**, or **Champagne Cove**. But hook right to the palms and false kamani and then ease on in to gently geothermally heated, sparkling clear (mostly fresh) water—and you will be smitten. Be sure to bring a mask to view turtles and fish, and reef shoes are a help. A lot of warm pools in this big wide world talk about healing powers, but this one really does the job.

56.   LAVA TREE STATE MONUMENT   HIKE

> **WHAT'S BEST:** Twisted lava statuary line a garden path beneath a towering canopy of leafy trees. Only birdsong and coqui frogs interrupt the hush in this park.
>
> **PARKING:** Take Hwy. 11 Hilo and turn on Hwy. 130 toward Pahoa. Take the Pahoa bypass and veer left on Hwy. 132. The park will be on your left, near mm2.5.

HIKE: Lava Tree loop (.75-mi.)

Begin the **Lava Tree loop** on the groomed path. The park's monkeypod trees, tower over hundred feet, creating a green, backlit dome. Ape, or elephant ears, creeps skyward up the tree trunks and ferns, ohia, ginger, and ti cover the buckled lava that opens here and there with mysterious earth cracks. In this setting are the 'lava trees,' created in the late 1700s when a fast-flowing pahoehoe eruption coated ohia trees up to a depth of 12 feet. The lava flowed away or down into the earth cracks, leaving the hot earth-goo congealed to the moist trunks, which eventually burned and rotted away leaving the lava molds. Dozens of these weird statues seemed to have been placed about by a curator. Add a little moonlit fog and you'd have a recipe for the willies. This dramatic effect is complimented by a cacophony of tweety birds which inhabit the ohia forest that surrounds the monument's 17 groomed acres.

More Stuff: Two nearby attractions will interest families and rainy-day sightseers. The first is the **Panaewa Rainforest Zoo**, a 12-acre county park, with free admission. The ruler of the roost is Namaste, a white Bengal tiger—although primates may beg to differ. The grounds include 100 varieties of palms, and a bamboo-and-rhododendron garden frequented by roving peacocks. *Driving:* Take Highway 11 from Hilo to mm4 and turn mauka on Stainback Highway. Continue 1.25 miles and turn right at signs, which also point toward an equestrian center. Hours are from 9 to 4, daily. Also, **Mauna Loa Macadamias** has a visitors center (with free samples) nearby. *Driving:* Continue from Hilo on Highway 11, passing mm4 and Ikaika Street, and turn left on Macadamia Road. The 2.5-mile drive in may be the trip's highlight on a country lane through 2,000 acres of fragrant orchards that are bordered by towering Norfolk pines.

57. HONOLI'I PAKA (BEACH PARK)   HIKE, SURF

WHAT'S BEST: Where have all the children gone? Hey brah, they're riding the tubes and chillin' at the east side's hottest surf scene. This park has big aloha.

PARKING: Go north from Hilo on Hwy. 19. Pass a scenic point and mm4, and turn right on Nahala St. Then go left on Kahoa, which reaches the park entrance after a short distance. *For Papaikou Landing,* continue north on the highway to mm6 and turn makai on Mill Rd. Pinky's store is on the corner. Drive .3-mi. to the end and park.

HIKE: Honoli'i Beach Park (.25-mi., 100 ft.); Papaikou Landing (.75-mi., 150 ft.)

HIKE/SURF: Around 2003 a nonprofit community group (Basic Image) took over care of this beleaguered county park to preserve it for the keiki (children) and future generations. The results have been astounding, thanks to Bradda Skibs and hundreds of volunteers. On nice weekends, surfmobiles line this quiet street at **Honoli'i Paka (Beach Park)**. A long flight of stairs leads down to the beach and past the park's show-piece: terraces of taro, yellow hibiscus, heliconia, and palms. Walk left on the sand, past heliotropes and palms, to the stream mouth, where many of the surfers enter. Bodyboarders and board surfers ride the offshore tiers, which are normally larger during the winter. A shore break combines with a north-side point break to give surfers a choice. *Be Aware*: A rip current heads out to sea and then circles to the left. *More Stuff:* If going north from Honoli'i Paka, continue on jungly, scenic Kahoa Street. Not far is 50-foot waterfall and pool on a narrow bridge over **Honoli'i Stream** Thrill seekers make the leap. The road loops out to the highway south of Papaikou.

For the quick, sublime getaway to **Papaikou Landing**, duck through the hiker's ease-ment along the lava wall. Down to the right, a stream cascades through pools with banana plants at its banks. You reach the grassy landing—site of old mill ruins, in a parklike setting that features towering royal palms. Take a side-trip to the left if you like, and then double back to drop down to the stream. Go left a short distance to the coral-rubble cove on **Mokihana Bay**.

Mauna Kea

THE SHADOW OF MAUNA KEA AT SUNSET FROM THE SUMMIT

You might say Mauna Kea is as close to heaven as you can get on earth. For the native Hawaiians it is Wakea's Mountain, sired by the god who is the expanse of the sky—The Famous Summit of the Land. Lake Waiau, near the summit, is the umbilicus, or piko, connecting all generations of people on all the islands to the heavens. For scientists from all over the world, the summit is the eye to the heavens where a dozen powerful telescopes explore the far reaches of the universe.

At 13,796, Mauna Kea is not only the highest peak in the Pacific, but, when measured from its base on the ocean floor, the highest in the world—close to twice as high as Mount Everest. Although born of fire, by the many millions of tons of magma that have surfaced from the earth's core, Mauna Kea was in the Pleistocene era capped by 300 feet of solid ice. Permafrost remnants still lie beneath its soils. A trip around the mountain takes you from forests inundated with up to 200 inches of annual rainfall to deserts, lucky to get 10 inches. With all these extremes in elevation, temperature, and moisture it should come as no surprise that a circumnavigation of Mauna Kea is akin to a spin around the globe, taking in some 11 of the world's 13 climatic zones.

On the windward side, Onomea Scenic Drive is in a rain forest, where you can roam the Hawaii Tropical Botanical Gardens and take the historic Donkey Trail to a wild bay. You can get delightfully lost in the garden for hours. Just up the road is Akaka Falls State Park, in the lush upcountry. An easy loop trail that takes in Akaka as well as Kahuna Falls is cut through a tangle of greenery and towering trees that will have you looking for dinosaurs. Nearby, you can depart tourist world at Kolekole and Hakalau beach park, both set in lush stream gorges alongside crashing waves.

Umauma Falls is north of Akaka on the Hamakua Coast. Here the high shoulders of Mauna Kea supported the island's sugar cane fields during the 1800s and well into the 1900s. Above the fields are forests reserves, a thicket of greenery sliced by dozens of streams. The falls are a sight that will impress even Yosemite veterans. The beat goes on as you continue north on the Hamakua Coast, passing verdant cliffs. Side trips over one-lane bridges and tight turns on the Old Mamalahoa Highway allow you to put the dripping flora at arm's length.

The coast yawns open to a huge gulch at Laupahoehoe. You can drop down to see one of the most ruggedly scenic beach parks in the Islands. Notoriously large waves lash against a lava point created by one of Mauna Kea's last eruptions, and a garden of trees decorates a flat bench set below sea cliffs. The scenic beauty is fittingly dramatic for a point best known for the tragic loss of school children and teachers that took place when a tsunami struck on April Fool's Day of 1946. Stay awhile at Laupahoehoe and you'll never forget it.

MAUNA KEA OBSERVATORIES

On the northeast slopes of Mauna Kea are gulches carved not by lava, or even rain, but primarily by ice during the mountain's glacial period. A number of bumpy roads lead up to forest reserves in this area, but the best place to explore is Kalopa Native Forest State Park—one the Big Island's underrated-attractions. Pick from nature strolls and forests treks in this groomed arboretum, which is set within 500 acres of forest. Another forest reserve, Ahualoa, will bring about the adventurer among hikers particularly attracted to these forests. The Ahualoa reserve takes in some of Mauna Kea's north slopes, which are the pastoral lands of the Parker Ranch, rolling grasslands dotted with eucalyptus and conifers lying at the foot of Waimea's Kohala Mountains.

Mana Road, near Waimea, takes a 45-mile contour around Mauna Kea, ending at Saddle Road. At this north end, even passenger vehicles can drive in for miles. Hikes are available toward the green pu'us and, a few miles later, the arid gulches that fall from the summit. Compare this rural greenery to the high plains on the south side of Mauna Kea, accessible from Saddle Road. That dry, lava-scoured zone shared with Mauna Loa gets 15 inches of rain in a good year.

At an elevation of just 6,000 feet, the Kilohana trailhead is an opportunity to explore the native forests that thrive in this harsh environment. Expeditionary trails rent skyward from Kilohana, but birders and strollers can sample the interesting lowlands of this remote region. A hike here will serve to acclimatize visitors headed for higher altitudes, as will the short hike to Pu'u Huluhulu, which is square in the saddle between the world's highest peaks. The short hike to this native tree sanctuary will take you a long way towards appreciating the geography of the Big Island.

If you head up Mauna Kea Observatory Road from the saddle, you pass the southern entrance to Mana Road, called Keanakolu Road on this end. During good weather,

KALOPA NATIVE FOREST STATE PARK

passenger cars can get in quite a distance on this old cowboy trail that leads to the lush Hakalau National Wildlife Refuge. It's tough to see all of the Big Island on a week's vacation, but local hikers can dedicate days to exploring these hinterlands.

The road is excellent to the Onizuka Center for International Astronomy, which is set amid a half-dozen pu'us at the 9,000-foot level. You'll have great views and learn more than you can handle about Mauna Kea. But it's well worth the effort (and four-wheel drive or tour van) it takes to get the final few miles to the top, where you will learn in short-of-breath moments what words could never impart.

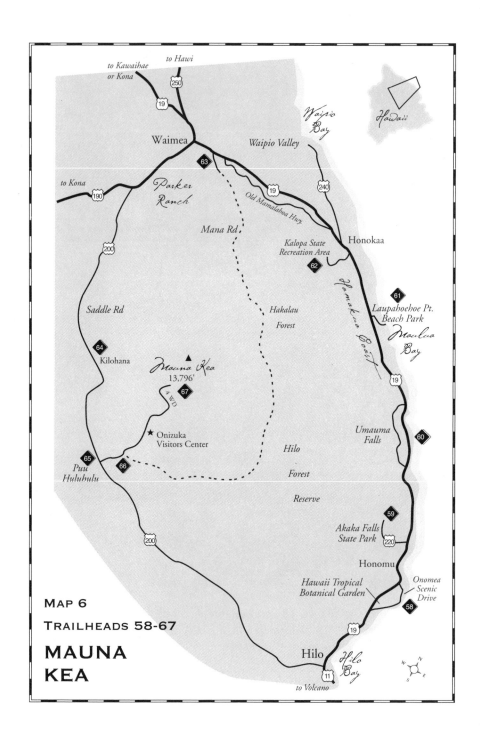

to Kawaihae
or Kona

to Hawi

250

19

Waipio Bay

Hawaii

Waimea

63

*Parker
Ranch*

Waipio Valley

240

to Kona

190

Old Mamalahoa Hwy.

19

Mana Rd.

Kalopa State
Recreation Area

Honokaa

200

62

Hamakua Coast

Saddle Rd

Hakalau

Forest

61

Laupahoehoe Pt.
Beach Park

*Maulua
Bay*

64

Kilohana

Mauna Kea
13,796'

4 WD

67

19

★ Onizuka
Visitors Center

Hilo

Umauma
Falls

60

65

*Puu
Huluhulu*

66

Forest

Reserve

59

Akaka Falls
State Park

220

200

Honomu

Onomea
Scenic
Drive

*Hawaii Tropical
Botanical Garden*

58

MAP 6

TRAILHEADS 58-67

MAUNA
KEA

Hilo

19

*Hilo
Bay*

N
W   E
S

11

to Volcano

TRAILHEADS

58-67

TH :	TRAILHEAD
HIKE :	HIKES AND STROLLS
SNORKEL :	SNORKELING, SWIMMING
SURF :	BOARD, BODYBOARD, BODYSURF
MM :	MILE MARKER; CORRESPONDS TO HIGHWAY SIGNS
MAKAI :	TOWARD THE OCEAN
MAUKA :	INLAND, TOWARD THE MOUNTAINS

ALL HIKING DISTANCES IN PARENTHESES ARE ROUND TRIP. ELEVATION GAINS OF 100 FEET OR MORE ARE NOTED. SEE RESOURCE LINKS FOR CONTACTS AND TELEPHONE NUMBERS.

58. ONOMEA SCENIC DRIVE   HIKE

WHAT'S BEST: Along a lush, four-mile scenic byway are the Big Island's best tropical garden and short hikes to several wild coves. Anyone with a green thumb will want to put a gold star on the map and spend the afternoon.

PARKING: *From Hilo*: Take Hwy. 19 north past mm7 and veer makai on the scenic route, toward Onomea Bay. Continue 1.75 miles to the Hawaii Tropical Botanical Gardens. *Note:* An admission of about $15 is charged. *For the Donkey Trail* to the beach, park at a small turnout just north of the garden offices. *From Kona:* Going south on Hwy. 19 toward Hilo, turn left at mm10.5 at the scenic road (Kulaimano) in Pepe'ekeo. Follow Old Mamalahoa Hwy. about 2.25 mi. *For Pepe'ekeo Point,* see below.

HIKE: Hawaii Tropical Botanical Gardens (1.25 mi., 150 ft.); Donkey Trail to Onomea Bay and Turtle Cove (1.25 mi., 150 ft.); Pepe'ekeo Point (1 mi.)

The experience begins at the **Hawaii Tropical Botanical Garden** as you descend a 500-foot boardwalk through a streamside Eden, under the welcoming limbs of monkeypods, mangos, and tree ferns—all lovingly tended by the garden's dedicated staff. You'll get help from a trail guide, as well as a tasteful array of signs and markers. Begun in 1978 by Dan and Pauline Lutkenhouse, the nonprofit garden has blossomed into Big Island's finest. You'll find more than 2,000 different species, including a plethora of palms, gingers, orchids, and heliconias—the garden is extremely profuse, yet meticulously maintained. The **Palm Jungle Trail** ends at a waterfall that makes three gushing drops to pools before cascading under a footbridge. The **Lily Lake** koi pond would inspire Monet, and kids will squawk when they see the big multicolored macaws at the **Founders Birdhouse**. At the lower end of the garden, a path fronts a shelter at a wild seascape. To the left is **Onomea Bay**, and **Turtle Cove** is to the right. Sit on one of many benches and you'll be surprised how the sights, sounds, and smells start to emerge.

The **Donkey Trail** descends a slippery root network under a cathedral of elegant Alexandria palms. Alongside is **Onomea Stream**, the garden boundary. At rough **Onomea Bay** a finger of land protrudes like a gangplank into oncoming waves. Check it out and then go right, crossing the stream to follow a fenced public easement to **Turtle Cove**, a.k.a. Kukilu Bay. You'll get a peek into the lower gardens. *Note:* Another trail to Turtle Cove is at mm1.5 south of the garden entrance. *Talk Story:* The Donkey Trail is so named for the beasts that would haul sugar down to the bay in the late 1800s. The Kahili'i fishing village, formerly at this site, was wiped out by the big wave of 1946.

The wild fishermans' perch at **Pepe'ekeo Point** is one of only a few access points on the south Hamakua Coast. *Driving:* Continue north from Onomea on Old Mamalahoa Highway until this segment ends at Sugar Mill Road. Go right downhill for 1.5 miles to public parking at Beach Road. (If coming from the north, turn left on Sugar Mill Road at mm11.) Walk left on a paved road (where large-parcel homes are planned) and then go right on a grassy path toward the Coast Guard light. From the light, a trail leads to a nook in the ironwoods just above a usually turbulent ocean. You can wander the shoreline bluffs (mindful of big waves) and come across old sugar mill ruins.

59. AKAKA FALLS-HAMAKUA BEACHES   HIKE, SNORKEL, SURF

WHAT'S BEST: The Big Island's famous tropical waterfall is easily accessible. Nearby scenic beach parks in stream gorges are relatively deserted.

PARKING: Pass mm14 while heading south on Hwy.19 toward Hilo. Turn mauka on Hwy. 220, Akaka Falls Rd. Follow the signs uphill for 3.75 mi. to a large paved lot. A fee of $5 per car is charged; free parking just outside the gate. A $1 per person hiking fee for persons not using the pay lot. Directions to Kolekole and Hakalau beach parks below.

HIKE: Akaka Falls loop (.5-mi., 125 ft.); Kolekole Beach Park (.25-mi.); Hakalau Paka (Beach Park) (up to .5-mi.)

Akaka Falls State Park is on the tour-bus circuit and if you hit the trail at midday you might feel like you should be wearing a cowbell. Still, Akaka and Kahuna Falls deliver the scenic goods. The path makes an oval around 65 acres alongside **Kolekole Stream**, passing a who's-who among tropical flora—bamboo, plumeria, ferns, ti, bird of paradise, and red ginger to name a few. All crowd the trunks of large trees. Heading down to the right on the path, you cross the stream and reach **Kahuna Falls** overlook, which bursts from a side canyon to make its 125-foot fall in two pitches. You the pass an enormous banyan before reaching the railed viewing area for **Akaka Falls**. Meaning "split" or "crack," the 440-foot free-fall of water demonstrates the later stage of the Mauna Kea volcano, when runoff gouges gorges. The final leg of the loop crosses a footbridge and passes philodendrons with leaves as big as card tables. The park was spruced up (trail maintenance, new restrooms) by a 2009 project.

HAWAII TROPICAL BOTANICAL GARDENS, AKAKA FALLS

Kolekole Beach Park is a dramatic inlet along cliffs, where the stream waters of Akaka Falls meet the sea. *Driving:* Go north on Highway 19 from the Akaka Falls turnoff and look left (mm14.25) at the start of a highway bridge. In traffic, you may want to cross the bridge and hang a U-turn. When coming south, pass mm15, cross the bridge, and make an immediate right. The .25-mile scenic road down, part of the **Old Mamalahoa Highway**, passes huge monkeypods. The park's calling-card is a cascade and swimming pool that gets frosted by foam during high surf. A pebble-and-rock beach fronts the rough shore way beneath the highway bridge.

Hakalau Paka (Beach Park), a family-picnic pleaser, is set on either side of a stream at a small bay, connected by a spillway road. This former sugar town gets high marks for both dramatic scenery and aloha. *Driving:* From Kolekole Beach Park, continue north on the old highway across several bridges to sleepy Wailea, where you join Highway 19 at mm15.25 and a pedestrian overpass. Cross the highway and take the .25-mile road down past the sugar plantation village. Or, go north on Highway 19 to the overpass at mm15.25 and turn right. At the park, to the right across the spillway are palmy

picnic tables and a mural that says it all: on a white wall are red, yellow, and green handprints of the many volunteers who created and now maintain the park. If you say hello to locals, they'll treat you like a guest. At the fringe of the picnic area are ruins that speak of Hakalau's bygone days as a sugar town.

More Stuff: A half-dozen forest reserves lie mauka the highway on the Hamakua Coast—above green cane fields and below the arid shoulders of Mauna Kea. One of the easiest to see via passenger car is the **Kaiwiki Forest Reserve**, accessible via **Chin Chuck Road**. It's left on Highway 19, at the pedestrian overpass where you turn right to Hakalau. The road makes a 3-mile run to an elevation of 2,000 feet, where adventures hikers can explore forested wilds.

SURF: Although boulders and surf are a dangerous combination, experienced bodyboarders ride the shore break at **Kolekole Beach Park**. The better bet for surfers, is **Hakalau Bay**. A near-shore break lies off the coarse, black-boulder beach, the best surf spot on the Hamakua Coast north of Hilo.

UMAUMA FALLS

OLD MAMALAHOA HIGHWAY

WHAT'S BEST: Two next-door neighbors vie for tourist attention with garden walks, swimming, kayaking, segways, and ziplines. Umauma Falls is the star of the show.

PARKING: Going north on Hwy. 19 from Hilo, turn left at mm16 on Leopolino Rd. *For World Botanical Gardens visitors center:* Turn right on Old Mamalahoa Hwy. and look for the center on your right. *For Stream Rain Forest:* Continue .25-mi past visitors center and look for the trailhead on the left side. *For Umauma Experience:* Continue about .2-mi. past the Stream Rain Forest trail, and turn left up a signed concrete driveway. (If coming from the north, you can turn right after mm17 on Kauniho Rd., and then left on Old Mamalahoa Hwy.) *Notes:* All activities are subject to an admission fees.

Scenic route: Driving south on Hwy. 19, turn right just before mm19 in Ninole. The **Old Mamalahoa Hwy.** passes jungly **Waikaumalo County Park**, after which adventurers can turn right Pihia-Kahuku Rd. and drive up to the **Pihia-Makai Forest Reserve**. Or just stay on the old highway as it takes a lush, 3.5-mile route to both the garden offices, crossing several streams. (If continuing north, remain on Old Mamalahoa Hwy. after your visits.)

HIKE: Umauma Experience: Garden & Riverwalk (up to 3 mi.). World Botanical Gardens: Garden Stroll (up to .5-mi.); or Stream Rain Forest (1.25 mi., 225 ft.)

The new and deservedly most-popular kid on the block, **Umauma Experience**, has a spectacular zipline, a visitor center with deli and intriguing gift shop (plus deck with a river view), and a walk (or drive) to the area's main event, the **Umauma Falls Overlook**. Umauma could be the cover shot for Glamour Falls magazine. At a photogenic distance away, three falls, punctuated by pools, spew from the jungle gorge. The overlook is best done with the **Garden & Riverwalk**, a stroll with a river view through a palm-and-flower forest. Viewing decks and footbridges accent a serene path. Umauma's zipline, though pricey, delivers the goods with a thrilling ride. Check in at the visitors center, and they'll fill you in on these adventures, plus guided swimming, hiking (try the **Flume Trail**), and kayaking.

Sprouted in 1995, the **World Botanical Gardens** is just starting to grow up to its name. In the lower garden's **Rainbow Walk**, are a hedge **Children's Maze** and a Japanese garden, as well as a host of profuse flowers and shrubs, arranged by species. Segway rides and a zipline is also on hand. *More Stuff:* The price of admission includes a short drive (take the road across from garden offices and turn left in the pastures after about .75-mile) to an overlook of **Kamae'e Falls**, a 60-footer not too distant.

For the pleasant hike along the **Stream Rain Forest** take the left-bearing concrete drive, called the **Rainforest Trail**. With **Honopueo Stream** tumbling by, the paved path curves beside ginger, orchids, and heliconia that will have flower freaks pointing. After .25-mile, the concrete path ends, but the road continues to a view of **Mauna Kea**. Bring bug juice. Many visitors will feel this is this garden's best offering.

LAUPAHOEHOE POINT PARK, HAMAKUA COAST

61.   LAUPAHOEHOE POINT BEACH PARK   HIKE

WHAT'S BEST: This wild point resonates with scenic beauty and the somber memory of the school children who lost their lives here in the great wave of 1946.

PARKING: Drive south from Honoka'a on Hwy. 19. About .75-mi. after mm28, turn makai just north of a small gulch at a signed road to Laupahoehoe Point. A one-lane paved road curves down a scenic 1.25-mi. to a developed lot at the county park.

HIKE: Laupahoehoe Point Beach Park (up to .75-mi.)

To the right at **Laupahoehoe Point Beach Park** is a beefy wharf and boat ramp. On the hill above the ramp is the memorial to the 32 people who were killed, including 21 school children, by a tsunami on the morning of April Fool's Day, 1946. *Talk Story:* "The Day the Sea Went Berserk," locals have named it. A 35-footer struck, bringing boulders and rocks churning in whitewater. Schoolteacher Marsue McGinnis survived by scrambling to the top of the schoolhouse, which became a raft that she was able to clutch until she was rescued at sea that evening. One of her four rescuers was Dr. Leabert Fernandez, a man with whom she had scheduled a first date that night. Needless to say, they later married. Most rescue crafts had been destroyed by the tsunami.

Gardeners groom the spacious lawn dotted with ironwoods and palms that sprawl along this wildly beautiful seacoast. The lava stacks and tide pools that fan out to form the point resulted from an eruption of Mauna Kea that sent lava down the gulch and into the sea. "Leaf of Lava," the ancients called the new point. *More Stuff:* The koa-rich, 8-thousand acre **Laupahoehoe Natural Area Reserve** extends to the 4,000-foot level inland. Try **Homestead Road**, just north of post office and south of the park turnoff—and good luck. You'll find lots of winding roads that see few visitors.

62.   KALOPA NATIVE FOREST STATE PARK   HIKE

WHAT'S BEST: Tree-huggers can choose between a trek in a large forest reserve or a walk in a pretty park. Kalopa is among the top state parks in Hawaii.

PARKING: *From Kona:* Take Hwy. 19 through Waimea and south, passing the Hwy. 240 junction to Honoka'a and mm42. Turn mauka on signed Kalopa Rd. Following signs, continue 4 mi. to the state park. *From Hilo:* Head north on Hwy. 19, pass mm39, and turn mauka at Papalele Rd. and a sign for Kalopa. Follow signs for 2.5 mi.

HIKE: Nature and Arboretum-Polynesian trails (1.25 mi., 150 ft.); Forest Reserve to: Blue Gum Lane loop (1.75 mi., 250 ft.) or Kalopa Gulch loop (4 mi., 475 ft.)

A hundred, well-kept acres of the **Kalopa Native Forest State Park** adjoin 500 additional acres of the **Kalopa Forest Reserve**, a union that will satisfy both exercise trekkers and aimless strollers. *Driving:* For both the **Nature Trail and Polynesian-Arboretum Trail**, pass the campground and enter the groomed grounds. Park to the left above the cabins; a map of the park is located here. Kalopa's central grounds have immediate appeal, with rolling lawns under towering ohia and large koa trees. Showy hibiscus add colorful accents, amid several fern varieties. The **Nature Trail** begins to the left, as you face the upper cabin. Watch your footing on a rooty, .75-mile exercise loop through a thicket of younger trees. The **Polynesian-Arboretum** is a left-veer across the lawn as you face downhill looking at the cabins. Koa is the star of the show, standing

at nearly 100 feet after being planted from seed in 1978. To preserve the native species that grow at 2,000 feet and above is the mission of the state park. One area has a fenced garden, to the right going downhill. *Be Aware:* It's surprisingly easy to get lost in the forest once you lose sight of the park's lawns.

The memorable **Kalopa Forest Reserve** hikes are a journey into the green wilds. *Driving:* Park to the left of the campground entrance, after the caretaker's house. Start walking left on the **Robusta Lane**. Cross the **Perimeter Horse Trail** and about .25-mile later go right on the **Gulch Rim Trail**, which ascends along the edge of the green 300-foot deep gulch. Then, heads up, because not far up the trail you need to cut left across a bedrock dip (don't cross during heavy rains), after which is a trail marker. The ascent continues, amid a variety of large non-native trees as well as a few loulou palms, Hawaii's only fronded native. For the shorter hike, hang a right at the sign for **Blue Gum Trail**. You cut across .5-mile of some of the reserve's planted trees, perhaps seeing a streaking pheasant or two amid the eucalyptus, ironwoods, and paperbark. The trail joins the **Old Jeep Road** (trail); turn right on the road to complete the loop.

For the **Kalopa Gulch Loop**, continue past the **Blue Gum Trail**, ascending for the next mile, at times steeply in deep, rich forest, where 5-foot trunks rise from a tangle of ginger and ferns. You'll veer right along the **Hanaipoe Gulch** and pass **Silk Oak Lane**. Continue up .4-mile to the park boundary and go right on **Ironwood Lane**. Keep your bird eyes peeled for the 'io, the Hawaiian hawk, and the auku'u, a heron. Stay along the fence for .25-mile to join the **Old Jeep Road**, across from a pasture gate on the left. Turn right to descend for 1.5 miles through the non-native tree plantings, an erosion control project of the CCC in the 1930s. Keep trucking down and you'll eventually hit the park. *Be Aware:* Don't let rain or mosquitoes be a surprise.

63. MANA ROAD-WAIMEA   HIKE

WHAT'S BEST: The old cattle trail contours the pastures several thousand feet above the ocean, in the shadow Mauna Kea, which rises an astonishing 10,000 feet higher. Follow the hoof prints of the paniolos, the Hawaiian cowboys.

PARKING: Take Hwy. 19 east from Waimea. Pass the Hawaiian Homelands office on your left near mm55, and then turn right on Mana Rd. Go left at a T-intersection. Pave-

ment ends 2.75 mi. from hwy. *Notes:* Mana Rd. continues for 45 miles to the Mauna Kea Observatory Rd. (see TH65). This trailhead covers the first 15 miles, which in decent weather can be driven by intrepid passenger vehicles. If weather blows in during your trip, sound the bugle and retreat. Regardless, Mana Road becomes a bona fide 4WD about midway. *Be Aware:* Private property borders the road; heed signs.

HIKE: Mana Puʻus (up to 3 mi., 300 ft.); Hanaipoe Gulch (up to 5 mi., 850 ft.)

Talk Story: Until a corporate transition took place in recent years, **Parker Ranch** was the largest privately held cattle ranch in the United States—a quarter-million acres. The paniolos were roping doggies in the early 1800s, 50 years before their American counterparts. **Mana Road** was the cattle trail, circling around Mauna Kea and across the saddle to Mauna Loa on the Puʻu Oʻo Trail, and then down to ships in Hilo harbor. Mana Road begins at nearly 3,000 feet, over the gentle green contours of the saddle between Mauna Kea and the Kohala Mountains.

About 4 miles from the highway you'll reach the first of Mana Road's many unlocked but closed cattle gates: secure all gates behind you. To walk the rolling pastures upslope toward the **Mana Road Puʻus**, continue until crossing a cattle guard, after 5 miles into the drive. Roadside fences should be absent and you'll be able to see a trio inland; from right to left they are Puʻu Io, Puʻu Makahalau, and Puʻu Kale, forming a triangle. Now pastoral hillocks, they once spewed Mauna Kea's boiling lava. Look mauka after 6 miles for a dirt tract. Okay, giddyup.

At 6.3 miles into the drive you'll pass a water tank and power line, on a nice red-dirt route. The pastoral scene continues for another 1.5 miles as you go by an old farmhouse and reach a hunter's station, at about 8 miles. Wiliwili trees dot rocky slopes, whitish now rather than reddish. After two more gates and some rutted road—14 miles in — you'll reach **Hanaipoe Gulch**. You're standing at 5,000 feet when Mana Road crosses the gulch, and **Kalopa Gulch** is close by. Two Jeep trails lead up the gulch for about 6 miles, to join a goat road that encircles the volcano. The grade is tolerable and you can pick your way up. On the mountain slopes above are more than a dozen former lava vents, strewn on the steeper, arid cliffs that jut toward the 13,796-foot summit. Pick your own turnaround.

64. KILOHANA   HIKE

WHAT'S BEST: If you came to Hawaii to hike the hinterlands of Mauna Kea, here's your chance. Casual hikers can explore down lower in the birdland forest.

PARKING: From Kona or Waimea, take Hwy. 190 to mm6.25, and turn onto Saddle Rd., Hwy. 200. At mm43.3 (limited sight), turn mauka toward the Kilohana hunter checking station that sits just above the highway. (When the Waikaloa extension of Saddle Road is completed, you will have to turn left at its junction with the old Saddle Road.) *Be Aware:* Avoid Kilohana on weekends when hunters may be present. Also, the state *may* require a hunting permit to enter.

HIKE: Pu'u La'au Road (from .25-mi. to 32 mi.)

From an elevation of 5,600 feet at the Kilohana hunter's station, **Pu'u La'au Road**, a.k.a. Skyline Road, climbs gradually, then steeply, on the upper shoulders of Mauna Kea. In good weather, most passenger cars can make it the first 4.25 miles to the ranger station that sits near Pu'u La'au. This lower section of cinder road, however, has the best hike, through the **Kaohe Forest Reserve**, a dryland Mamane-Iliahi forest that is habitat for native birds. At the ranger station, the road forks. The left fork takes a hairy, 32-mile circumnavigation of the peak, winding up near Hale Pohaku at the Onizuka Visitors Center. Even in a chunky SUV, the route takes about 5 hours, climbing 3,000 feet. Trekking trailblazers who drive to the old ranger cabin can get a taste of this trail, but prepare for both blazing sun and snow. The road skirts the lower boundary of the scraggly **Mauna Kea Forest Reserve**. The right fork at the old ranger cabin heads seriously up, and eventually climbs almost 5,000 feet over a ragged 12 miles. This right fork will give you some exercise, plus spectacular views of Mauna Loa, Hualalai, and Maui on the downward leg. About a mile from the ranger cabin, the road forks again; the right fork climbs to about 10,000 feet. The left fork bears toward the observatory stations at Pu'u Pohaku, near the summit. *More Stuff:* You'll see picnic tables at **Mauna Kea State Park**, on a dry, windswept plain at mm34.

65. PU'U HULUHULU   HIKE

WHAT'S BEST: It's not just fun to pronounce. This mini-hike in the middle of the saddle offers spectacular vistas and is a smart way to acclimatize to the altitude.

PARKING: From Kona or Waimea, take Hwy. 190 to mm6.25, and turn onto Saddle Rd., Hwy. 200. Continue to mm28 and pull off to the right at a paved parking lot and hunter checking station. The trailhead is directly across from the Mauna Kea Access Road.

HIKE: Puʻu Huluhulu (.75-mi., 200 ft.)

A ten-minute traverse takes you atop **Puʻu Huluhulu**, a bump almost dead center in the lava-scoured **Humuʻula Saddle** between the Big Island's two big mountains. With its summit above the lava flows of 1843 and 1935, and also beyond the chomping teeth of range cattle, Puʻu Huluhulu has grown into a native tree sanctuary. On top are a picnic area and a few mamane and wiliwili trees, along with other flora. Take the time to do a slow 360-degree spin on this place of geographical significance.

66. MANA ROAD-HUMUʻULA SADDLE   HIKE

WHAT'S BEST: Lush forests reside below Mauna Kea at 7,000 feet, with blue water views and chilly trade winds. If you want a slice of wild nature, here it is.

PARKING: From either Hilo or Kona, head to the middle of Saddle Rd., Hwy. 200. At mm8, turn on the Mauna Kea Access Rd. Continue 2 mi. and veer right on an unpaved, public road where a sign reads "4-Wheel Drive Recommended."

HIKE: Hakalau National Wildlife Refuge (up to 3 mi., 650 ft.); Dr. David Douglas Monument (.75-mi., 275 ft.)

Mana Road, called **Keanakolu Road** on this side of the mountain, circles for 45 miles around Mauna Kea to Waimea. Passenger cars creeping along in lower gears normally can navigate all but the middle 5 or 10 miles of the unpaved cattle road, *if* wind, rain, or fog are not present, and no big rain storms have created serious ruts or mud. Four-wheel drive vehicles are preferable. Plan for 3 hours of round-trip driving. The road swerves through the puʻus around the **Puʻu Oʻo Ranch**, roughly maintaining a

6,800-foot elevation. After 16 miles, the road dips down a grade, and you'll find a gate for the **Hakalau National Wildlife Refuge**. Some 7,000 of the refuge's 32,000 acres are open to the public, while the rest are reserved for the endangered species of birds.

The **Dr. David Douglas Monument** is about a mile beyond the refuge road, at 18 miles in on the dirt road. Go downhill across tree-fringed pasturelands to a gate in the **Humu'ula Forest Reserve**. The monument, erected in 1934, is a short distance after the gate. *Talk Story:* The famous yet unfortunate botanist after whom the Douglas fir is named was inspecting the forest plantings when he fell into a

MAUNA KEA SUMMIT LELE (OFFERING PLATFORM)

pit, dug to trap wayward cattle. Sadly, the pit was occupied already by an enraged bull. Douglas died at age 35. Some say triple-D was pushed into the pit by escaped Aussie convict Ned Gurney. *More Stuff:* For the nearby **Pu'u O'o Horse Trail**, see page 137.

67.   MAUNA KEA SUMMIT   HIKE

WHAT'S BEST: What can you say about the top of the world? Scientists and spiritualists can join hands on the sacred summit. Mauna Kea is a high-impact experience that requires some planning.

PARKING: From either Hilo or Kona, head to the middle of Saddle Rd., Hwy. 200. At mm28, turn on the Mauna Kea Access Rd. Continue 2,500 ft. over 6 mi. on this excellent road to the Onizuka Center for International Astronomy Visitor Information Station.

Driving Notes: All visitors should stop for 30 to 45 minutes to acclimatize to high altitudes at the visitors center, which sits just below 9,300 ft. The road continues from the center, climbing more than 4,000 ft. over 8 mi. to the summit trail and observatories. The first 5 mi. is unpaved washboard, with grades up to 15 percent. The last 3 miles is paved again. Four-wheel drive is highly recommended by park rangers. Tour vans will take you up for varying prices. Two of the better are Hawaii Forest & Trail (Kona side) and Arnott's Lodge (Hilo side). One disadvantage to taking a tour is that they are not allowed visit Lake Waiau and the Mauna Kea Ice Age Natural Area. So, consider renting a four-wheel drive vehicle, which will be cheaper anyway for 2 passengers or more. See *To Four-Wheel or Not To Four-Wheel?* on page 214.

HIKE: Onizuka Center (up to .75-mi.); Mauna Kea Summit and observatories (.75-mi., 225 ft.); Lake Waiau and Mauna Kea Ice (.75-mi., 200 ft.)

Be Aware: Bring warm clothes, as low temps are common. The summit is arid, with clear skies 325 days a year, but it does get snow and high winds. The likelihood of a symptom of altitude sickness is fairly common—oxygen is 40 percent less than sea level (see *Free Advice and Opinion*, page 213). Slooooooow down.

Perched at 9,000-plus feet and surrounded by a handful of pu'us, the **Onizuka Center for International Astronomy** is a destination unto itself. The volunteer staff is very knowledgeable, although a crush of visitors can leave them with little time for extended queries. Every evening a stargazing telescope is set up, and on weekends, the staff leads a tour to the top—transportation not included. It's all free. The center honors Hawaii's favorite son, Ellison Onizuka, an astronaut killed in the Challenger Space Shuttle disaster of 1986. Spend your acclimatizing time by walking toward the far end of the parking lot, on the short **Hale Pohaku Trail** to a some rare silversword plants. Only several remain here. Longer walks in the area lead to the tops of several pu'us, all visible from the center's outside patio. The tallest, at 9,394 feet, is **Pu'u Kalepeamoa**, which you can get to by crossing the road and veering right on a trail. *Note:* Center hours are from 9 a.m. to 10 p.m. daily. *More Stuff:* Trekkers who want to say they walked all the way to the top of Mauna Kea, by God, can take the **Summit Trail** that begins near the center. Average hike time is 8 hours, round trip.

If you're taking a tour to the **Mauna Kea Summit**, be sure to ask if you are allotted the 20 or 30 minutes that it takes to do the hike. If you are travelling independently, set your trip odometer, stick it in gear, and go. After 7 miles, keep right as the road makes a hairpin right. Chug another mile up a switchback and then keep right again where another road drops left to the Keck and NASA observatories. Just after this junction, park on the left, near the University of Hawaii and United Kingdom buildings. The trail to the summit is across the street. The red-cinder summit trail crosses a little saddle and makes the short climb to **Ka Piko Kaulana o Ka Aina**, "The Famous

Summit of the Land." A shrine at the top is for Hawaiians to worship at this sacred spot, also known at **Wakea's Mountain**, the mountain begat by the god of all the heavens. In recent years, Hawaiian groups and their supporters have begun to seek limits to the ever-expanding telescope emplacements on the mountain's crater rims, which now number over a dozen. The view from the top is fabulous to the nth degree.

The **observatories** of Mauna Kea are for working scientists, but a few will let you inside to take a peek. Try the **University of Hawaii Telescope** at the parking area, from behind which you can also get a view of the 10 or more telescopes that encircle the mountain. Just up the hill, the **Gemini Telescope** will wow you with its gigantic retractable roof. To make a driving loop, head down and turn right after 100 feet. Proceed to the **Keck Observatory**, which has two white domes connected by a long building. Enter the left-side dome, where, between 10 and 4 on weekdays, you can duck inside to a public alcove to see the intricate and massive workings of the telescope. The shiny dome to the right of the Keck is the **NASA Infrared Telescope**. Then drive to the right of the Keck to circle around the detour road which takes you by the flat-topped **Subaru Telescope**. It is able to observe squeaks of light up to 15 billion light years into the universe.

The 4,000-acre **Mauna Ice Age Natural Area Reserve** boundary is just 1.5 miles up the dirt road from the Onizuka Center. In the recent geologic past, perhaps only 8,000 years ago, a 300-foot thick, 25-square-mile cap of ice covered Mauna Kea, extending down it slopes to within a few thousand feet of sea level.

The heart of the reserve is between 6 and 7 miles as you drive up, where you'll see a paved turnout on the right. This area is sometimes called **Moon Valley**, since it was used to simulate the moon's landscape before the Apollo missions—and woo-woo theorists proclaim that photos taken on the moon were actually shot here. Yeah, here and outside of Vegas. One trail to quirky **Lake Waiau** begins across the street from the turnout. Although it's a short hike, conserve your energy. Resting at the base of Pu'u Poliahu, the milky green lake is thought to be the third highest in the U.S., at 13,020 feet. It's about 10 feet deep, set in a cinder crater and devoid of vegetation. The lake's main claim to fame is that it is fed by a gradually melting permafrost beneath Mauna Kea's desert slopes— a vestige of the Ice Age. For the ancient Hawaiians, Lake Waiau was the "umbilical cord to the heavens," where birth offerings were made. For certain ceremonies, would-be ali'i would scale Mauna Kea as a test of courage and skill, and bring the sacred water down to coastal villages. The harrowing trek to the summit was also made for more prosaic reasons.

Sort of nearby is the **Keanakakoi Crater**, which was a quarry for basalt that was used for adzes and weapons. Volcanic glass, a black rock very similar to the obsidian, was also gathered in this area—and nowhere else in the Pacific universe that was ancient Hawaii. The old quarry is 700 feet in elevation down from the lake, on the **Humu'ula Trail**.

BIG ISLAND
Driving Tours

BIG ISLAND DRIVING TOURS

About twice the size of the other Hawaiian Islands combined, the Big Island doesn't surrender its charms to a leisurely day trip. Circling just the perimeter roads is nearly a 300-mile jaunt that only Indy wannabes can make in less than 7 hours without pit stops. The Big Island is like visiting five islands in one, literally. Driving from Hilo to Kona, or from Kohala to Kau, has all the impact of an inter-island flight. Although traffic can be congested in a 20-mile segment around Kailua-Kona, and to a lesser extent for a few miles around Hilo and Waimea, much of the driving will call forth fantasy car commercials. Getting off the scenic highways onto numerous country lanes and byways will be pleasantly lonely. The following three driving tours are designed to depart from the Kona-Kohala area. Cross-reference the trailhead sections for more details.

TOUR ONE: PARKER RANCHLANDS & KOHALA VALLEYS

WHAT'S BEST: The Kohala valleys surrender the scenic wonders most sought by many Hawaii visitors—green chasms laced with waterfalls that open to remote beaches. The high pastures and rolling hills of Parker Ranch around Waimea are soothing to the eyes. Shoppers and snoopers will love the sugar-town storefronts of Hawi and Kapaʻau, on the north Kohala coast, ideal places to settle in for lunch. Then drive back through sunny South Kohala, with the opportunity to duck in at several history parks and sunset beaches.

DRIVING TIME FROM KONA: 4 to 7.5 hours, depending on stops (165 miles). **ROADS:** Paved state highways. **BEST DAYS:** Any day is okay. Use caution on Hwy. 190, where lack of shoulders and speeding drivers pose hazards. **START TIME:** Start early to avoid the cloud layer that often rises to Waimea later in the day. If you encounter foul weather in Waimea, bail out. Go west and find a sunny beach in South Kohala.

START EARLY, KAILUA-KONA, TAKE HWY. 190, PALANI RD., TOWARD WAIMEA

Highway 190—also called the **Mamalahoa Highway** or **Belt Road**—climbs to about 3,000 feet and opens up to expansive seaward looks toward the South Kohala coast. On the mauka side, you'll have a sunrise panorama of the Kohala Mountains, Mauna Kea, and Hualalai Volcano. Much of the 38-mile run on Highway 190 is over lava flows from 1859 and earlier, where ohia grasslands are springing to life. A few miles from town (the mile markers click down) you'll enter some of **Parker Ranch's** quarter-million acres of green pastures. Just a mile before Waimea, on the left, is **Puʻuopelu,** "the meeting place," John Palmer Parker II's attractive French Provenical homestead., built in 1862. Next door to Puʻuopelu is **Mana Hale,** the 150-year-old, koa-interior home of patriarch John Parker Palmer. *Note:* Unfortunately these sites will probably be closed. But **Camp Tarawa,** a memorial to a WWII training site, is open. It's located on the highway near the ranch entrance.

IN WAIMEA, GO RIGHT, OR EAST ON HWY. 19. CONTINUE FOR SEVERAL MILES. BEFORE MM52, VEER RIGHT ON OLD MAMALAHOA HWY. (Tour will double back to Waimea)

The old highway, now a country lane, curves on a 10-mile contour through choice ranchlands with blue-water views. At a downhill S-turn that is 3.75 miles from the main highway, look on the right for a reminder that you're on a volcano. Dripping ferns mark the entrance to a cavern, the result of a collapsed lava tube of an old Mauna Kea eruption. Then you'll pass large eucalyptus groves and the lush **Ahualoa Forest Reserve**, before the old road rejoins the highway.

MIDMORNING. TURN RIGHT ON HWY. 19. THEN TURN LEFT, NEAR MM42, ON HWY. 240 TOWARD HONOKA'A AND WAIPIO VALLEY

Honoka'a, whose several blocks of storefronts are designated as an official "Main Street USA" town, is a good place to snag another cup of coffee. Paniolos made this an Old West town in the cattle heyday. Today you'll find several browser's stores. Walking the whole town is recommended, but your best bet is **Honoka'a Marketplace**. Highway 240 passes coastal fields and ironwood groves before ending at **Waipio Valley Lookout**. On a nice day, you may be tempted to blow off the driving tour and walk down there. Upon leaving the lookout, you have the option of veering left on Kukuihaele Road, a 2-mile scenic byway that passes the old social hall, sugar shacks, and the island-style gifts at **Waipio Valley Artworks**.

BACKTRACK ON HWY 240 TO HONOKA'A AND HWY. 19. TURN RIGHT AND RETURN TO WAIMEA

Waimea, which is also called **Kamuela** to avoid postal confusion with Kauai's town of the same name, had its origins as a company town for Parker Ranch. John Palmer Parker had the brains, pluck, and the luck of being in the right place in the right time. After arriving in 1809 from Massachusetts, he jumped ship. He then married a Hawaiian chiefess and became acquainted with Kamehameha the Great. Parker was handy with a gun and horse, and he was able to help the king in subduing the wild cattle that were ruining agricultural lands. This arrangement netted Palmer a small plot of land, that was parlayed in the following years to a ranch larger than any in America.

WAIPIO LOOKOUT, HONOKA'A MARKETPLACE

'ROAD' TO WAIPIO, CHURCH ROW

Although lacking a central charm (Parker Ranch seems to have disdain for tourists) Waimea has several spots of interest. As you enter town, after mm56, pull off to the right on **Church Row**. You'll find several historic churches, including Buddhist, Baptist, and congregational—a calabash that is Hawaii. **Imiola Congregational**, at the end of the row, was built in 1855 and features koa and other hardwoods from floor to ceiling. The bad news: the churches aren't always open. Continuing on the highway, on the left is the shopping center that houses the **Parker Ranch Museum and Visitor Center**, a stop that may appeal to people with a special interest in ranching.

AT THE SHOPPING CENTER, TURN RIGHT ON HWY. 19-HAWI AND KAWAIHAE

On the right at address 65-1692 is the Big Island's top art museum, the **Issacs Art Center**. Housed in an airy, historic school building, you'll find works of Hawaii's finest, including Herb Kane, Madge Tennet, Jean Charlot, and Jules Tavernier. The staff know their stuff and you will get a complete experience—without being overwhelmed.

ABOUT 2 MI. FROM WAIMEA, VEER RIGHT ON HWY. 250-KOHALA MOUNTAIN RD.

SIDE TRIP: Highway 19 continues left at the above junction. Immediately to the left on Highway 19—look for a tall rock wall—is the **Kamuela Museum**. After many decades, this family operation closed in 2008. The remarkable collection reflected Parker Ranch, ancient Hawaii, and vintage Waikiki—totally eclectic. TV comedian Roseanne Barr, oddly enough, bought the place in 2011; let's hope she reopens it .

Highway 250 twists downhill for 20-plus miles through the pastoral **Kohala Mountains**, with blue-water views and through lovely tunnels of eucalyptus and ironwoods. Those green hills inland midway on the drive are part of the **Pu'u Umi Natural Area** Reserve, million-year-old volcanic vents that became the island's first land.

NOON & LUNCH. REACH HAWI AT JUNCTION WITH HWY. 270

The historic sugar mill town of **Hawi** is a block or two on either side of the junction; **Kapa'au**, is 2 miles to the east, or right. In Hawi, people flock to the **Bamboo Restaurant**. In Kapa'au, check out the **Nanbu Courtyard**.

POLOLU BEACH, KAMEHAMEHA STATUE IN KAPA'AU

These towns combine to make the Big Island's best runs of shops and galleries. In Hawi, the Bamboo has a gift gallery, and, nearby, **As Hawi Turns** is crammed with island delights. Don't overlook Hawi's back alleys, where you'll fine quirky stuff.

Window shoppers won't be finished after Hawi. In Kapa'au stop on the right at the **North Kohala Center** to see the **Kamehameha Statue**, the famous painted-bronze likeness that was lost at sea near the Falkland Islands on its voyage from Italy, where it was crafted. A new statue had already been re-commissioned for Honolulu when an enterprising sea captain arrived with the original, which he had fished from the drink. The eight-foot, six-inch original giant became an extra, and was erected in Kohala, where the king was born and reared. Across the street look for jewelry and fine gifts at **Elements**, and for artworks, check out **Ackerman Galleries**, which has shops on both sides of the highway. You'll find more stuff by wandering around town and checking out the back streets.

AFTERNOON. CONTINUE EAST, TOWARD THE END OF THE ROAD AND POLOLU VALLEY LOOKOUT ON HWY. 270

The road east of Kapa'au, about 7 miles long, enters lush tropical forests with a few one-lane bridges. You'll pass the orignial art and local slack key CDs at **Rankin Gallery**, which is next to and the colorful **Wo Tong Society Building**. The lazy highway comes to an end where a guardrail marks the **Pololu Valley Lookout**, a stunning sight.

BACKTRACK ON HWY. 270 TOWARD HAWI. CONTINUE TO KAWAIHAE

Along the 28-mile run from Pololu Valley to the coast at Kawaihae is a transition from rain forest to a grassland desert. At mm24.5, you can turn right on Lighthouse Road to see the new **Hawaii Wildlife Center**, the Islands' only bird hospital. A half-mile later, turn left on Iole Road to roam the 2,400 acres of lush gardens and historical buildings of **'Iole Foundation.** After leaving Hawii are potential stops at three of Hawaii's best history parks. At mm19 is the Old Coast Guard Road to the trailhead for the

Kamehameha Birthplace and **Moʻokini Heiau**. Then, well marked to the south near mm14, is Lapakahi State Historical Park, with a drive-up interpretive center. Finally, right at Kawaihae is a national historic park, **Puʻukohola Heiau**, a massive structure where Kamehameha finally achieved dominion over all of the Big Island. Nearby, at Kawaihae Harbor, canoe teams may be putting in for practice. At **Kawaihae Village**, check out **Island Herbal**, where you can find locally made soaps, lotions, and other delights for the skin and nose.

SUNSET. AT THE JUNCTION WITH HWY. 19, TURN SOUTH TOWARD KONA

The vast lava fields of **South Kohala** are never more pleasing to the eye that when the big red Kona sun is melting into the Pacific. At the north end of this homeward leg is a view inland of the island's panorama of high volcanoes, looming like far off lands. On a highway that is wide and straight, you can kick back and cruise control over a seemingly extraterrestrial landscape. People longing to do magic hour with bare feet on sand will have several easy opportunities. **Hapuna Beach State Park** is a good choice at the north end of the drive. Midway is **Anaehoʻomalu Bay**, home to on-the-beach cocktails and top-end bar food at **Lava Lava Beach Club**. Or try **Honokohau Harbor**, a quick pull-off with plenty of 'seating' available for the sunset show.

TOUR TWO: COFFEE COUNTRY AND
KEALAKEKUA BAY

WHAT'S BEST: World-renowned Kona coffee will fuel this half-day trip of tasting rooms, along a green corridor as rich in history as it is in agricultural bounty. With spring in your step, stroll Holualoa, the artist's enclave in the hills. Then drop down to visit Old Hawaiian-style towns of Kealakekua and Captain Cook, with their heritage stores, quirky shops, living museums, and botanical gardens—and coffee tasting. Then, teeth chattering, head down to dramatic Kealakekua Bay, for ocean time (more coffee) and a visit to a national historic park. As a finale, plan for a late-day snorkel and a tropical picnic dinner.

TOUR TIME FROM KAILUA-KONA: 3.5 to 6 hours, depending on stopover time and traffic (72 miles). **ROADS:** Paved highways and rural roads, in small towns with moderate-to-heavy traffic. Among the 600 growers in Kona, some 50 have coffee farms and tasting rooms. Keep your eyes peeled for your own discoveries. **BEST DAYS:** Holualoa's streets roll up on Sundays. Try Saturday or any weekday other than Monday, when some attractions are closed. **START TIME:** Since this tour includes stops at businesses and museums, beginning around 10 will give them a chance to be open.

START MID-MORNING. GO SOUTH FROM KAILUA-KONA ON HWY. 11 FROM HENRY DR. AND TURN MAUKA ON HUALALAI RD.

Hualalai Road ascends about 1,000 feet through 3 miles of gardenscape, before reaching **Holualoa**. Now an rustic artist's enclave, this agricultural zone was home to pre-contact Hawaiian farms. Later, a string of family-owned stores were built. They bartered coffee and other farm products with the passing ships that put in at the small harbors of the Kona Coast. During the late 1800s the sugar industry established its only Kona stronghold here, but it was soon eclipsed by coffee. Don't expect anything too spiffy or commercial. It's easy to miss things driving by. Just before Hualalai reaches the highway, is **Blue Sky Coffee** where you can sip and pick up a bag of beans.

TURN LEFT AT THE JUNCTION OF HUALALAI RD. AND MAMALAHOA HWY. 180. CONTINUE FOR ABOUT 3 MI.

Much of Holualoa's attractions are strung along the road, including the galleries and old heritage stores. Earlier stores were manned by Europeans, later by Hawaiians and Chinese, and finally by Japanese. About a dozen of the stores still stand along this 3-mile stretch. Among them are the **M. Onizuka Store** (now a private residence) in Keopu, begun in 1933 by the family of Hawaii's beloved astronaut (Ellison), and **K. Komo Store**, open for nearly a century. Open 24/7, these were mom & pop places, with families living in the back with the pigs, chickens, and gardens. Customers would use one of a store's donkeys, called **Kona Nightingales**, to haul stuff up the mountain.

KAINALIU, DRYING COFFEE BEANS

The **Kona Arts Center** is mauka after you make the turn, just north of Holualoa School. Bright pink, you can't miss it. Up the road, on the mauka side past the library, is perhaps the best gallery in the area, **Ululani**, which features works of former resident painter, the late Herb Kane. Then, a little farther on the mauka side past the post office, is **Holualoa Gallery**, another pay-off stop with paintings, glasswork, and Raku ceramics. Studio 7, featuring pottery and a garden room, is on the other side of the road, as is **Holualoa Ukulele Gallery**, known for fine locally made ukuleles and other collectibles. Nearby is **Paul's Place**, a mom-and-pop mercantile.

BACKTRACK ON HWY. 180. THROUGH HOLUALOA AND REACH JUNCTION WITH HWY. 11. GO SOUTH, AND CONTINUE THROUGH CAPTAIN COOK

Before the junction with Highway 11 you'll have opportunity to bust your mouth on salty-sweet crack seed at **Doris' Place**, and to take a taste and tour at the estate orchards of the **Holualoa Kona Coffee Company**, pleasantly set on the hillside.

Kainaliu is the first set of old-style storefronts you'll pass on Highway 11. Look for the Deco **Aloha Theater**, still playing after all these years. Some two-dozen heritage buildings are scattered on both sides of the road over the next dozen miles, 7 of which are still running after 50 or more years. Fabric lovers will want to stop in to see the collection at **H. Kimura**, which is located on the makai side just as you get into Kealakekua, just down the highway from Kainaliu.

The oldest structure is the **H. N. Greenwell Store**, which opened in 1875 and has housed the **Kona Historical Society** since 1976. Look on the right before mm112, as you're leaving Kealakekua. Henry Nicholas Greenwell brought his gold fortune from California in the late 1800s, and became the daddy of Kona coffee in 1873, when his Kona brew took home a medal in Vienna. Staffed by helpful docents, the store re-creates the experience of what shopping was like in the old days. Admission is $7, less for kids and seniors; hour are Monday through Thursday, 10 to 3. A short walk down the hill from the historical society is **Greenwell Farms**, where you can sample some java and tour some of the 35-acre orchard and low-tech roasting facility that started it all. Tours are free, daily from 8:30 to 4:30. One of the island's best.

South of these places on the highway, you'll pass Napoʻopoʻo Road, one route down to the bay. Just past Napoʻopoʻo Road (right at mm110) is a memorable family outing, the **Kona Coffee Living History Farm**. You'll want to pull into the 7-acre re-creation of the Japanese immigrant coffee and macadamia farm that thrived for about 20 years, beginning in 1925. Open weekdays, 10 to 2; admission is $15 for adults, $5 for kids.

Then, anyone interested in Polynesian agricultural life, should look for **Amy B. H. Greenwell Ethnobotanical Garden**, located on the mauka side, also near mm110 in Captain Cook. Run by Bishop Museum, the 15 acres are landscaped in terraces, with the 30 or so plants that the Hawaiian voyagers brought with them. Above the gardens is an example of the Kona Field System, where forests with trees like koa and hau were used in the making of canoes and dwellings. Hours are 9 to 4, closed Mondays, and admission is $7. Across the street is the venerable, funky **Manago Hotel**.

Past Captain Cook the road enters **Honaunau**, where shops are less frequent and you'll have views down to the bay. For a highly scenic coffee stop, pull in before mm107 on the makai side at the red **Royal Kona Coffee**. They have an outside deck, set up with many Kona coffee varieties. Also on the makai side, about a half-mile after Royal Kona, is **Super J's**, a home-kitchen where you can pick up an authentic plate dinner for later consumption. Look closely, since it's easy to pass by. On the makai side near mm106 is **Coffees ʻN Epicuria**, with more tasting, but also lots of stuff that will end your quest for gifts. Another hot tip: Just past Epicuria, at Middle Keʻei Road, is the **Kona Coast Macadamia Factory**. This low-key place offers deals on big bags of reject nuts, when available. It's open Tuesday through Friday 10 to 5, and Saturday 10 to 4.

NEAR MM104, TURN MAKAI ON HWY. 160 TOWARD PUʻUHONUA O HONAUNAU NATIONAL PARK. AFTER ABOUT 1 MI., TURN RIGHT ON PAINTED CHURCH RD.

SIDE TRIP: If you continue straight for a few miles, instead of turning right on Highway 160, you'll reach **Kealia Ranch Store**, home to lots of reasonably priced arts and giftware, as well as the addictive Mauna Kea Icecap, a creamy shave ice concoction. Look for the old ranch buildings on the makai side at mm101.

PAINTED CHURCH, MANINI BEACH PARK

PUʻUHONU O HONAUNAU CREATORS OF MAUNA KEA ICECAP AT KEALIA RANCH STORE

On wide Highway 160 you leave the Kona commerce behind, beginning a 1,500-foot descent to the Big Island's remarkable bay. **Painted Church Road** is the scenic route down, where, shortly after making the turn you can stop to see the route's namesake. Established in 1898 as St. Benedict's Catholic Church, it became the Painted Church after the artistic Father John Berchman Velge adorned its wooden walls with tropical-themed Christian murals. The spacious grounds feature breadfruit, Norfolk pines, a garden, as well as a spiritually inspiring view. Speaking of which, check out the panorama at **Bay View Farm's** tasting room, which is a half-mile past the Painted Church, on the makai side. A coffee gazebo overlooks the farm's rolling orchard. *Note:* The tasting room may still be closed, due to the sad passing of owner Roz Roy.

CONTINUE, TURN LEFT ON MIDDLE KEʻEI RD, KEEP LEFT ON NAPOʻOPOʻO RD.

Try to save room for one last shot, since partway down on Napoʻopoʻo Road is the **Kona Pacific Farmers Cooperative**—a large facility standing alone at a bend in the road. The co-op's top-of-the-line brew, made with a special step that removes the tiniest of husk impurities, may well win your taste test. The company processes and roasts the offerings of some 300 local growers. Hours are 9 to 4:30, closed Saturdays.

CONTINUE DOWN NAPOʻOPOʻO TO A STOP SIGN. TURN RIGHT, CONTINUE A SHORT DISTANCE TO THE KEALAKEKUA BAY HISTORICAL PARK

Across from the stop sign is **Napoʻopoʻo Wharf**, where kayakers used to put in for the paddle to the Cook Monument. The scene got out of hand, and park officials closed the wharf. The **Kealakekua Bay Historical Park**, just a block to the right, is known for **Hikiau Heiau**, where the ancients were celebrating the fertility season of Makahiki when Captain Cook's ship sailed into the bay in 1779.

BACKTRACK FROM THE PARK, TURN RIGHT ON MANINI BEACH RD.

This little side loop passes an undeveloped park with an exquisite view across the bay toward Kealakekua's famous cliffs. You'll see the white obelisk that is the **Cook Monument** near the point—not to be confused with the farther seaward lighthouse.

The single-lane paved road along the bayshore crosses an a'a lava field where Kame-hameha won a decisive victory at the Battle of Mokuohai, strengthening his reputation as a would-be king. The road widens just before reaching **Pu'uhonua O Honaunau National Historic Park**. One of the Hawaiian Island's best snorkeling spots is just to the right, before the park's entrance station. **Two Step** is the local name for the lava benches that lead to the waters of Honaunau Bay. One dip in Two Step and you'll be hooked. Thus refreshed, loop around on the one-way road, and head into the park. Inside are the remains of a former place of refuge, where miscreants and vanquished warriors could sojourn for short periods to escape more severe punishment. Queen Ka'ahumanu, Kamehameha's favorite wife, once did a night here, and you can bet there were two sides to that story. The pretty site was also an enclave for royalty, and features the largest stone wall you'll find in Hawaii.

By now, the sun should be setting in the Pacific, a sight to behold at the **Pu'uhonua Beach Park**—a spot tourists overlook. To get there, take the unpaved road that is to the left at the lower end of the large parking lot. After a short distance you'll reach a line of palms strung along a strip of sand and a lava reef. A coastal trail leads south from the park. Or, take a stroll out to the reef to catch a peek at a turtle, dolphin, or whale, if you're lucky.

TOUR THREE-HILO HERITAGE COAST

WHAT'S BEST: You won't see the heart and soul of the Big Island until tak-ing Saddle Road to green Hilo. On the back, the Hamakua Coast is cleaved by dozens of stream valleys choked with flora. Tucked away are heritage sugar towns, with blue-water views on open slopes. Hilo's historic old town is host to a huge farmers market with exotic fruits and flowers, and an imagination-defying selection of ethnic clothing, jewelry, musical instruments and crafts.

TOUR TIME FROM KAILUA-KONA: 6 to 10 hours, depending on stops and side trips (215 miles). **ROADS:** High speed scenic highways and paved scenic byways. **BEST DAYS:** Try Saturday or Wednesday to see the Hilo Farmers Market. Although the entire market is covered and many other attractions are indoors, bring an umbrella if you have one. Rain walks are part of Hilo, so don't let weather deter your trip. **START TIME:** Arriving in Hilo between 8 a.m. and 10 a.m. is optimum to catch the market on the upswing, which calls for a 6 a.m. to 8 a.m. departure. In so doing, you leave Kona in no traffic and catch Mauna Kea at sunrise, up high in Waimea.

START EARLY MORNING. TAKE HWY. 19 NORTH FROM KAILUA-KONA TO MM75 AND TURN MAUKA (RIGHT) ON WAIKALOA ROAD. CONTINUE UP ABOUT 10 MILES, TURN LEFT ON HWY. 19 MAMALAHOA HWY, AND TURN LEFT. AFTER A FEW MILES TURN RIGHT ON SADDLE RD., HWY. 200. NOTE: WHEN THE NEW SADDLE ROAD EXTENSION IS COMPLETED, YOU CAN CONTINUE FROM WAIKALOA RD. STRAIGHT ACROSS HWY. 19 AND ONTO SADDLE RD.

In the recent past, narrow and pothole-pocked **Saddle Road** was a no-no for tourists, prohibited by rental car companies. These days, except for the curves and dips of the first 10 miles on the west side, the route is a smooth-sailing highway across the lunar landscapes that separates **Mauna Kea** and **Mauna Loa**.

AFTER MM14, AS SADDLE ROAD DROPS AND CURVES DOWNWARD, TURN LEFT ON KAUMAU-MA DRIVE. KAUMANA MERGES WITH WAIANUENUE AVE. AT A STOP LIGHT. FOLLOW WAIANU-ENUE UNTIL IT ENDS IN HILO. ARRIVE HILO

At the end of Waianuenue Avenue, go right on Kamehameha Avenue. You'll see a public parking lot across the street that extends for several blocks. To avoid congestions later, you're better off parking there and walking a block or two. The market and a walking tour of historic Hilo are described on page 145.

NOON. LUNCH IN HILO

You'll find a number of eateries along the main drag and side streets, ranging from the gourmet **Café Pesto** to rice plates and a burger spa. A better option, particularly in fair weather, is to gather goodies at the market or nearby at **Abundant Life Natural Foods**. Then head to one of two parks, both less than a mile away off Kamehameha Avenue. One option is **Waiakea Fishpond**, at **Wailoa River State Recreation**, the island's largest lake. Huge trees dot a large lawn sprinkled with picnic tables. The better choice for a noon break is **Moku Olu** at Queen **Liluokalani Gardens**. A footbridge leads from near the Japanese-style gardens across to the tiny island, with its palm-lined shore and portrait-quality view across the bay to Hilo. (See page 151 for directions.)

CARLSMITH BEACH PARK

After lunch, you have some choices to make. The scenic route back to Kailua takes about 3 hours; with side trips, you can figure up to 5 hours. So, add those times to what your watch reads as you wistfully contemplate your immediate fate on Moku Olu. If you have time, one sightseeing option is an hour-long trip to see the beach parks that run along the south side of **Hilo Bay**, outside the breakwater. These are described beginning on page 152. Another choice is to check out touristy **Rainbow Falls** and **Boiling Pots**, which are a couple miles above Hilo on the **Wailuku River State Park** (page 148). A third choice, if you have at least two hours to fritter, is to head down to the Puna coast, a beautiful region that most tourists miss. That region is described in trailheads 49 through 55. Okay, mull it over. Or don't mull it over, and forget all of the above by sticking with the program, which continues below.

TAKE HWY. 19 NORTH FROM HILO. PASS A SCENIC POINT AND MM4, TURN MAKAI ON NAHALA ST., AND THEN GO LEFT ON KAHOA

This scenic detour passes **Honoli'i Paka** (Beach Park) where the east-side surf scene amps up on sunny weekends. You get a great view of it from the stairs that lead down to the beach. Then continue on this side road, past the beach park and over the one-lane bridge with a waterfall view. Kahoa Street reaches Kulana Street and then rejoins the highway.

CONTINUE NORTH ON HWY. 19 PAST MM7 AND VEER RIGHT ON THE SCENIC ROUTE, TOWARD ONOMEA BAY.

The **Onomea Scenic Drive** is a verdant 4 miles that passes through the **Hawaii Tropical Botanical Gardens**—the Big Island's best. Not far after beginning the drive, look on the right for the modest digs of **Hawaiian Artifacts**, where artisan Lynn Gephart can offer you some bargain-priced hardwood treasures, including rare replicas of ancient weaponry. The botanical gardens are a mile or so farther. Then continue on the old highway and you'll rejoin the main road.

CONTINUE NORTH ON HWY. 19

SIDE TRIP (30 TO 60 MIN.): TO AKAKA FALLS AND HONOMU. AT MM13 TURN MAUKA ON HWY. 220 A 4-mile mauka drive gets you to **Akaka Falls State Park**. When tour buses arrive, you may have to elbow your way down the short, paved trail to the 440-foot ribbon of white water. But the green amphitheater is striking, backed by a dense arboretum of tropical trees. **Honomu**, the little town near the highway, has an appealing historic block that includes a temple and old shops, frequented by locals and not all cutesied up. For lunch, check out the **Woodshop Gallery Cafe**, or try the cookies, jams, and puffy baked goods at **Mr. Ed's Bakery** up street. In the 1940s this quiet village had a raucous air and was known as "Little Chicago." *Note:* After rejoining the highway from Akaka Falls, look for a sneaky left-turn just before reaching the bridge and mm15. This turn takes you down to **Kolekole Beach Park** where you can snake along the old highway and come back out to the main highway before mm16.

CONTINUE ON HWY. 19. TURN MAUKA AT MM16 ON LEOPOLINO RD.

Here's another choice 4-mile run of the **Old Mamalahoa Highway**, twisting through an all-star assortment of tropical greenery over several narrow bridges. You'll pass the **World Botanical Gardens**, which still have some growing to do, and, not much farther, come to the **Umauma Experience**, a chance to view the queen bee among scenic cascades, **Umauma Falls**. Near the end of this segment, the old highway passes the streamside flora of **Waikaumalo Park**, a hidden surprise.

CONTINUE ON HWY. 19

Along the green margins of the makai side of the road, near mm24, is the former mill camp of **Papa'aloa**, a chance to take a quiet swing by sugar shacks. Nearby the camp dwellings is the old mercantile, still in business, the **Papa'aloa Store**. Then, just a mile farther, past mm25 on the mauka side of Highway 19, is **Laupahoehoe Train Museum**. Long before there were roads on the Hamakua Coast, railroad tracks and bridges spanned the deep gulches, carrying freight cars that were filled with donkey-loads of cane destined to satisfy America's sweet tooth. The train museum's grounds include a schoolhouse, former jail and police station, and post office. South of the museum—on the old highway—is the small **Big Island Bakery**, where bargained priced bread is sold out the back screen door, if you ask.

SIDE TRIP (30 MIN.): TO LAUPAHOEHOE POINT BEACH PARK. TURN MAKAI PAST MM27. You'll reap a healthy interest in fond memories by investing a half-hour of your life on a mile-long trip to the **Laupahoehoe Point Beach Park**. A poignant memorial to the school children and teachers who lost their lives in the giant tsunami on April Fools Day, 1946 is set beside lovely grounds and crashing waves.

CONTINUE NORTH ON HWY. 19

KALOPA NATIVE FOREST STATE PARK

The green gulches you see mauka the highway were carved mostly by the ice cap that covered Mauna Kea eons ago. A number of unpaved tracts lurch mauka through the former cane fields to forest reserves that ring the mountain. On the makai side, near mm36, is **Pa'auilo**, a former plantation town. The field manager's home and workers camp sit above the abandoned mill site. A landing is way farther down, at sea level. If you want to learn more, ask and get an earful at **Earl's Pa'auilo Store**, which is just mauka the highway, next to the post office.

SIDE TRIP (30 TO 60 MIN.): TO KALOPA NATIVE FOREST STATE PARK. PASS MM39, AND TURN MAUKA AT PAPALELE RD. TURN RIGHT ON KALOPA RD., FOLLOW SIGNS UP TO THE PARK. A 5-mile round-trip ride takes you to the upcountry forest reserve and the groomed grounds of **Kalopa Native Forest State Park**. Birders, botanists, and campers will award high marks. You won't have to be a tree-hugger to enjoy a stroll around the luscious gardens that surround the park's cabins, set at a refreshing elevation of 2,000 feet. Then roll back down the hill, keeping left on country-road options that will rejoin the highway, slightly north of the road you came up on.

SIDE TRIP (45 TO 60 MIN.): TO WAIPIO VALLEY LOOKOUT. AT MM42, VEER RIGHT ON HWY. 240 TOWARD HONOKA'A. If you won't otherwise see **Waipio Valley**, it's worth a family squabble to extend the tour to the lookout that would have King Kong pounding his chest. Pick up a tall beverage or ice cream cone in **Honoka'a** to soothe the 9-mile scenic ride to the end of the road. Waipio is a classic green fissure that gives way to a long beach, once the playground of kings.

CONTINUE ON HWY. 19. PASS MM42 AND PIKAKE ST. NEAR MM43 TURN MAUKA ON MAUNA LOA RD. THEN TURN RIGHT IMMEDIATELY ON OLD MAMALAHOA HWY.

A mellow 11-mile segment of the **Old Mamalahoa Highway** runs mauka the new road and then rejoins it just east of Waimea. You'll swerve through open ranch country, rolling hills with copses of eucalyptus and cypress trees. This bypass doesn't add much time but, if you're up to your eyeballs with scenic stuff, just stay on Highway 19.

FROM WAIMEA, TAKE EITHER HWY. 190 TO KAILUA, OR STAY ON HWY. 19 TO KAWAIHAE AND THEN GO SOUTH TOWARD KAILUA.

$\mathcal{Strategies}$ FOR VISITING THE BIG ISLAND

You can get anywhere on the island in one day, but in some cases it will be a long day of driving with little time for hikes and stops. You'll need a very active week to be able to see most of the best stuff. With two weeks, you will still have to choose which featured attractions will have to be postponed until the next trip. A visit of three or four weeks or more is required to take a thorough gander. Depending on the type of visit you'd like t, you can choose from among four different strategies for where to stay and for how long.

KONA BEACH HOG

Stay your whole visit in Kailua-Kona or Kohala resorts, choosing from among the modest to the swank. This option takes advantage of beaches and snorkeling. You can easily spend a week exploring beaches from Miloliʻi north to Hapuna. On alternating days, take day trips to Hawaii Volcanoes National Park, Mauna Kea, Hilo, Mauna Loa, and Waipio Valley. This may be the best strategy if you only have one week. *Downside:* You won't see much of Hilo and the Puna coast, and traffic from Kailua to Captain Cook is almost always congested.

KONA-HILO YIN-YANG

Stay about half the time in Kona and half the time in Hilo. While in Kona, focus on the Kohala beaches, Kealakekua Bay, North Kohala, and South Point. While in Hilo, see Hamakua and Waipio, Mauna Loa and Mauna Kea, Hawaii Volcanoes, and the Puna coast. As a variant on the yin-yang, rob a day or two from Hilo and stay in Volcano, which is one mile from Hawaii Volcanoes National Park. Seeing sunrises and sunsets at the park is a big plus. You can pull off this strategy during a week's stay, but it is perfect for a 10-day stay, or longer. *Downside:* The west side is normally sunnier and has better beaches.

ISLAND HOPPER

Stay at several spots on a trip around the island. You'll enjoy mornings and evenings in different locales, and spend less time driving. For example, if you have 14 nights, spend the first 4 in Kona, the next 2 in Volcano, then 4 in Hilo, 3 or 4 nights in Waimea or Hawi. Island hoppers will also want to consider a night or two in Wood Valley, a serenely beautiful getaway. This strategy makes most sense for longer visits and people who aren't all about beaches. *Downside:* This is a lot of check-ins and checkouts. Two-night minimums are less hectic.

CAMP & INN HOPPER

The Big Island is ideally set up to circle around, spending some nights staying in rustic cabins and campgrounds, and then going modestly upscale in tasteful inns and B&Bs. Money-wise, you can do this for the price of a mid-level resort, or even less. See *Camping and Rustic Lodging* map, for these options. Look at *Where to Stay* to cherry pick among the top inns and B&Bs. *Downside:* Why does there always have to be a downside?

BIG ISLAND *Biking*

KEʻEI VILLAGE

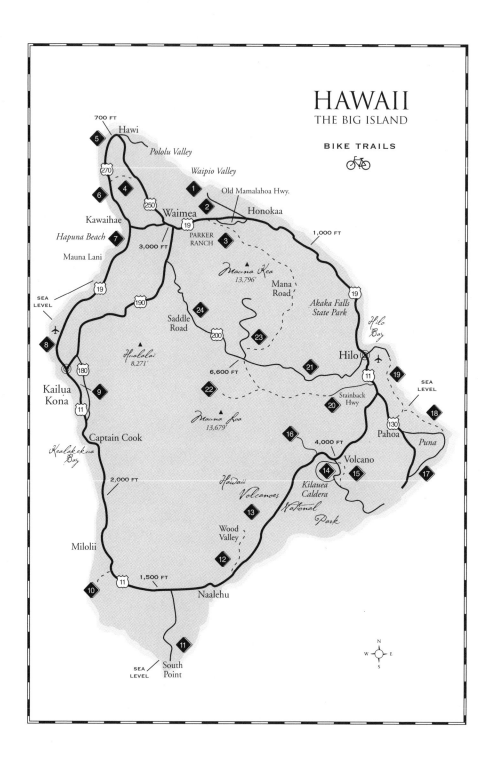

HAWAII
THE BIG ISLAND

BIKE TRAILS

700 FT

Hawi

Pololu Valley

Waipio Valley

270

Old Mamalahoa Hwy.

Honokaa

250

Waimea

Kawaihae

19

Hapuna Beach

PARKER RANCH

Mauna Lani

3,000 FT

1,000 FT

Mauna Kea
13,796'

Mana Road

Akaka Falls State Park

SEA LEVEL

19

190

Saddle Road

200

Hilo Bay

Hualalai
8,271'

6,600 FT

Hilo

19

SEA LEVEL

180

Kailua Kona

Stainback Hwy

11

Captain Cook

Mauna Loa
13,679'

130

Pahoa

Puna

4,000 FT

Kealakekua Bay

Hawaii Volcanoes

Volcano

2,000 FT

Kilauea Caldera

National Park

Wood Valley

Milolii

1,500 FT

Naalehu

11

N
W — E
S

SEA LEVEL

South Point

BIG ISLAND BIKING

Strap a mountain bike to the car and you'll be ready for island routes that will suit a wide-range of bicycling skills. Included are four-wheel drive roads, forested single-tracks, and coastal paths. Or forget the car, and lash the camping gear to the pedaling machine. The Big Island is well suited for hardcore cyclists who can handle some elevation and weather extremes. Cycling among campgrounds, B&Bs, and rustic lodging is very possible for adventure riders who want to muscle-power around the island.

CONSULT THE BIKE MAP FOR LOCATIONS OF THE RIDES LISTED BELOW. IN PARENTHESES ARE THE RIDE'S TOTAL LENGTH, ELEVATION GAIN, THE TYPE OF RIDE, AND THE TYPE OF RIDING SURFACE. PARKING DIRECTIONS ARE GIVEN LAST.

1. WAIPIO VALLEY (5 MI., 500 FT., OUT-AND-BACK, ROUGHLY PAVED)
Rolling down to the famed valley from the lookout is a third option to walking or driving. Ride deep into the valley or head right when you reach the bottom and hit the beach. *Parking:* See TH1, page 31 for driving directions and trail descriptions.

2. MUD LANE (10.75 MI., 2,100 FT. DOWN, CAR-SHUTTLE, UNPAVED ROAD AND SINGLE TRACK)
Ocean views toward Waipio are fantastic as you descend an ironwood-and-eucalyptus forest on a challenging ride. Descend 1.75 miles on a gravel road, and snake down on a twisting single track for another .5-mile—and then keep left at a junction. You'll soon reach Mud Lane, where you go right. Fallen trees and other debris, as well as mud, will test riding skills over the next 2 miles of descent. Then turn right at a junction with the Mauka Cane Haul Road, a paved-potholed road that takes you 5.5 miles to Highway 240. If you miss this junction, Mud Lane continues down for another mile and reaches a private road that takes you to the highway between mm7 and mm8. *Parking:* Take Hwy. 19 east, or toward Hilo, from Waimea. Turn left just before mm52, across from the junction with the Old Mamalahoa Hwy., and park near the golf course. Car-shuttle pick-up is on Hwy. 240, between Honoka'a and Waipio Valley, between mm3 and mm4. (Hawaii Forest & Trail has outings in this area; see *Resource Links*.)

3. MANA ROAD-WAIMEA (UP TO 20 MI., 2,000 FT., OUT-AND-BACK, UNPAVED ROAD)
Pastoral lands with blue-water views are at 3,000 feet, but still about 10,000 feet below looming Mauna Kea. *Parking:* See TH63, page 176 for driving and trail descriptions.

4. PU'UHUE ROAD (5 MI., 1,500 FT. DOWN, CAR-SHUTTLE, DIRT ROAD)
Coast down rolling hills with ocean views, in the heart of cattle country. From Highway 250, a .75-mile paved road leads to a pasture, where you go right past a cattle guard. Maui will rise offshore to enhance the view. Pu'uhue is a downhill thrill that doesn't

OLD MAMALAHOA HIGHWAY THROUGH PARKER RANCH

require a lot of technical skill. *Parking:* Take Hwy. 250 north from Waimea, headed toward Hawi. Look for Puʻuhue Rd. on the left, after mm17. Pick-up at the bottom is on Hwy. 270, headed north from Kawaihae. About .75-mi. after mm17, look mauka for Puʻuhue-Honoipu Rd. A stop sign marks the spot.

5. KING KAMEHAMEHA BIRTHPLACE (5 MI., 150 FT., SEMI-LOOP, UNPAVED ROAD)

This easy coastal pedal along open grassy bluffs takes you by the Kamehameha Birthplace and the Moʻokini Heiau. Using the hiking directions in TH5 as a guide, continue past these two attractions to the Upolu Airport, a fenced landing strip. Pass on the makai side of the airport and then loop around to your right for the return leg. For hardy riders wishing to explore more, the road continues past several gates for a few miles along the coast to Kepuhu Point, where Hoea Road climbs up to Hawi. *Parking:* Use the driving directions for TH5, page 38.

6. MAHUKONA BEACH KAPAʻA BEACH PARKS (3.75 MI., 300 FT., LOOP, UNPAVED AND PAVED ROAD)

Check out two beach parks that are connected by an old road along a rugged coastline. Lots of village ruins, overgrown by kiawe trees, will be in the area as you make your way north from Mahukona to Kapaʻa. Be sure to hang a left when you reach the paved road to see Kapaʻa Beach Park before pedaling up to the highway to make the return leg. *Parking:* Park near the old mill ruins near the wharf, as described in the *More Stuff* of TH6, page 40.

7. HAPUNA STATE PARK TO MAUNA LANI (6 MI., 200 FT., CAR-SHUTTLE, PAVED AND UNPAVED ROAD)

You start at the state park and take beachside back roads to the grounds of the luxury Mana Lani Resort. From Hapuna, follow Old Puako Road past Beach 69 and keep right on Puako Beach Drive. After 3 miles, you need to head into the last Shoreline Public Access and take a .25-mile connector single-track to Holoholokai Beach Park. Take pavement out from the beach park and keep making rights as you work your way to the resort. *Note:* This ride can be extended for several miles by starting farther north at Spencer Beach Park. From there, take the road south (not the Mau'umae Trail) to the Mauna Kea Hotel. From there, go right on Rockefeller Road and take Kauna'oa Drive to Hapuna. *Parking:* Park near the entrance to Hapuna Beach State Park, as described in TH10, page 52. Pick up is at the Mana Lani, as noted in TH12, page 56.

8. PINETREES AND KEAHOLE PT. (6 MI., LEVEL, OUT-AND-BACK, SAND AND LAVA ROAD)

This is a double out-and-back, as you head north from the beach park to Keahole Point, and then return to head south to Pinetrees. Be prepared to push the wheels through sand sections. This is a wild section of coast leading to historical sites and a popular surfer beach. See TH20 for trail descriptions. *Parking:* Start at the main lot for Wawaloli Beach Park, TH20, page 83.

9. WALUA ROAD (6.5 MI., 600 FT., OUT-AND-BACK, PAVED NEIGHBORHOOD)

Bike path segments connect with a rural neighborhood road that goes through a gardenscape with sea views. Turn around where Walua Road reaches the highway, about 1.5 miles past Kamehameha III Road. *Parking:* Head south on Hwy. 11 from Kailua-Kona and turn mauka on Lako St., just after mm120. Look for the bike path on your right.

10. ROAD TO THE SEA (14 MI., 1,900 FT., OUT-AND-BACK, 4WD ROCKY ROAD)

The bumpy drop to the sea is a Big Island classic, leading to two beaches on a remote section of coast. Bring plenty of water. The ride back up is a leg-burner. You'll see fewer vehicles on weekdays, which is not a good thing if you decide to mooch a ride back up. See the *More Stuff* section of TH31 on page 109 for detailed route descriptions. *Parking:* Head south of Manuka State Park and look mauka for the road at the corner near mm79.

11. GREEN SANDS BEACH (5 MI., 250 FT., OUT-AND-BACK, ROUGH UNPAVED ROAD)

The blustery and open coastal road to unique Green Sands Beach makes a better bike ride than a hike. Inland are views of Mauna Loa. See TH32, page 118, for a trail description. *Parking:* Take Hwy. 11 south from Kona, pass mm70 and turn right on South Point Rd. Continue 10 mi. and veer left toward Ka Lae.

12. WOOD VALLEY (4.5 MI., 400 FT., LOOP, PAVED AND UNPAVED ROAD)

These flowered rain forests are best seen from the seat of a bicycle. You can take off into the mountains on a network of old cane and forest reserve roads. This place is like an unlisted mountain biking park. *Parking:* See Wood Valley access in Kau Forest Reserve, TH35, page 123.

13. AINAPO TRAIL (UP TO 16 MI., 2,800 FT., OUT-AND-BACK, UNPAVED HUNTERS ROAD)

An 8-mile road winds through the pastures of Kapapala Ranch and climbs into indigenous woodlands that are home to the Hawaiian nene and other native birds. Prepare for cool weather and be sure to close gates after passing through. The road ends at the gate for the historic Ainapo Trail. *Parking:* See TH36, page 124, Ainapo Trail, for driving and access directions and more route descriptions.

14. CRATER RIM DRIVE (11 MI., 150 FT., LOOP, MOSTLY PAVED ROAD WITH CARS)

Take the big circle around one of America's most amazing national parks. The trailhead descriptions describe the turnouts and side-trips along the way. Near the beginning of the ride, you can leave the road and take the bike-friendly 2.25-mile section of the Crater Rim Trail. Access is across from the Kilauea Military Camp. *Parking:* Park at the Hawaii Volcanoes National Park Visitors Center, as described in TH37, Kilauea Caldera, page 125. (Portions of this road may be closed due to volcanic activity.)

BEGINNING OF MANA ROAD

15. ESCAPE ROAD (8 MI., 700 FT., OUT-AND-BACK OR LOOP, ROUGH LAVA AND CINDER)

Head partway down the Chain of Craters, enveloped by a lush ohia and tree fern forest. To access Escape Road, go right at the entrance to the Thurston Lava Tube trail and through a gate. You can also access the road outside the park, which will add 1.5 miles to the round-trip ride. The forest gives way to the open lava flows from the 1970s near the end of the ride. You'll come to Mauna Ulu Road, where you can turn right to reach Chain of Craters Road to ride back. *Parking:* See TH37, Kilauea Caldera, page 125. Park at the Kilauea Iki Overlook lot.

16. MAUNA LOA LOOKOUT (10 MI., 2,600 FT. DOWN, CAR-SHUTTLE, PAVED ROAD)

Make sure the brakes are adjusted and then enjoy the roll down from the 6,700-foot level on the shoulder of Mauna Loa. Views of Kilauea are superb as you pass through lava flows and native forest. *Parking:* See the driving directions for TH40, Mauna Loa Lookout, on page 132.

17. KEHENA-POHOIKI SCENIC COASTAL DRIVE (11 MI., LEVEL, CAR-SHUTTLE, PAVED HIGHWAY)

Ride the bluffs along the Puna coast, as lush a forest as you'll find in the Hawaiian Islands. Traffic can be heavy on weekends, but weekdays should be downright sleepy. The road undulates a little, but is basically straight and made for a brisk pedal. *Parking:* See driving directions for Kalapana Lava Bay, TH50, on page 156. Pick-up point is Isaac Hale Beach Park.

18. BEACH ROAD (UP TO 21 MI., LEVEL, OUT-AND-BACK, CINDER AND 4WD DIRT)

This is the best coastal jaunt on the island, through fields of wild orchids and rain forest. Expect to get moist and muddy. Weekdays are best for this route. *Parking:* Head south from Hilo on Hwy. 11 and turn toward Pahoa on Hwy. 130. Before Pahoa at mm4 turn makai on Kaloli Rd. Continue 4.25 mi. to Beach Road, turn right, and go another 1.25 mi. to road's end.

19. OLD PUNA TRAIL (UP TO 20 MI., 300 FT., OUT-AND-BACK, ROUGH CINDER)

This 1830s tract connects the Puna coast to the Hilo Airport. You'll pass Haena Beach, set in a grove of ironwoods and conifers, and ride through tropical fruit trees and flowers. Weekdays are best, since 4WD fishermen and locals like this route on weekends. It's a tough pedal in places, but improvements are planned to make the ride suitable for beginners. *Parking:* Use the driving directions above, only park when you get to Beach Rd. Go left on Beach Rd., or north, toward Hilo.

20. KULANI TRAILS (UP TO 10 MI., UP TO 900 FT., LOOPS AND OUT-AND-BACK, CINDER ROADS AND SINGLE TRACK)

Experienced riders will eat up the network of roads and single-track that are part of the Lower Waiakea Forest Reserve. Roots, mud, and tree-debris will keep you on your toes. Ferns and eucalyptus dominate these lush woodlands in this mountain biking

HAWAII VOLCANOES NATIONAL PARK

haven. Many options available for all levels of rider. *Parking:* Take Hwy. 11 south from Hilo, pass mm4, and turn mauka on Stainback Hwy. Continue 2.5 mi., passing the zoo turnoff. Park at the Waiakea Arboretum on the highway, or turn left, drive in .5-mi., and park at the quarry.

21. WAIAKEA TREE PLANTING ROAD (UP TO 22 MI., 500 FT., OUT-AND-BACK OR CAR SHUTTLE, PACKED LAVA AND CINDER)

While maintaining an undulating contour at an elevation of 3,500 feet, Waiakea Tree Planting Road runs straight over the lava flow of 1852. After 11 miles, the road joins Stainback Highway, coming up from Hilo, making the possibility of a car-shuttle. About midway, the route passes the Waiakea Natural Area Preserve, 640 acres of ohia forest that are rejuvenating after a 1942 flow. Prepare for extreme conditions. *Parking:* Head to Saddle Rd., just west of mm16, which is much closer to the Hilo side. Look for the big turnout on the Mauna Loa side of the road, crossed by a cable.

22. MAUNA LOA OBSERVATORY (17.5 MI., 4,500 FT. DOWN, CAR-SHUTTLE, POTHOLE PAVED)

Provided a Good Samaritan will drive you up, this downhill glide looking toward Mauna Kea and Maui is similar to that island's Haleakala ride. Sunrise or sunset will add drama to the panorama, and also avoid the glaring heat over a Marslike terrain of recent aʻa flows. Be prepared for cold weather.

Parking: The observatory road is off the middle of Saddle Rd. See TH44, Mauna Loa Observatory page 138 for directions.

23. MANA ROAD-HUMU'ULA SADDLE (UP TO 45 MI., 4,700 FT. DOWN, CAR-SHUTTLE, UNPAVED CINDER AND DIRT, SOME RUTTED)

A high-elevation ranch road wraps around Mauna Kea, from its arid north slopes, past forest reserves and into the pasturelands of Parker Ranch. It's a roller coaster, with plenty of dips in either direction, though you definitely want to start from this side if you're going to eat the whole thing. Most of the ride is easy, though weather extremes (fog, sun, wind, cold rain) can be a factor. All level riders will enjoy an out-and-back on this end.

Parking: The route begins on Mauna Kea Observatory Rd., just up from Saddle Rd. See TH66 on page 179 for driving directions and more trail descriptions. Pick up is off Hwy. 19 east of Waimea, as described in TH63 on page 176.

24. KILOHANA (UP TO 30 MI. AND 4,500 FT., OUT-AND-BACK, CINDER-ROCK AND DIRT HUNTER'S ROAD)

Starting at 5,500 feet, Pu'u La'au Road, which is also called Skyline Road, is ready-made for strong-willed riders who want to pedal to heaven. These are wild lands, so bring along plenty of water and weather protection. The first part is an easier forest ride that climbs to the ranger station. From there you have options, all of them upward. Kilohana, TH64 on page 178, gives more details. Loose rocks and cinder will be trying going up and require attention on the downhill slide. *Parking:* The trailhead is on the Kona side of Saddle Rd. See TH64 on page 178 for driving directions.

KAPA'A BEACH PARK

Trailblazer
KIDS

HAPUNA BEACH

In Hawaiian, the word keiki (KAY-kee) means both 'child' and also the green shoot of a new banana plant. Bananas are plants, not trees, and each year a new generation must be nurtured to maturity—just like children in the family. Is there anyplace in the world better suited than the Big Island for keikis to learn while having fun? Volcanoes, dolphin pools, tropical gardens, ancient petroglyphs, tide pools and lagoons, and stargazing are just some of the unforgettable wonders. In addition to the attractions listed below, most of the larger resort hotels have programs especially for kids. Create your own program by selecting from the categories listed below. Remember when you look over each category, trailheads that are close together numerically will be in the same area.

SEE THE VOLCANO HIKES
Jaggar Museum-Steaming Bluffs, TH37, page 126
Iki Crater-Thurston Lava Tube, TH37 page 128
Pu'u Huluhulu, TH38, page 129
Chain of Craters, bottom, TH38, page 130
Kalapana Lava Bay, TH50, page 156

PETROGLYPHS
Puako Petroglyphs, TH11, page 54
Waikoloa Petroglyph Preserve, TH13, page 60
Kaupulehu, TH17 (may be closed) page 68
Pu'u Loa Petroglyphs, TH38, page 130

BEACH PARK PICNICS
Keokea Beach Park, TH3, page 37
Holoholokai Beach Park, TH11, page 54
Kekaha Kai Beach Park, TH19, page 72
Pu'uhonua Beach Park, TH28, page 101
Richardson Ocean Park, TH49, page 154
Ahalanui County Park, TH53, page 158
Kolekole Beach Park, TH59, page 170
Laupahoehoe Beach Park, TH61, page 174

MUSEUMS & ATTRACTIONS
'Iole Foundation, TH3, page 35
Eva Parker Woods Museum, TH12, page 56
Hilton Resort, TH13, page 61
Onizuka Space Center, TH20, page 84
Hulihe'e Palace, TH23, page 89
Kona Historical Society, DT2, page 190
Mokupapapa Discovery Center for Hawaii's
    Reefs, Hilo, TH44, page 147
Laupahoehoe Train Museum, DT3, page 196

KOHALA FOREST RESERVE, DOLPHIN
QUEST, LEI MAKING

KAILUA, VOLCANO, KAHALUʻU BEACH

Free Advice and Opinion

FREE ADVICE & OPINION

DISCLAIMER
Think of this book as you would any other piece of outdoor gear. It will help you do what you want to do, but it depends upon you to supply responsible judgment and common sense. The publisher and authors are not responsible for injury, damage, or legal violations that may occur when someone is using this guidebook. Please contact public agencies to familiarize yourself with the most current rules and regulations. Posted signs and changes in trail status determined by public agencies supersede any recommendations in this book. Okay, be careful and go out there and have fun.

HIKING
Never walk downhill with your hands in your pockets ... Wet cowboy neck bandanas combat the heat... Stay on trails: cliffs, earth cracks, steam vents, loose rocks, collapsed lava tubes, dense foliage, and so forth ... Plan your return time before you start ... Don't get caught in the dark ... Begin mountain hikes early to avoid cloud cover ... Avoid hiking alone, and always let someone know where you're going ... Keep your hiking group together ... Wear sunscreen, hat, and sunglasses ... Lava turns the ground into a grill ... Always take your equipped knapsack on a hike; see *Packlist* ... Flashlights or headlamps are essential gear ...

Carry 2 liters of water per person, per day ... And drink it ... Stash water bottles half-way on out-and-back hikes to avoid having to carry it all ... The Cook Monument hike is a good one for this trick ... Bring your cell phone ... Wear white or bright colors ... Avoid hunter's roads on weekends ... Do not drink stream or pond water ... Don't climb cliffs; rocks are unstable ... If you lose the trail, backtrack immediately ... Don't attempt to make your own loop trail ... It's easier to get lost following rock cairns down a mountain that going up ... Pay attention ...

Don't try to hike out at night if you get lost ... Part of Pele's curse: Don't climb on ancient walls or heiaus ... Use a hiking pole ... Figure out a way to hang snorkeling gear on your knapsack ... Malama i na mea kahiko (Care for things of the past).

VIEWING FLOWING LAVA
All the usuals about sun and footing ... Volcanic fumes contain hydrochloric acid and sulfur dioxide, so don't be downwind ... Stay back about half-mile from the steam plume where lava enters the ocean ... Another reason to stay back is a steam explosion, which sends rocks the size of TVs hurtling through the air ... Stay back 100 yards from lava flowing through vegetated areas ... Methane from burning plants is trapped in underground lava tubes, until it goes kaboom ... Keep your balance at all times when close to flowing lava ... People fall in ... A'a can cut like glass ...The degree of difficulty for lava hikes is triple that of normal hiking on a trail or path ... While you're standing there gawking, that lava stream is moving somewhere, so don't get surrounded by an advancing stream ...

Stay well back from benches along the coast that are at all close to recent flows ... The overhanging benches fall in multi-acre chunks into the surf ... Bring one flashlight per person on night walks to see lava ... A hiking pole will greatly help, especially at night ... Fill up on drinking water and bring plenty with you ... There's no food down there either, usually ... Avoid trekking onto the lava fields in midday ... Stop at the visitors center at Kilauea Caldera to get latest conditions before heading down ... Make a mental offering to Pele before venturing to see the volcano ... And after.

ALTITUDE SICKNESS, A PRIMER BY DR. JOHN BARR

Causes: Can occur above 8,000 feet, due to decreased concentration of oxygen ... Rapid ascent and exertion increase your chances of getting sick ... *Symptoms*: Generally, a decreased tolerance for physical activity ... Minor symptoms include flatus expulsion (yes, farting), sore and dry throat, tunnel vision, and shortness of breath... More severe symptoms include headache, confusion, slurred speech, dizziness and fainting, and difficulty walking ... *Prevention and Treatment*: Acclimatize for an hour at a high altitude before ascending above 8,000 feet ... Drink plenty of fluid before ascending and during your stay ... Take aspirin or Tylenol ... Move more slowly when at a high altitude ... Pressure breathe by inhaling, compressing your diaphragm, then exhaling (you force oxygen to absorb) ... Rest or lie down ... When symptoms are severe, descend below 5,000 feet immediately.

SNORKELING & SWIMMING

Shore break can knock anybody down ... Don't turn your back on waves ... Never let children beyond grabbing distance ... Bigger surf means increased current ... Always float and watch the bottom to see if current is in force ... Current will release you offshore ... Don't panic and swim against it ... Swim with a buddy, or have a buddy watch from the beach ... Swim perpendicular to the direction of current ... Some rip currents go straight offshore through rippled openings in the waves, you can see them from shore ... Steep shores mean sudden drop-off and possible undertow ... If caught in an undertow, you will pop up on the backside of the wave ...

Complex shorelines and surf make for dangerous conditions in Hawaii ... If in doubt, stay out ... Always ask a lifeguard if one is on duty ... Don't step on or grab coral ... You'll kill it ... To disturb or touch a sea turtle is both impolite and illegal ... High waves roll in without high wind or storms ... If caught on burning sand in bare feet, scrape off the top few inches to stand on the cooler grains below ... Dry your towels by hanging them in rolled-up car windows (also keeps car cooler, hides the inside, and looks "local") ... To keep your mask from fogging up you can buy a squirt bottle of defogger, or just spit in it and rub it around ... Fins with heel straps and separate booties mean you have a surf shoe to aid in rocky entries ... surf shoes are the right thing for the island's many tide pool snorkeling spots ...

The entire coast of Hawaii is open to the public ... All beaches have public access ... Once you get used to snorkeling on clean, pahoehoe lava beaches, you may swear off sand forever ... Lack of streams and erosion on the Kona side means gin-clear water ... If you want to avoid sharks while swimming, stay out of the water at dawn and dusk, and avoid cloudy, murky water, such as near streams ... According to local lore, never swim when the wiliwili is blooming ...In April .

BIKING

Always wear a helmet ... Drink twice as much water in the subtropics ... Bring water with you in the car ... Allow time to adjust to high altitudes ... Carry first aid and treat minor scrapes right away ... Take extra care not to get lost in remote areas ... Bring a spare tube and a repair kit ... You ain't had road rash until you fall on a lava road ... Bikes are permitted on all highways, and most roads have extra shoulder width ... But watch out on Highway 11 south from Honaunau and especially watch out on Highway 190 from Kailua to Waimea: dangerous and no shoulders ... Highway 19 north to Kohala has nice wide shoulders.

DRIVING

Drive aloha … Allow turns and merges … Watch for pedestrians and cyclists … Don't leave valuables in the car … Never move valuables to the trunk while at a parking space … Vandals know they shouldn't rip off local cars: Put a bumper sticker in the back window, or a local newspaper; hang beads or a lei from your rearview mirror … Broken glass at a parking space indicates a prior break in … Generally, you are very safe parking on the Big Island … Parking directions for trailheads will indicate a less-safe spot … Road maps left out on the dash say, "I'm a tourist" … Be prepared for Nene Crossings, Banana Virus Areas, and Donkey Zones …

Watch out for speeders on mountain roads … Driving will be your most-dangerous activity, statistically speaking … Highway 11 north of Kona has long turn and merge lanes; don't use them for passing … Set the cruise control and mellow out … Make sure to pull safely off the road when sightseeing … You meet people by asking directions … Drive with your low-beams on … Carry towelettes (baby wipes) for instant refreshment … Carry drinking water and food along for the ride since finding either can be very inconvenient.

TO FOUR-WHEEL OR NOT TO FOUR-WHEEL?

Steep roads to two major attractions require four-wheel drive vehicles: The last 8-miles from the visitors center to the top of Mauna Kea, and the 1.5 miles from the Waipio Valley Lookout to the beach and valley below. (Technically, 2WD vehicles are premitted up Mauna Kea, but the drive is not safe.)To see these attractions without driving, you can sign on for tours—and you can walk down to Waipio Valley. You can also rent a four-wheel drive from an appropriate company for a day or two, which will be cheaper than a tour for two or more people. Plenty of other roads require four-wheel capability, but you'll be able to see all other major attractions without having one.

Many rental car companies used to prohibit driving on State Highway 200, a.k.a. Saddle Road, even though it was suitable for passenger vehicles. Improvements to this road— passing landes, wide pavement, yellow lines—have made this policy outdated. The road provides access to the visitors center at Mauna Kea, the highest trailhead at Mauna Loa, as well as several other hiking trails. No company should prohibit driving Saddle Road.

SOME TIPS: 1. Call your insurance company before booking a car to see if you will be covered. Full coverage will pick up the voids in rental car coverage. You won't need additional rental car coverage. 2. Rent passenger car for most days but trade it in for a Jeep on specific days to get to the top of Mauna Kea, Waipio Valley, Road to the Sea, and other bumpy byways. 3. Rent a four-wheel drive for the entire trip from Harper, which allows driving to Mauna Kea, Waipio Valley, and everywhere else. 4. Book a tour to Mauna Kea and walk to Waipio Valley, and forget about the other obscure roads. Only repeat visitors will have time to devout to seeing the hinterlands of the Big Island.

Saddle Road is smoothly paved all the way, from the Kona side to the Hilo side. Passing lanes help speedy drivers get by—delivery vans and cross-island commuters like to make time. A new (2014) extension actually makes Saddle Road one of the Big Island's mellow drives. The Belt Highway from Kona to Waimea is narrow with no shoulders; be aware of high-speed vehicles and find someplace to let them get around you.

BIG ISLAND *Calabash*

BIANCA SORIANO, HALAU NA PUA 'O ULUHAIMALAMA OF HILO

A CALABASH, OR GOURD, WAS USED IN ANCIENT TIMES AS A WATER VESSEL. IN HAWAII TODAY,
THE CALABASH IS A GROUP OF FRIENDS, LIKE FAMILY, THOUGH NOT BLOOD-RELATED.

VOLCANOES

Hawaiian volcanoes result from billions of tons molten magma roiling into the sea from the Hot Spot, a crack in the earth's crust in the middle of the Pacific. Very fluid magma (see *Lava* below) piles up and eventually breaks the ocean surface and continues to pile up thousands of feet above sea level. These are called "shield" volcanoes, because as seen on the horizon this gentle piling up of lava looks like the profile of a shield. The Hawaiian volcanoes differ from other volcanoes in the Pacific's "Ring of Fire," such at Mt. Fuji and Mt. St. Helens, which are called "composite" or "strato" volcanoes. These are formed by friction between tectonic plates grinding together to melt rocks. Strato volcanoes produce viscous lava and violent eruptions.

Most experts say the Big Island is comprised of five volcanoes whose flows have joined them together—Mauna Loa, Mauna Kea, Hualalai, Kilauea, and Kohala. Ninole, which is on the southeast coast, used to be considered a separate volcano, but now is thought to be an ancient subformation of Mauna Loa. Another volcano, Loihi, is in its submarine stage, erupting 20 miles offshore Hawaii's southeast coast. Several thousand feet under the surface, its coming-out party is scheduled about 10,000 years from now. Since 1983, about 800 acres of new land have been added to the Big Island by Kilauea's Pu'u O'o eruption.

Recent observations show the swelling of Mauna Loa's surface to be related to subsequent eruptions on Kilauea, indicating that the underground plumbing of Kilauea and Mauna Loa may be related. Some volcanologists dispute this theory. Three volcanoes are active: Kilauea, which has been erupting since 1983; Mauna Loa, which sent lava to within four miles of Hilo in 1984; and Hualalai, whose most recent eruption was in the early 1800s. All these volcanoes don't erupt from a single crater, but along rift zones that themselves have a series of cones or vents that release lava. On Hawaii there are many dozens of these vents, each called a pu'u (poo-oo).

The life of a Hawaiian Volcano has six stages, most of which are occurring today on the Big Island. Loihi is in the submarine stage, and headed toward the second, emergent stage, when steam blows sky-high but no dry land is present. The third stage is the shield building, when frequent eruptions occur on rift zones, such as is occurring on Mauna Loa and Kilauea. The fourth stage, only recently discovered, is the giant landslide phase, when up to one-third of a shield volcano can slide into the sea. Scientists speculate Kilauea has this to look forward to. Mauna Kea is an example of the fifth stage, the capping phase, when viscous lava covers and stops flows. The erosional stage comes next, as evidenced in Kohala, where streams carve valleys and canyons, and ocean waves produce sea cliffs. A renewed volcanism phase can follow, like on Maui's Haleakala, where activity can begin again after eons of dormancy. The final destiny for Hawaiian volcanoes is the atoll stage. Moving northwest along with the earth's crust, the volcanoes wear down to sea level and coral reefs grow, forming a low island with a lagoon in the middle. An example is the Kure Atoll that is 1,500 miles northwest of the Big Island.

LAVA

Magma, the molten rock that is at the core and below the crust of the earth, is called lava when it reaches the surface. Magma that cools beneath the earth's surface is called igneous rock, such as basalt and granite. Worldwide, Hawaiian names are used to classify lava into two types, which are very different looking but have basically the same chemical composition. Hawaiian lava is more than half silicon and aluminum oxides, about one-quarter iron and magnesium oxides, and also has small amounts sodium and potassium. The result is usually a dark red or brown color, although fresh-cooled lava is often black, with a gleaming, oily surface.

Hawaiian lava also contains lots of gas that is driven into the atmosphere during cooling. Most of the gas is harmless: Two-thirds is steam, or water. About 13 percent of the trapped gas is carbon dioxide, and some 8 percent is nitrogen. The stuff that can kill you is the 9 percent sulfur dioxide and the 1 percent carbon monoxide. The markedly different physical characteristics between the two types of lava result from gas content and cooling rate. Surface temperatures of lava range from about 1,800- to 2,200-degrees Fahrenheit. Toss a rock on hot lava and it will melt. The two types of lava are:

A'A (*ah-ah*) erupts and cools in rough, jagged piles. Walking across this stuff is a nightmare. (Remember: "Oh-oh, it's a'a.") A'a lava contains less gas and cools faster. It flows in jumbled, clinking, and crumbling piles, and has no sheen on its surface.

PAHOEHOE (*pa-hoy-hoy*) erupts and cools in smooth streams and ribbony waves. Although collapsed lava tubes can be a hazard, walking over these surfaces is generally safe and easy. (Remember: "Oh boy, it's pahoehoe.") Pahoehoe contains more gas and cools more slowly. It flows in ropy sheets and bulging drips, looking like thick cake batter. The surface of fast-moving pahoehoe streams often cools and hardens while a subsurface stream continues. When the eruption stops, the subsurface stream drains, leaving a hollow tube, or long cave. The ceiling of tubes near the surface will often collapse. The entire mass of Hawaii is riddled with tubes and cracks.

TSUNAMI

Often mistakenly called tidal waves, the deadly tsunamis have no relation to waves that are generated by the rise and fall of the tide, or with hurricane-generated high seas that come ashore with great force. "Tsunami," a Japanese word meaning "harbor wave," refers to a series of waves traveling across the ocean with very long wavelengths, up to 100 miles between crests. In the open sea, a tsunami wouldn't upset your drink, since the wave's height is a few feet or less. When approaching shallow waters near land, the wave's speed decreases and its size drastically increases, rearing up to an ugly 30- to 50-foot wall of water that carries boulders and sea debris with it in a destructive assault on the coastline.

Oceanographers say tsunamis are the result of a sudden rise or fall of the earth's crust on the ocean floor, such as an earthquake, landslide, or volcanic eruption. Hilo is known as the tsunami capital of the world, with 13 of the monsters coming ashore in the 20th century. In 1946 and 1960, behemoth waves wiped out coastal communities and killed more than a hundred people. The 1960 wave, generated by an earthquake in Chile, traveled 10,000 miles to Japan at 500 miles an hour, and struck with enough force to kill 150 people. In Hawaii, these tragedies have led to the establishment of a detection and warning system, as well as new coastal building codes.

Unfortunately, regional tsunamis can be generated by local earthquakes, of which the Big Island has a hundred or more yearly. Most quakes don't make waves, but the ones that do strike before a warning can be issued. In November of 1975, an earthquake dropped a miles-long section of coastal bluff some 10 feet at Hawaii Volcanoes National Park, generating a wave that swept 32 campers into the sea, two of whom didn't make it back. Don't put this high on your things to worry about, but if you do experience a trembler at the beach, head to high ground pronto.

ANCHIALINE PONDS

To nature's subtleties that are peculiar to the Big Island, add anchialine ponds, which you'll find primarily on the North Kona-South Kohala coast, as well as on the Puna coast. What these coastlines have in common is a lack of streams, since the land is so new that rain has not yet eroded the surface into valleys. The mauka showers percolate down through the porous lava slopes of Mauna Loa, creating a vast aquifer that sits at about sea level under the mountain.

At coastal depressions, this fresh water daylights, creating little ponds that were crucial for survival for the ancients, used for drinking water, agriculture, and raising fish. At some locales, such as the fishponds at the Mauna Lani, canals with fish gates were dug to enhance nature's handiwork. At many other places, like the ponds near the Hilton at Anaeho'omalu, the ponds are unaltered. The ponds are always brackish, more so at high tide when underground sea water intrudes, and less so farther ashore and after heavy rains, when freshwater percolates in greater volume. So, don't bother looking for inlets or outlets for these little lakes. There are none, above ground anyway.

PETROGLYPHS

Of the 150 known petroglyph sites in the state, most are on the Big Island—due to its size, availability of smooth pahoehoe lava on which most pictures are etched, and the fact that foliage has not had time to overgrow the fields. The rock carvings, called ki'i pohaku in Hawaiian, are a combination of a newspaper, diary, and mural. The etchings span centuries. A few are a mystery, made by artisans before the Polynesian migrations. Most depict events during the 1,000- to 1,500-year period before Western culture arrived in the late 1700s. But many are post-contact, depicting such things as whalers, horseback riders, and rifles.

Petroglyphs are best viewed during the morning and late afternoon hours, when slanting light casts shadows that highlight the indentations in the rock. Photographers should stand with the sun at their backs. Many ki'i pohaku are in remote locations, but several fields are marked and easily accessed. Some of the best are the Puako Petroglyphs at Holoholokai Beach Park, the Kulia Petroglyphs at the Mana Lani, the Waikoloa Petroglyph Preserve, the Kaupulehu Petroglyphs at the Kona Village, and the Pu'u Loa Petroglyphs off Chain of Craters Road. One vast site harder to get to is the Pu'u Ki Petroglyph field in Ocean View. (All sites are referenced in the index.)

When viewing a field, note that the oldest drawings are usually clustered in the center, and the most recent efforts are on the periphery. Some fields are at regional boundaries, where waylaid soldiers and travelers etched away the hours. The exact story told by many of these etchings will never be known, but others, such as sails, fishermen, paddlers, and surfers are less obscure. Circles with dots are thought to commemorate the birth of boys, while semi-circles with dots denote girls' births. Avoid stepping on petroglyphs.

KAMEHAMEHA THE GREAT

A fair number of history's heavy hitters have earned the title "great," but if you lined them all up in some kind of pageant that measured composite skills, the smart money would be on Hawaii's Kamehameha to be a favorite to take home the top prize. To clone a replica of this man, the first ruling monarch of the Hawaiian Islands, you'd need big doses of charisma, intelligence, skill, modesty, and foresight. And then put all of it in the jumbo package—pushing seven-feet and around 400 pounds. This is the guy, Kamehameha the Great, whose bodily gifts were matched by a peculiar convergence of historical events.

Intrigue surrounded his birth. He had been slated as a future king by his uncle, the Big Island's Chief Kalaniopu'u, but another chief in Hilo had other plans, and had vowed to slay the infant. To save the baby's life, Kamehameha's mother was secreted away to a forlorn, windswept spot in north Kohala. The birth took place in 1758, a date later confirmed by the passing of Haley's Comet. Kamehameha spent his youth in hiding but hardly in hardship, since much of his time was spent frolicking on his surfboard and with the wahines of Waipio Valley.

His training for leadership began early also. A famous warrior from Napo'opo'o in Kealakekua Bay, named Kekuhaupio, was enlisted to train the boy. Even as a youth he towered over his five-foot-eight mentor, but it would be years before he matched his teacher's skills. Kamehameha learned the Hawaiian martial arts of the lua, and as a teenager he was a one-man army—able to catch spears thrown at him and artfully deploy his ikoi, a type of bolo that would bring down a running man. He mastered the wrestling art of "bone-breaking," for which the lua is renowned. The Hawaiians had no metal weapons or complex armaments, but they may have been the most fearsome hand-to-hand combatants the world has ever seen. Their skills were matched by tremendous size: Bone records indicate some ancient warriors were closer to eight feet than seven. In his day, Kamehameha was a standout. As a graduation test, he had to jump off an outrigger with a pointed stick and kill a large tiger shark.

At age 20, he and Keuhaupio were on the fringes of a great battle in Maui, the Battle of the Sand Hills, at which the Big Island's army ignored the advice of the kahunas and were killed in great numbers. Kamehameha and his mentor defeated a small army of Maui warriors in the nearby village of Olowalu. Then, as they retreated from this foray, offshore they sighted the towering white sails of the *Endeavor*, the ship of British Captain James Cook. Coincidentally, Cook had returned to the islands after making the first contact with Hawaii a year earlier, 300 miles north in Kauai. Kamehameha and Keuhaupio decided to approach and board this alien vessel.

Three days later, as the people of the Big Island lamented the loss of their young warrior to this bizarre visitation, Kamehameha and his mentor appeared. The young warrior, beaming, was stuffed into a red British officer's jacket. Far from being fearful, Kamehameha had seen at once that the apparition that was Western contact was an opportunity for his future. He had seen steel and iron, and to a Hawaiian warrior these were like assault rifles.

In the next few months, Cook was to land in Kealakekua Bay during the peace-and-fertility festival of Makahiki. The British captain was heralded as the god Lono—only to be bludgeoned to death on the bay's shores just weeks later in a scuffle over a stolen dory. Western ships would not return to the islands for six years.

In 1780, based on his exploits thus far—and his ability to move the mammoth, ceremonial Pohaku Naha stone—Kamehameha was commissioned with custody of the war god, Kukailimoku, by his uncle, Chief Kalaniopu'u. The chief's son, Kiwalao, received land. Though ultimately wise, the chief's decision stirred enmity, both between his son and Kamehameha, and among other island chiefs. This bad-blood rose to a full-scale battle when the Chief Kalaniopu'u died. In

1782, Kiwalao and other chiefs, met Kamehameha and his forces, along with Keuhaupio, in the Battle of Mokuohai, near Napoʻopoʻo in Kealakekua. Using superior knowledge of the terrain, Kamehameha prevailed against a larger force and his legend ramped up a notch. He was 24.

By 1785, Western ships had begun stopping in the islands to provision for trading journeys to China. Conflicts arose, one of which resulted in the massacre of scores of villagers on Maui in 1790. As revenge, and also for his own personal gain, Kamehameha's warriors captured a vessel, the *Fair American*, offshore the Big Island. Conscripting two of the ship's officers as aides, Kamehameha sailed the *Fair American* to Maui. Using the ship's cannon, he routed the forces of the Maui Chief Kahekili's son, Kalanikupule, in the famous battle of the Iao Valley. The bodies of fallen warriors were said to dam the stream and turn its waters red.

A year later, upon the advice of his kahunas, Kamehameha built Puʻukohola Heiau in Kawaihae, laboring alongside the workers to complete the task. Then, Kamehameha's cousin from the Hilo side Keoua, was invited to an opening ceremony. Keoua also had been groomed as a youth to be king, by the same branch of the family who conspired to kill Kamehameha at birth. Upon Keoua's arrival, a skirmish ensued—perhaps a planned subterfuge—and the cousin was killed. Although later that year he had to defend the island from invaders from Maui and Oahu, Kamehameha's control over the Big Island was now unquestioned.

Kamehameha did not attack Maui until 1794, after the death of its Chief Kahekili, a man who claimed to be Kamehemeha's father. (The intrigue among the aliʻi is Shakespearean.) The following year, his forces took Oahu. A year later, in 1796, a huge storm thwarted his invasion of Kauai. To prepare for another invasion that would bring all of Hawaii under his rule, Kamehameha and his sprawling retinue went to Lahaina on Maui, where a fleet of 1,000 war canoes was constructed, and where the young leader also reacquainted himself with life's pleasures, such as surfing and cavorting. Once again using conscripted Westerners, he built himself a brick palace. Showing his humility, he labored in his gardens alongside the commoners.

In 1804, another attempt to invade Kauai failed, this time due to disease brought by Europeans that depleted his army. By this time, Honolulu, the only deep-water port in the islands, was frequented by Western ships, and Kamehameha moved the capital to that village in order to better control trading. Not a squealing pig was traded for a single nail without the great man's approval. In 1810, Kamehameha and Kauai's Chief Kaumualiʻi entered into a treaty that gained Kamehameha control over all the islands as the first Hawaiian monarch. Both men could see that the Hawaiian people were dying in great numbers due to new diseases, and that the Western sailing ships were arriving in great numbers.

In 1812, the 44-year-old king returned to his Big Island home, and made Kailua the capital of Hawaii. He appointed governors for all the islands' major land areas, and supervised the sandalwood trade with ships bound for China. (The fragrant sandalwood was Hawaii's first cash crop, but the forests were denuded within a decade.) Kamehameha's heir, Liholiho was educated in Kona, and his youngest boy, later Kamehameha III, was born in 1814. In nearby villages, Kamehameha built huge fishponds that were a marvel to Western visitors.

In May of 1819, the great king died, and his remains were spirited away to a location that remains a mystery to this day. Liholiho became Kamehameha II, and, at the urging of his mother, Queen

Keopuolani, and Kamehameha's favorite wife Queen Ka'ahumanu, he immediately abolished the kapu system that, among other provisions, treated women unfairly. Liholiho struggled with trying to fill his father's huge sandals, and also with the onslaught of Western culture. Change came in the same year of his father's death, in the form of missionaries and whaling ships. While on a trip to London to further educate himself on these matters, Kamehameha II died in 1824.

The rule of the islands was left to Kamehameha III, then only 11 years old. The queen mothers stood watch over the boy until he matured into Hawaii's longest-ruling monarch. He died in 1854. The native population diminished from some 800,000 people to around 60,000 during the 70 years of European and American contact. In an effort to adapt, the royal family embraced Western religion, and established the best school system west of the Rocky Mountains. The literacy rate was among the nation's highest after only a few years, although the Hawaiians previously had no written language. The Hawaiian nation was able to withstand the raucous whalers and traders, but the emergence of the sugar cane industry in the late 1800s, to make a long story short, was to do in the monarchy. Hawaii was annexed as an U.S. Territory in 1893.

PELE

If the Big Island is this planet's giant wedding cake, then Madame Pele, the Goddess of Volcanoes, is the bride standing on top—all by her lonesome. She is the maternal goddess of lust, impetuousness, and violence to be respected and feared—Pele, the "woman who devours the land," while at the same time adding new land to the earth.

Legends say Pele's first Hawaiian home was the little island of Ni'ihau off the northwest coast of Kauai, but the volcano goddesses' sister, Namakaokahi, the goddess of the sea, was angry and caused her to move. Over the millennia, move she did, first to Kauai, then Diamond Head Oahu, followed by Molokai and then Maui. But each time the sea goddess put a damper on things, causing Pele to move—until she found her present home, in the Halemaumau Crater in the Kilauea Volcano on the Big Island. Here she resides with her fiery sisters, each called Hi'iaka. From the look of things, both scientists and kahunas agree that Pele isn't going anywhere for a long time. (The ancient legend of Pele's travels mirrors the geophysical observations made by contemporary science.)

There are many legends and curses surrounding the volcano goddess. Tourists think they're quaint stories. Locals think differently. In 1801, Kamehameha the Great, who was not known for being hen-pecked by any of his 20-plus wives, went to his knees with offerings to save a Kona village from a Hualalai eruption. Prayer answered. In 1881, same story with Princess Ruth Ke'elikolani, who traveled from Honolulu to Hilo to divert a Mauna Loa flow. In 1960, the Cape Kumukahi Lighthouse survived an east-rift eruption days after the keeper gave food to a hungry, lone woman (a typical Pele incarnation).

The nearby village of Kapoho, which had turned the woman away, was destroyed. On March 30 of 1984, many observers saw a fireball shoot across the sky between Kilauea and Mauna Loa, a white streak that the ancients call a popoahi, which Pele issues to announce an eruption. Following the popoahi came the first dual blast from these two volcanoes in more than 130 years. Today, Pele is revered at yearly fetes, including the Merrie Monarch and Aloha festivals, as well as by daily offerings left at Halemaumau Crater—which blew its cork again in 2008.

Pele's existence will never be proven, but you cannot be on the Big Island for long without feeling her presence. Sometimes, she does appear, taking different forms, such as that of a shapely young woman with coils of dark hair, or, more commonly, a gin-swilling gray-haired tutu (old woman), often walking lonely trails on the mountains or seacoast. If you see someone who meets that description, play it safe and be nice. If you see her hitchhiking, pick her up.

Scores of tourist scoff at the notion of Pele, and break the curse against taking lava rocks, or na pohaku, home for souvenirs. Ha, ha, they think, only to be inundated with a run of bad luck. Should this happen to you, or any of your loved ones, know that Pele may forgive you. Each month, on the first Wednesday at high noon, a ceremony is held on the grounds of the Outrigger Waikoloa Beach resort, where, in an area called a Hoaka Ho'omalu, the rocks are placed in a shrine, called an ahu paepae. You can ship your ill-gotten souvenir to the resort (which gathers all such stones from around the island) and it will be added to the shrine and returned to Pele via a piko, or navel, which travels to the surrounding mountains. Laugh if you dare.

COFFEE

Kona coffee worshipers can thank Kamehameha's interpreter, Don Francisco de Paula y Marin, who planted the first scraggly tree nearly 200 years ago. Homage must also be paid to Reverend Samuel Ruggles whose arabica-bean orchards took hold in 1828, and to Henry Nicholas Greenwell, whose Kona blend took a medal in Vienna in 1873. But to give credit where credit is due, 600 small-time growers and small companies that comprise today's market also must be honored. When the world coffee market crashed in 1899, coffee orchards were sold off in 3- to 5-acre parcels, many to Japanese and later to Hawaiians, Chinese, Filipinos, and growers from the mainland. The backbone of today's Kona coffee industry remains this calabash of smaller growers.

In the spring, coffee trees (technically bushes) issue white flowers called Kona snow, which aromatically reveal the tree's relation to the gardenia flower. The flowers give way to red berries, called cherries, that are picked by hand. It takes seven pounds of cherries to make one pound of ground coffee. Top pickers can snare about 300 pounds of cherries a day, or, if you do the math, several cherries per second over the course of an 8-hour day. After being picked, the cherries are rolled and washed, separating the beans from their red husk and a whitish pulp that is underneath it. Then, most beans are dried the old-fashioned way, by spreading them out in the sun for about a week and raking periodically. Roller dryers are also used. The dried beans are called parchment.

Not yet roasted, the beans are sorted into grades. About one-fifth make the top grade, Kona Extra Fancy, which has two flat seeds. About a third of the parchment is bagged as Kona Fancy, and another third as Kona Number One, the third-best grade. Ten percent of the coffee is Kona Prime (apparently there is no Kona Krummy), while five percent is Kona Peaberry, a bean that has only one seed. Many of the beans are sold on the world market prior to roasting. Roasters are like vintners, using their eyes, nose, and even ears to achieve the perfect roasts. Lighter roasted coffee—which contains the most caffeine—is allowed to make one 'pop' during the roasting. The darker roasts, like Italian, French, and espresso, 'pop' twice.

Kona coffee is grown along a 20-mile stretch of the coast, at an elevation of 800 to 2,000 feet, on lands that during ancient times produced breadfruit, bananas, sugar cane, and taro. Worldwide, demand far outstrips supply. Like wine, Kona coffee taste can vary from year to year. The large number or growers also results in a varying product. To find the perfect cup, take the coffee tour described in *Driving Tours*, or see the growers listed in *Resource Links*. Don't bother to buy a Kona blend coffee, as the distinctive flavor will be lost.

ORCHIDS AND EXOTICS

Drive to the green slopes of Puna and you'll understand why the Big Island's nickname is the Orchid Isle. Most of the world's supply of this flower, as well as other tropical flowers, is flown out daily from the Hilo Airport. This region can also take credit for 95% of the state's papayas, and nearly three-quarters of the bananas. Virtually all of the ginger grown in the United States, about 8 million pounds per year, also comes from the lush slopes of Puna. Also grown in abundance are guava, anthuriums, carnations, roses, and protea. The Big Island is the nation's exotic fruit-and-flower basket.

Many flower growers, situated around Pahoa, are set up to receive visitors. A drive around the upper slopes of Puna will also reveal large papaya and other fruit orchards. Orchids can be seen growing along the coast of Puna. (See the Beach Road bike tour, number 18, on page 205 for driving directions.) A convenient place to see scads of orchid varieties is at the Akatsuka Orchard Gardens, near Volcano. To get there from Hilo, take Highway 11 to .5-mile past mm22. Volcano Orchid Farms is located between mm20 and mm21.

MACADAMIA NUTS

You can't chomp a big, meaty mac nut without thinking of Hawaii, but the snack treats are a native of Australia and were not harvested here in any great volume until the late 1950s. The nuts were named to honor an Australian doctor, John Macadam, but it was a Massachusetts man, Baron Ferdinand von Muller, who first planted a tree in Honolulu in 1921. To Muller's chagrin, nut quality varied hugely from tree to tree, and from year to year. It took botanists from the University of Hawaii 20 years to study thousands of different trees and come up with today's variety. Unlike coffee, small growers account for only fraction of the island's macadamia production. Big companies like Castle & Cooke (Dole) and C. Brewer and Company got into growing the subtropical trees, which can reach a height of 40 feet. Brewer's Mauna Loa brand orchards cover more than 2,000 acres near Hilo. Smaller growers harvest nuts along the Kona coast. The only organic nuts are grown in the orchards of 'Iole, in Kohala.

Trees may produce a nut after about 5 years, but it takes 15 years until large quantities can be harvested—at four or five different times through the year. The nuts have a leathery outer husk that covers a thin smooth shell that is known as a tough nut to crack. In the old days, orchard workers would lay boards over the round, in-shell nuts and drive over them in cars. Nowadays, mechanized rollers are used, as you can see at the Mauna Loa Macadamia Visitors Center. Most of Hawaii's sweet meats are produced on the east side, where 130-plus inches of rain, porous soil, and the right combination of sun and clouds combine to make nut heaven. But you'll find plenty of acres of orchard in southern Kona, and you can crack your own at the Kona Coast Macadamia Factory, just south of Captain Cook.

Climate

RAINFALL, AVERAGE INCHES PER YEAR

Kailua-Kona 40	Puna coast 100
South Kohala 20	Hawaii Volcanoes Park 85
Kawaihae 10	Wood Valley 90
Hawi 42	Naʻalehu 45
Honokaʻa 125	Manuka State Park 55
Hilo 150	Mauna Kea summit 10

LAVA FLOW RISK

Lava flows from eruptions occur slowly and are not an immediate threat. Vog, or volcanic smog, is most prevalent in South Kona, and occurs occasionally in North Kona and Waimea. Taking into account all locations on the island, vog density exceeds healthful standard set by the Environmental Protection Agency about 20 days per year.

1 = HIGHEST LAVA RISK, 9 = LOWEST LAVA RISK

Kailua-Kona 3-4	Hilo 3	Mauna Kea 7
South Kona, Kau 2	Hamakua 8	Mauna Loa 2
Hawaii Volcanoes Park 1	Waimea-North Kohala 9	
Puna 1-2	South Kohala 3-4	

TEMPERATURES
OCEAN
Low, late February to March:
73 degrees Fahrenheit
High, late September to October:
80 degrees Fahrenheit

AIR
Average high temperatures on the
Big Island, at sea level range from
a low of 78 degrees in January to
a high of 85 degrees. In Waimea,
daytime temps are normally in the
mid-60s to low-70s. At Hawaii
Volcanoes National Park (4,000
feet in elevation), 60 degrees
is an average high, with night-
time temps dropping to the 50s
and high 40s. Atop Mauna Kea,
expect temperatures in the high
40s to low 50s, with a potential
to drop below freezing at night.
Mauna Loa is generally 10 degrees
warmer.

WIND
Trade winds occur about 300
days a year, hitting the east side
of the island with speeds hovering
around 20 mph. The winds are
more prevalent in the summer. The
winds normally are stronger as the
day progresses, and then die down
at night. Kona winds, buffeting
the west side of the island, bring
warmer air and occur mostly in
the winter and spring.

POPULATION
Nearly 160,000 people live on the Big
Island, about double the number since 1970 and some 12 percent of the state's total
population of 1.2 million. (With an area of 4,030 square miles, the Big Island has
almost two-thirds of the state's landmass.)

PACKLIST

If your closet is lacking any of the items, consider picking them up once you arrive. All the surf-and-sun stuff and Alohawear is readily available at budget prices. Don't overpack. Leave room in your suitcase for the Kona coffee and macadamia nuts.

ONE OR TWO-WEEK VACATION
Shoes
> Slippers (a.k.a. zoris, sandals, go-aheads, slappers, flip-flops)
> Plane & hotel shoes (clean athletic shoes, sandals, or boat shoes)
> Hiking shoes (light weight hikers or cross-trainers)
> Surf socks (recommended for tide pool snorkeling)

Khaki pants plus Aloha shirt for plane, hotels. Women can bring a lightweight no-iron dress or go with short sleeved shirt, light jacket and comfortable pants.
Swimming suit
Sarong to wrap around waist (women)
Two or three pairs shorts
3 or 4 short sleeve tops (quick-dry polypropylene preferred)
1 or 2 long sleeve tops (mountain hikers bring 2 for layering, polypro)
Gore-Tex shell, or equivalent, rain jacket
Fleece vest, lightweight (optional)
Sun hat, sunglasses
Gloves (optional, for warmth on Mauna Kea and Mauna Loa, and to protect hands on lava hikes.)
Retractable hiking pole
Mask, fins, snorkel
Umbrella (optional, but the retractable model tucks into a knapsack and provides instant shelter for rain forest strolls)
Knapsack (most everything below can be picked up in Kona or Hilo)
> Antibiotic ointment
> Antibacterial handwipes
> Band Aids
> Binoculars
> Camera (disposable waterproof varieties available on island)
> Cell phone and GPS (won't work everywhere, but good for emergencies)
> Energy bars, emergency food (nuts, jerky)
> Flashlight or headlamp (one for each person, if planning nighttime, lava-viewing hikes)
> Handkerchief/bandana
> Mosquito repellent
> Motion sickness tablets
> Small bottle hydrogen peroxide
> Sunscreen, lip balm
> Swiss Army Knife
> Water bottles
> Water purification tablets or pump
> Whistle

Resource Links

RESOURCE LINKS

All area codes are 808 unless otherwise noted

AIRPORTS

Hilo International, 934-5838, Kona International, 329-3423

AIRLINES

American, 800-433-7300
Continental, 800-523-3273
Delta, 800-221-1212
Hawaiian, 800-367-5320
United, 800-241-6522

CAR RENTALS

Alamo, 800-327-9633, 836-3000
Avis, 800-367-3367, 840-2847
Aloha Car Sales, 935-9958
AA Aloha Cars-R-Us (quotes for all companies), 800-665-7989
Budget, 800-527-700
Dollar, 800-367-7006, 329-2744
Harper Car and Truck (4WD), 800-852-9993, 969-1478
Island Safari RV Rentals, 800-406-4555
National, 800-227-0891
Thrifty, 800-367-5238, 329-1339

BUSES AND SHUTTLES

Mass Transit Agency (public) 961-8343
Speedishuttle, 329-5433

BLUE HAWAIIAN HELICOPTERS

Features the quiet Eco-Star, tours all over the Big Island, and departs from both the Hilo Airport and on the Kona side at Waikaloa. This is as close as you can get to the eruption at Pu'u O'o, as well as the green valleys of Kohala. Blue Hawaiian may not be the cheapest, but this is something you don't want to skimp on. You get luxurious, well-maintained flying machines, as well as first-class narratives from the pilots. 800-786-2583, 961-5600, Hilo, 886-1768, Waikaloa.

PUBLIC PROPERTY

COUNTY

Beach Parks and Camping, Hilo, 961-8311,
   Kona, 323-4322
Aquatics, 961-8694
Culture & Arts, 961-8706
Information, 961-8223
Recreation Programs, 961-8740

VOLCANO TRACKING

http://hvo.wr.usgs.gov/
http://volcano.und.edu/vw.html
http://www.soest.hawaii.edu/
   GG/HCV/kilauea.html
http://virtual11.pgd.hawaii.edu/goes/
http://www.nps.gov/havo/

STATE
State Parks (Department of Land and Natural Resources), 961-9540
Na Ala Hele Trail System (Division of Forestry and Wildlife), 974-4382, 587-4175
Hapuna Beach State Recreation Area, 882-6206
Kalopa State Park, 775-8852
Lapakahi State Historical Park, 327-4958
Mo'okini Heiau, 591-1170
Pu'u Wa'awa'a Forest Reserve, 333-0084
Wailoa River State Park Art Center, 933-0416

NATIONAL
Hawaii Volcanoes National Park, 985-6000, 961-8093, 985-6019 (lava flow info.)
    Hawaiian Volcano Observatory, 967-7328
    Volcano Art Center (nonprofit) 967-7565
Hakalau National Wildlife Refuge, 443-2300
Kaloko-Honokohau National Historic Park, 326-9057
Pu'uhonua o Honaunau National Historic Park, 328-2326
Pu'ukohola Heiau National Historic Site, 882-7218

PRIVATE HIKING PERMITS
Kamehameha Schools-Bishop Estates, 322-5300
Kapapala Ranch (Ainapo Trail), 928-8403
Parker Ranch, 885-7311
Surety Kohala (Hawi), 889-6257

VISITOR INFORMATION
About.com: http://gohawaii.about.com; http://trailblazerhawaii.com
Big Island Visitors Bureau, 800-648-2441, Hilo, 961-5797, Kona, 886-1655
Bus schedules, 961-8744
Destination Kona Coast, 328-0614
Destination Hilo, 935-5294
Governor's State Information Office, 327-4953
Hawaii Tourism Authority, Honolulu, 973-2255
Mauna Kea Management Office, University of Hawaii, Hilo, 933-0734
Mauna Kea Observatories, 974-4205, Roads, 974-4203
    Keck Observatory, 935-8693, 935-6268
Mauna Loa Observatory, Hilo, 933-6965
Waiola Center (includes state parks), 933-4390, 933-0416
Weather, island-wide, 961-5582, Hilo, 935-8555

MUSEUMS, CULTURAL EVENTS, ATTRACTIONS
Amy Greenwell Ethnobotanical Garden, Captain Cook, 323-3318
East Hawaii Cultural Center,
Eva Parker Woods Cottage, Mauna Lani, 881-7911
   Danny Akaka's creation is a Big Island treasure
Hawaii Nature Center, Kohala, 887-6411
Hawaii Kupuna Hula, Kona, 322-1812
Hula Halai Na Lei O Kaholoku, 883-9005

Hulihe'e Palace, Kona, 329-6558
Imiloa Astronomy Center, Hilo, 969-9700
'Iole Foundation, Kohala, 889-5151
  Historic estate set on lush acres
Isaacs Art Center, Waimea, 885-5884
  One of the best Hawaiian painters'
  collections outside of Honolulu
Jaggar, Thomas A. Museum, Volcano, 985-6000
Kaupulehu Cultural Center, 323-8520
Kealakowa'a Heiau, Kona, 329-7286
Kona Coffee Living History Farm, 323-2006
Kona Historical Society, 323-3222
Ku'ulei Keakealani Interpretive
  Center, Kona, 987-9365
Lapakahi State Historical Park, 587-0300
Laupahoehoe Train Museum, 962-6300
Lyman House Museum, Hilo, 935-5021
Mokupapapa Discovery Center for
  Hawaii's Reefs, Hilo, 933-8195
Mo'okini Heiau, 591-1170
Na Mea Hawaii Hula Kahiko, Volcano, 967-8222
Onizuka Space Center, Kona, 329-3441
Onizuka Center for International Astronomy, Hilo,
  961-2180, Mauna Kea, 935-7606, 935-6268
Pacific Tsunami Museum, Hilo, 935-0926
Queen's Marketplace Hula, 886-8822
Volcano Art Center, 967-8222, 967-7565
  Historic building in the park; hula performances are unforgettable

SUPPLEMENTAL MAPS
Free maps are widely available in shopping centers, on the plane, and from the visitors bureau. National park maps are included with the price of admission. This book's maps and directions are enough for you to get around the island, but having a street map and detailed, all-purpose map is a good idea.

Map of Hawaii, The Big Island. University of Hawaii Press. James A. Bier, cartographer. Full Color Topographic, 2840 Kolowalu Street, Honolulu, HI, 96822. *Best all-purpose map. Indexes place names and shows unpaved roads. Be sure to get the 2002 copyright, since over-inking on earlier versions make them almost unreadable. Widely available at mainland and Hawaii stores.*
Island of Hawaii Recreation Map. Department of Land and Natural Resources, 974-6200, 587-0300. *May not be available. Shows hunter's reserves, state hiking trails, and public lands.*
The Ready Mapbook of West Hawaii, East Hawaii. Odyssey Publishing, 888-729-1074, 935-0092. *Best street maps. In book form, one for each side of the island. The choice if you plan of doing a lot of exploring by car. Does not include Saddle Road, however.*
A Guide to Public Parks. County of Hawaii, Department of Parks & Recreation, 961-8311. *Includes current facility information and is useful in planning your trip.*
Big Island Mountain Biking. Big Island Mountain Biking Association, 961-4452
  Not a 'must-have, but cyclists may wish to request this free map.
Map of the Neighbor Islands, Hawaii, Maui & Kauai, Compass Maps, 800-441-6277
  Fold-up street map. Needs update. Includes neighbor islands.

USGS Topos, 800-ASK-USGS. *Set of 3 topographical maps covers the island at a 1:100,000 scale. Shows roads and trails, but place names are not marked well enough for all-purpose use.*

NEWSPAPERS, NEWSLETTERS
Big Island Gold (visitors guide), 593-9404
Hawaii Herald Tribune, 935-6621
Hawaii Island Journal, 328-1880
Ka Wai Ola OHA, 800-468-4644
North Hawaii News, 930-8675
This Week Big Island (visitors guide), 961-5797
Volcano Art Center Gazette, 967-8222
West Hawaii Today, 329-9311

PRESERVATION AND CULTURAL GROUPS
Friends of Ho'okena Beach, 328-8430
Hawaii Natural History Association,
    Volcano, 985-6051
Hilo-Hamakua Heritage Coast, 966-5416
'Iole Foundation, Kohala, 889-5151
Kahikolu Congregational Church, 328-8110
Ka Ohana O Honuapu (Whittington) 929-8454
Kaupulehu Cultural Center, 325-8520, 325-8467
Kona Historical Society, 323-3222
Mauna Kea Management, University of Hawaii, Hilo, 944-0734
Mokuaikaua Church, Kona, 329-1589
Na Opio O Halelea (hula group), 635-0281
Paniolo Preservation Society, 887-6059
Pulama Ia Kona Heritage Council, 323-3222
Queen Liliuokalani Trust, 935-9381, 329-7336, 329-0503
ReefTeach, 329-2861

GARDENS AND ORCHARDS
Akatsuka Orchid Gardens, Volcano, 967-8234, 888-967-6669
Hawaii Tropical Botanical Garden, Papaikou, 964-5233
    On the short list of best in the state.
Hilo Farmers Market, 933-1000
Hilo Forestry Arboretum, 974-4221
Kona Coast Macadamia, 328-8141, 800-242-6887
Mauna Loa Macadamias Visitors Center, Hilo, 888-628-6556
Nani Mau Gardens, Hilo, 959-3500
Panaewa Rainforest Zoo (county), Hilo, 959-7224, 959-9233
Puna Kamalii Flowers, Inc., *(training the mentally challenged)* 982-8322
Sadie Seymour Botanical Gardens, Kona, 329-7286
Volcano Winery, 967-7772
Umauma Experience, Hamakua, 930-9477
World Botanical Gardens, Hamakua, 963-5427

KONA COFFEE

Bay View Farm, 328-8400
Coffees 'n' Epicuria, 328-0322
Greenwell Farms, 323-2275
Heavenly Hawaiian, 322-7720
Kona Blue Sky Coffee, 322-1700
Kona Pacific Farmers Co-op, 328-2411

CULTURAL GIFT STORES, BOOKS, GALLERIES
Ackerman Galleries, Kohala, 889-5971
As Hawi Turns, 889-5023
Basically Books (Maps), Hilo, 800-903-6277, 961-0144
Outdoor and nature selections among the best in the state
Hawaiian Artifacts, Hamakua Coast, 964-1729
Hawaii Tropical Botanical Garden, Hamakua, 964-5253
Hawaiian Force, Hilo, 934-7171
Hawaiian Quilt Collection, Waikoloa, 886-0494
Hilo Bay Books, 935-9234
Holualoa Gallery, 322-8484
Holualoa Ukulele Gallery, 324-4100
Honoka'a Marketplace, 775-8255
Kealia Ranch Store, Honaunau, 328-8744
Paul's Place, Holualoa, 324-4702
Rankin Gallery, Kapa'au, 889-6849
Suisan Fish Market, Hilo, 935-9349
Third Dimension Gallery, Mauna Lani, 885-6280
Ululani Gallery, Holualoa, 322-7733
Under the Koa Tree, Waikoloa King's Shops, 886-7444
Victoria Fine Art, Kapa'au, 889-1711
Volcano Art Center, 967-8222, 967-7565
Waipio Valley Artworks, Honoka'a, 775-0958
Woodshop Gallery-Café, Akaka Falls, 963-6363

OUTFITTERS, TOURS, HIKES, AND GROUPS

HIKE/DRIVE
Arnott's Lodge & Hiking Adventures, 339-0921
Green Lakes, Puna, 965-5500
Mauna Kea Summit Adventures, 322-2366, 888-322-2366
Hawaii Ecotourism Association, 877-300-7058, 235-5431
Hawaii Forest & Trail, 331-8505, 800-464-1993, 334-9555
The Big Island's premier outdoor tour company
Hawaiian Walkways, 775-0372
'Iole Foundation, Kohala, 889-5151
Kona Historical Society, 323-3222
Waipio Valley Shuttle, 775-7121

BIKES

Big Island Mountain Bike Association, 961-4452
Dave's Bikes and Triathalon Shop, 329-4522
Hawaiian Pedals, 329-2294
Kona Coast Cycling Tours, 327-1133
Mauna Kea Mountain Bikes, 883-0130
PATH (People's Advocacy for Trails Hawaii-bikes),
    326-9495, *Plenty of advice & info. available*
Top of Waipio, 775-9393

ZIPLINES

Big Island Eco Adventures ('Iole) Kohala, 889-5111
    Flying high over a tropical stream and arboretum
Umauma Experience, Hamakua , 930-9477

SNORKEL, BOATS, KAYAKS, WATER SPORTS

Adventures in Paradise, Kealakekua, 800-979-3370
Big Island Divers, Kona, 800-488-6068
Big Island Water Sports Snuba, Kona, 324-1650
Captain Zodiac, 329-3199
Dolphin Quest (kids, Hilton), 886-2875, 800-248-3316
Dolphin Discoveries, 322-8000
Fair Wind (Cook Monument), 322-2788
Flumin' Da Ditch Ride, Hawi, 889-6000
Kamanu Charters (night manta ray), 329-2021
Kohala Divers, Kawaihae, 882-7774
Kohala Kayak, 882-4678 (Cheryl & Sian)
Kona Honu Divers, Kailua, 324-4668
Red Sail Sports, 886-2876
Sea Quest Raft & Snorkel,
    Keauhou, 329-7238

SURF

Ocean Eco Tours, Kona, 331-2121
Kona Surf Company, 217-5329
Surfer Bear Hawaii, Kona, 936-3654

HORSES

Dahana Ranch, Waimea, 885-0057
Kapapala Ranch, Volcano, 928-9811
Kealia Ranch, Honaunau, 328-8777
Kohala Na'alapa Stables, 889-0022
Mauna Kea Beach Stables, 882-5707
Paniolo Adventures, Waimea, 889-5354
Waipio on Horseback, 775-7291
Waipio Ridge Stables, 775-1007

GOLF

Kohala
Hapuna Golf Course, 921-2808
Hilton Waikoloa Seaside, 886-5172
Big Island Country Club, 325-5044
Francis H. I'i Brown North and
    South Courses, 885-6655
Waikoloa Kings' Course, 886-7888
Waimea Country Club, 885-8777

Kona/Keauou
Kona Country Club, 322-2595
Makalei Hawaii Club, 325-6625

Hilo
Hilo Municipal Course, 959-7711
Naniloa Country Club, 935-3000

Honokaa
Hamakua Country Club, 775-7244

Punaluu/Volcano/South Point
Discovery Harbor, 929-7353
Sea Mountain Golf
    Course, 928-6222
Volcano Country Club, 967-7331

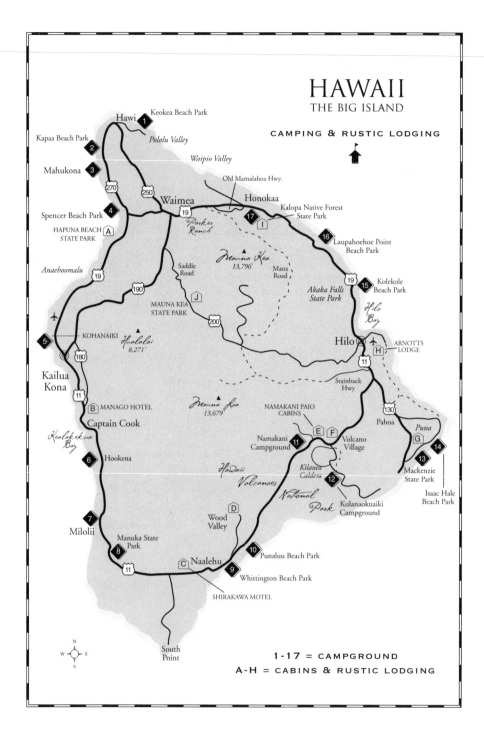

HAWAII
THE BIG ISLAND

CAMPING & RUSTIC LODGING

Keokea Beach Park

Hawi **1**

Kapaa Beach Park **2**

Pololu Valley

Mahukona **3**

Waipio Valley

270 250

Old Mamalahoa Hwy.

Waimea Honokaa

Spencer Beach Park **4**

19

HAPUNA BEACH STATE PARK **A**

Kalopa Native Forest State Park **17** **I**

16 Laupahoehoe Point Beach Park

Anaehoomalu

19

190

Parker Ranch

Mauna Kea 13,796'

Saddle Road

Mana Road

Akaka Falls State Park

19 **15** Kolekole Beach Park

Hilo Bay

MAUNA KEA STATE PARK **J**

200

KOHANAIKI **5**

Hualalai 8,271'

Hilo **H** ARNOTTS LODGE

180

11

Kailua Kona

11

B MANAGO HOTEL

Captain Cook

Mauna Loa 13,679'

NAMAKANI PAIO CABINS

Stainback Hwy

130

Pahoa

Puna **G**

E **F**

Kealakekua Bay

Namakani Campground **11**

Volcano Village

14

6 Hookena

Hawaii Volcanoes

Kilauea Caldera

13 Mackenzie State Park

12

Isaac Hale Beach Park

7

National Park

Kulanaokuaiki Campground

Miolii

Manuka State Park

8

D

Wood Valley

11

C Naalehu

10 Punaluu Beach Park

9 Whittington Beach Park

SHIRAKAWA MOTEL

N
W — E
S

South Point

1–17 = CAMPGROUND

A–H = CABINS & RUSTIC LODGING

Camping & Rustic Lodging

SPENCER BEACH PARK

The Big Island has the state's best camping, with beach and forest sites spread around the island. You'll also find cabins and rustic lodging,. When planning your trip, also take a look at *Where to Stay* for budget-priced hotels, as well as reasonably priced inns and B&Bs. Some of the prices are as cheap as cabins.

Duffel Bag Campsite:
Most of what you need for a night's camping will fit into a duffel bag, checked with the rest of your airplane luggage: a backpacking tent, very lightweight sleeping bags, kitchen set, and cook stove that takes readily available fuel. One stop at a super market will complete your camp set: a Styrofoam cooler, picnic dinnerware, stove fuel, and gallon water jugs.

See the *Camping Map* for locations of campgrounds and cabins. Call ahead for reservations where necessary and to inquire about specific amenities. Thumbnail descriptions follow each listing, but you can read the trailhead descriptions to get a better handle on the area. Use the *Trailhead Directory* in the front of the book for a quick reference to page numbers.

CONTACTS AND PERMITS

All area codes are 808

Hawaii County: Department of Parks and Recreation, 101 Pauahi Street, Suite 6, Hilo, HI, 96720. Phone: 961-8311, Fax: 961-8411. County fees are $5 a night, per adult. Permits available online

State of Hawaii: Department of Land and Natural Resources, Division of State Parks, P. O. Box 936, Hilo, HI, 96721. Phone: 974-4343, 974-6200, Wailoa Center, 933-0416, Honolulu, 587-0300. No fees for campgrounds.

National: Hawaii Volcanoes National Park, P.O. Box 52, Hawaii National Park, HI, 96718. Phone: 985-6000, 985-6017. Two no-fee, no reservation campgrounds are within the park.

CAMPGROUNDS

1. Keokea Beach Park (county) – Set on a remote bay, with good access of Pololu Valley. Pavilion, lawn, showers, drinking water. Popular with neighboring Filipino community, particularly on weekends. Directions are in TH3, Polulu Valley.
2. Kapaʻa Beach Park (county) – Beautifully situated on a rugged coastline. More remote-feeling than most coastal camping. Basic rest rooms and pavilion. No drinking water or picnic area. See TH5, Mahukona, for directions.
3. Mahukona Beach Park (county) – Nice lawn camping with good snorkeling nearby. Large pavilion with tables. Shower, but no drinking water. Doesn't get a lot of local use, but popular among travelers. See TH5, Mahukona.
4. Spencer Beach Park (county) – Beautiful stone pavilion, drinking water, indoor showers. Shaded large camping area next to swimming beach and a short walk to excellent snorkeling beach. Gets a lot of use. See TH7, Puʻukohola Heiau.
5. Kohanaiki Coastal Park (county)- Newly developed north Kona park at site of Pinetrees sufring beach is the *quid pro quo* for the big swank development built inland. Camping status may still be in limbo.
6. Hoʻokena Beach Park (county) – 'Cozy' beachside camping at this popular park, the closest to Kailua-Kona. Rest rooms, showers, picnic tables. See TH28.
7. Miloliʻi Beach Park (county) – Not many tourists spend the night in Miloliʻi, and the campground feels more like a day-use area. You'll have more privacy on weekdays. May feel too 'local' for some. See TH29 for directions.
8. Manuka State Park (state) – Beautiful native forest, midway between Kona and Hawaii Volcanoes. Set at about 2,000 feet, cooler but not cold. One of the more woodsy, quiet camping experiences available. See TH30 for directions.
9. Whittington Beach Park (county) – Remotely located, this is one of the least used county parks, in spite of its scenic charms. Rest rooms, showers, and pavilion, but no drinking water. Directions are in TH32.
10. Punaluʻu Beach Park (county) – Set on a hillside next to the Big Island's most popular black sand beach. Wind can be a factor. Locals like the pavilion for parties, particularly on weekends. See TH33 for directions.

11. Namakani Paio Campground (national) – Located 3 miles west of the entrance to Hawaii Volcanoes National Park on Highway 11. Nice lawn surrounded by lush forest. Full facilities. Can be damp and chilly, set at 4,000-feet. No fees or reservations required. Closed until early 2012 for renovations.

12. Kulanaokuaiki Campground (national) – Located within Hawaii Volcanoes National Park, on Hilina Pali Road. Will be warmer and drier (at 2,700 feet) than Namakani Paio, but also in an arid setting. Usually quiet and more private than most Big Island campsites. Nice views and new tent pads. Restroom and fire grates. No fees or reservations required, although you need to pay the park admission.

13. Mackenzie State Recreation Area (state) – Set within a huge coastal ironwood grove along the lush Puna coast. Has picnic area, pavilion, and rest rooms, but no drinking water. Frequented by fishermen, mostly on weekends, and not many tourists. Some spillover from Isaac Hale Beach Park. See TH50 for the driving directions.

14. Isaac Hale Beach Park (county) – Not the greatest facilities. Gets a lot of local use, particularly on weekends. Some permanent blue-tarp campers. Ahalunai hot pool is nearby. See TH51 for a description.

15. Kolekole Beach Park (county) – In a lovely jungle gorge, fairly close to Hilo and very near Akaka Falls State Park. Nice lawn with pavilion, picnic facilities, and showers. Gets local action, particularly on weekends, due to proximity to Hilo. See TH58, Akaka Falls, for directions.

16. Laupahoehoe Point Beach Park (county) – Beautiful, well-kept coastal setting. Nice lawn area with plenty of trees and full facilities. On weekend evenings, locals like the gather at the park, but the place usually is not overcrowded with campers. Details are given in TH60.

17. Kalopa State Park (state) – Among the best sites, set around a large meadow in a native forest. Full facilities. Can be damp and chilly, at 2,000 feet. Usually uncrowded and quiet. Also has cabins, which are listed below. Directions are in TH61.

NAMAKANI PAIO CAMPGROUND

CABINS AND RUSTIC LODGING

A. Hapuna Beach State Park (state) – About a half-dozen A-frames are nicely spaced on an arid, windswept hillside above the island's most-popular beach. A communal cooking pavilion is nearby. Don't expect anything fancy, but the cabins were rehabbed in 2012. Great location for Kona and Kohala. Rent is about $50.

B. Manago Hotel (private, 323-2642) – Basic but hardly rustic, the Manago is a Big Island classic. Views of Kealakekua Bay. Easy Kona access from Captain Cook. Japanese restaurant attached, and stores of the town are nearby. Double rooms are still under $60, with weekly rates available.

C. Shirakawa Motel (private, 929-7462) Most likely closed for the forseeable future.

D. Wood Valley Temple (private, 928-8539) – Rustic, private rooms and a share-kitchen on the lovely grounds of an internationally known Buddhist retreat. Rooms are around $50.

E. Namakani Paio Cabins (private, 967-7321) – Ten cabins next to the camp-ground, 3 miles west from the Hawaii Volcanoes National Park entrance. Communal rest rooms and showers. Bedding included, but it gets chilly, so bring an extra blanket. About $40 gets you a cabin. Operated by Volcano House Hotel. These cabins will be closed until early 2012 while the hotel is being renovated.

F. Holo Holo Inn (private, 967-7950) and Kulana Retreat (private, 985-9055) – To call the modest Holo an Inn is generous, but they have clean rooms. Dorms are about $21, and privates are up to $75. Kulana is an artist retreat with cabins, rooms, and camping. Prices range from $25 to under $50. Both places are near the national park and Volcano Village restarants, in the ohia birdlands.

G. Kalani Retreat (private, 965-7828, 800-800-6886) – A range of choices—$40 campsites, $140 rooms, and cabins up to $250. Not cheap for sure, but the retreat is set on 100-plus verdant acres on a lovely part of the Puna Coast.

H. Arnott's Lodge and Hiking Adventures (private, 339-0921) – Enterprising Aussie Doug Arnott has tent spaces for $11, dorm beds for $28, and private rooms for around $75—with suites up to $180. Walking distance to good beaches in Hilo. Shuttle service from the airport, plus cross-island excursions. You're bound to meet interesting people, many of them Euro-style and student travelers. A television series could be set in and around this quirky place. See TH48; Arnott's is on Apapane Street.

I. Kalopa Native Forest State Park – Large cabins on the manicured grounds of the park, set at 2,000 feet. Can be chilly and damp, but these cabins are a find. Cabins are about $90 a night for nonresidents. See TH61.

J. Mauna Kea State Park – A rather forlorn location, off Saddle Road at 6,000 feet, and next to a military training area. Still, spending the night between Mauna Loa and Mauna Kea is a memorable experience. Cost is around $80.

Where to Stay

FAIRMONT ORCHID HAWAII,
HILTON WAIKOLOA VILLAGE,
SHIPMAN HOUSE,

All listings are recommended but **bold** type indicates a preferred lodging. Give them a call to inquire about amenities and location, and anything else that is important to you. Listings range from large destination resorts to single-room lodgings in private homes. In all cases, be sure to ask if you're getting the lowest rate. You'll find that most people in Hawaii will have time to talk to you. Also see *Camping & Cabins*, page 235, for economy lodging; and *Strategies For Visiting The Big Island*, page198, for tips on booking your stay. For island-wide bed & breakfast referrals, try Hawaii's Best Bed & Breakfast, 800-262-9912. Area codes are 808, unless otherwise listed.

(P) = PRICEY, $200 AND WAY UP
(M) = MODERATE, $100 TO $200
(C) = CHEAP, AROUND $100

KONA COAST

Kailua-Kona is the island's most-developed coast, with a 4-mile run of moderately priced resorts and condominiums situated mostly along Ali'i Drive. Captain Cook, Holualoa, and Kealakekua are a few miles from downtown Kailua and lodgings are set among vintage storefronts or in rural area. You're guaranteed sunshine, and excellent snorkeling is nearby, but Kona doesn't have big beaches.

ROYAL KONA RESORT

Areca Palms, (B&B) Captain Cook (C-M), 800-545-4390, 323-2276
Black Bamboo Hawaii (agent, B&Bs, homes) Kealakekua (M-P) 800-527-7789
Bear's Place Guest House, Kailua (C), 990-1383
Captains Suite-Bamboo Hideaway, Honauau (C-M), 866-328-8686, 328-8687
   Beautifully designed, quiet studios with kitchens have a panoramic view of Kealakekua Bay.
Cedar House B&B, Captain Cook (C) 328-8829
A Hale Lanai (cottage), Holualoa (M) 530-583-6062
Holualoa Inn (breakfast) (M) 324-1121, 800-392-1812
   Spectacular view, private, in the rural hills above Kona.
King Kamehameha (Courtyard) Beach Hotel, Kailua (M-P)
Kona Bali Kai Resort (condos) (M-P) 329-9381
Kona Magic Sands (condos) (C-M) 244-4752
Kona Tiki Hotel (breakfast) (C) 329-1425
   Oceanfront, unpretentious, great value, book way ahead.
Manago Hotel, Captain Cook (C) 323-2642
   A Big Island classic, some rooms with views of Kealakekua Bay, family owned since 1917, a real deal.
Nancy's Hideaway, Kona mauka (B&B) (M) 325-3132
Royal Kona Resort (M), 329-3111
Sea Village (condos) (M) 326-7434, 326-2252
Sheraton Keauhou Bay Resort & Spa (P) 888-488-3535, 930-4900
   Quietly one of the best luxury resorts on the Big Island. Oceanfront setting and well situated to visit Kona, Kohala, Kealakekua Bay, and the national parks.
Tara Cottage, Kealakekua (M) 328-9607, 800-527-7789

SOUTH KOHALA

Hawaii's best beaches and its luxury resorts lie in green oases along the coast of this 25-mile stretch of barren lava flows. You'll also find several wild beaches. These swank destination resorts are exquisitely beautiful. You can visit this area on easy day drives from Kona or Hawi-Waimea.

Aldridge Associates (agent) (C-P) 883-8300
Fairmont Orchid Hawaii (P) 885-2000, 800-845-9905
Four Seasons Resort Hualalai (P) 325-8000, *Pamper yourself in understated luxury.*
Hawaii Vacation Rentals (agent, Puako) (C-P) 882-7000, 800-332-7081

MAUNA KEA

Hilton Waikoloa Village (P) 886-1234, 800-445-8767
Opulent family fun. Waterslides, monorail, Dolphin Quest program, hop on a motorboat to your room.
Lava Lava Beach Club (cottages) (P) 769-5282
Kaunu Cottage (Kawaihae) (C-M) 233-8124
Three miles up Kawaihae Road from South Kohala beaches—ideal base camp for active visitors
Mauna Kea Beach Hotel (P) 882-7222, 800-882-6060
Mauna Lani Resort (P) 885-6622, 800-367-2323, *La creme de la creme.*
Outrigger Waikoloa Beach (M-P) 886-6789, 800-922-5533
Sea Turtle Villa (C-P) 949-766-0374, 949-283-8153 (owner), 800-662-5642 (agent)
Deluxe unit 1101 at Fairways Mauna Lani is quiet but close to the beach action.

HAWI-WAIMEA

At nearly 3,000 feet in elevation, Waimea, a.k.a. Kamuela, is set in rolling pasturelands. You're able to drop down easily to the beaches of Kohala and Waipio Valley, and also to the Hilo-Hamakua Coast. Cool weather rolls through Waimea, which is in a saddle between Mauna Kea and the Kohala Mountains. Hawi is in rural north Kohala, with easy access to Pololu Valley and not far from the beaches of South Kohala. Obviously, you won't get oceanfront at either location.

Cabin in the Treeline, mauka Hawi (M) 884-5105
Hawaii Palm Properties (agent), Hawi, 889-1295
Booking information as a courtesy to locals
Hawi Haven (cottage) (M) 884-5345
Country cottage with birds as neighbors.
Kamuela Inn (Waimea) (C-M) 885-4243,
Kohala Club Hotel, Kapaau (C) 889-6793
Kohala Village Inn, Hawi (C-M) 889-0404
A find for budget travelers.
Hale O Kohala (home), Kawaihae
(M) 822-7022
Paniolo Cottage, Waimea
(M) 866-399-5842

HILO-HAMAKUA

They're aren't many accommodations on the lush Hamakua Coast, nor in Hilo, relative to Kona. Banyan Drive hotels are underrated, and the Shipman House is one of the best places in the Hawaiian Islands. This is the green side of the island, with easy access to Waipio, Mauna Kea, and Hawaii Volcanoes National Park. The Puna coastline has excellent snorkeling, and Hilo's beach parks are a pleasant surprise. Hilo is known for its rainfall, but it comes in downpours, followed by tropical sunshine.

Shipman House (B&B), Hilo (M) 934-8002, 800-627-8447
   Jack London stayed here, one of the state's premier historic accommodations; lavish breakfast.
Arnott's Lodge (hostel, rooms), Hilo (C) 969-7097
   For the Euro-adventure travel set, close to beaches. Organized group tours to volcano and Mauna Kea.
Dolphin Bay Hotel (M) 935-1466
Hale Kukui Orchard Retreat (cottages), Honoka'a (M) 775-1701, 800-444-7130
Hilo Hawaiian Hotel (M) 935-9361
   Oceanfront resort hotel dated but value.
Hotel Honoka'a Club (dorm, rooms) (C)
   775-0678, 800-808-0678

Inn at Kulaniapia Falls (M) 935-6789
Luana Ola B&B Cottages, Honoka'a (M)
   775-1150, 800-357-7727
Old Hawaii B&B, Hilo (C) 961-2816,
   877-961-2816
**Palms Cliff House (B&B) Honomu
   (P), 963-6076**
   Luxurious and quiet, right on an ocean bluff.
Plantation Bungalow, Pepe'ekeo
   (C) 866-328-8686, 328-8687
Waipio Ridge Vacation Rental (cottage),
   Honoka'a (M), 775-0603

VOLCANO

Within a mile of the national park, Volcano is a quiet burg with several excellent B&Bs, fabulous Kilauea Lodge and also several fun choices for

WOOD VALLEY TEMPLE

dinner. Birds flock to the ohia and fern forest, set at a chilly 4,000 feet. You get to enjoy evenings and mornings at the park, and see it at its most serene.

Hale Ohia Cottages (B&B) (M) 800-455-3803, 967-7986
   Lots of intriguing options on these historic beautifully groomed grounds.
Kilauea Lodge (includes breakfast) (M) 967-7366
   Great to come home to after a day at the volcano; ambiance matches excellent cuisine.
Guesthouse at Volcano (cottages, B&B) (C-M) 967-7775
Holo Holo Inn (C) 967-7950
Volcano House (renovated historic hotel on crater rim) (P) 756-9625, 866-536-7972
Volcano Rainforest Retreat (cottages, B&B) (M-P) 985-8696, 800-985-8696
My Island Bed & Breakfast (C-M) 967-7216, 967-7110

KAU-WOOD VALLEY

Not many people stay is this section of the Big Island, in spite of several excellent lodging choices. A rain forest is close by, and you have access to the coast at several places—although snorkeling is generally not good. You're within range to visit Hawaii Volcanoes National Park, as well as South Point, Wood Valley rain forest, and Miloli'i.

Hale Aloha Aina (Big Island Cottage), Wood Valley (C-M) 888-256-4206, 541-382-7659
Good people, garden setting. Try this side of the island for a getaway.
Macadamia Meadows Farm B&B, Waiohinu (C-M) 929-8097, 888-929-8118
Orchard setting, family farm in lush valley.
Pahala Plantation Cottages (C-P) 928-9811, 937-9965
SeaMountain at Punalu'u (condos) (M) 928-8301, 800-488-8301
Oceanfront value near Black Sand Beach.
Wood Valley Temple & Retreat (C-M) 928-8539
Peace and contemplation in a rain forest; modest decor

HALE OHIA COTTAGE, VOLCANO HOUSE'S 'PERPETUAL' FIRE, SHIPMAN HOUSE BREAKFAST, KILAUEA LODGE

Where to eat

Whether you hunger for Pacific gourmet or island-style grinds, pupus or a full-on luau, you can end the quest at one of these Big Island winners. Call ahead to see if they suit your tastes. Not all serve dinner. All area codes are 808.

(C) CHEAP OR TAKE-OUT
(LESS THAN $10)

(M) MODERATE, FAMILY
($10 TO $20)

(P) PRICEY, SPECIAL
OCCASION ($20 AND UP)

KAILUA
Ba-le Sandwiches & Bakery (C) 327-1212
Humpy's Big Island Ale House (C-M) 324-2337
Da Poke Shack (C) 329-7653
Huggo's, Kailua (P) 329-1493
Kau Kau Kona (C) 334-1698
   Hawaiin plates, Aisan and American favorites
Kona Inn Restaurant (M-P) 329-4455
   Great food since Don Ho was a keiki. Peacock chairs, view of Kailua Harbor. Watch the sunset.
PineTree Cafe (C) 327-1234
Royal Kona Resort (luau) (P) 329-3111
Sam Choy's (P)333-3434

KEALAKEKUA-CAPTAIN COOK
Evie's Natural Foods, Kainaliu (C) 322-0739
Manago Hotel, Captain Cook (C) 323-2642
   Try the pork chops and potato-mac salad. A taste of Old Hawaii.
Kaalo's Super J's, Honaunau (C) 328-9566
   Aunty and the keikis prepare authentic Hawaiian take out plates.
Teshima's, Kainaliu (C-M) 322-9140, *Japanese food is a magnet for locals.*

KOHALA-SOUTH KOHALA

Bamboo Restaurant, Hawi (P) 889-5555
Just look for the crowds.
Cafe Pesto, Kawaihae (M-P), 882-1071
Kohala Coffee Mill, Hawi (C) **889-5577**
CSC Cafe, Kapa'au (C) 889-0208
Lava Lava Beach Club, Waiakoloa (M-P) 769-5282
Pricey bar food. but great beachside atmosphere
Minnie's, Kapa'au (C) 889-5288
Kawaihae Harbor Grill (M) 882-1368
King's Shops Food Court, Waikaloa (C-M) 886-8811
Nanbu Courtyard, Kapa'au (C) 889-5546
Lots of homemade goodies.
Sansei Seafood & Sushi, Waikoloa (P) 886-6286

WAIMEA-HONOKA'A

Hawaiian Style Café, Kamuela (C) 885-4295
Tex Drive-in & Restaurant, Honoka'a (C) 775-0598
Tour buses pull in for the sugary malasada balls
Lilikoi Cafe, Waimea (C-M) 887-1400
Merriman's Restaurant, Kamulea (P)
885-6822 *Enjoy an evening at this gourmet hideaway.*
Pau, Waimea (C-M) 885-6325
Paniolo Country Inn (M-P) 885-4377
Waimea Coffe Company (M) 885-8915

HILO-HAMAKUA

Abundant Life Cafe, Hilo (C-M) 935-7411
Baker Tom's, Papaikou, 964-8444
Roadside attraction; try the cheese malasada ball
Cafe Pesto, Hilo, (M-P) 969-6640
Hilo Bay Cafe (M-P) 935-4939
Don's Grill, Hilo (C-M) 935-9099
Neighborhood eatery. Spirited service and great value.
Ken's House of Pancakes (C-M) Hilo, 935-8711
Nightly specials on wide-ranging menu. Hilo institution
Lucy's Taqueria, Hilo (C) 315-8426
Mr. Ed's Bakery, Honomu (C) 963-5000
Miyo's, Hilo (C-M) 935-2273
Romance on the pond without paying through the nose.
Moonstruck Patisserie, Hilo(M) 933-6868
Naung Mai Thai Kitchen, Hilo, (C-M) 934-740
Puka Puka Kitchen, Hilo (C-M)933-2121
What's Shakin', Pepe'ekeo (C) 9 64-3080

VOLCANO-SOUTH POINT

Cafe Ono(C-M) 985-8979
Cafe Ohia (C-M) 985-8587
Large gourmet sandwiches
Hana Hou Restaurant, Naalehu,
(C-M) 929-9717
You won't be alone at this well-known locals' cafe
Kilauea Lodge, Volcano (M-P)
967-7366
Fireside gourmet cuisine where you can bring along a healthy appetite.
Punalu'u Bake Shop-Visitor Center
(C-M) 929-7343

Hawaiian Glossary

VOLCANO ART CENTER

The Hawaiian language was first written by Big Island missionaries in the 1820s, who transcribed phonetically. *Hawaiian Grammar*, which is now out of print, was published by Lorrin Andrews in 1854. Only 12 letters were needed—A, E, I, O, U, plus the consonants, H, K, L, M, N, P, and W. Note that there is no B and S in Hawaiian.

Hawaiian can be thought of as a dialect of the Polynesian language; others include Samoan, Tahitian, Marquesan, and Maori. The original home of the Polynesians was India, and after a long period of migrations they reached the South Pacific, as their language transformed with their travel.

Vowels may follow each other, but consonants stand alone. A "W" is sometimes pronounced as a "V," when in the middle of a word. Words always end in a vowel. The funny apostrophe (') between some vowels is called an okina. It creates a glottal stop in the word; for instance, in "ahupua'a," the ending is pronounced "ah-ah." Among all words, stress is usually placed on the second to the last syllable, unless the word only has two syllables, in which cast the last is stressed. Today, an increasing number of schools in Hawaii are centered around teaching the language, as well as the time-honored crafts, dance, and legends.

a'a – sharp, broken lava
ahupua'a – a division of land from the mountains to the sea around which a
   village lived; watershed
aina – land, country
aka'aka – to laugh
akua – god, deity
akua ki – image of a god
ala – path, way, or trail
ali'i – chief or chiefess descended from original chiefs or nobles
aloha – hello or goodbye, welcome or farewell, love and best wishes
aumakua – ancestral spirit, personal or family god
hale – house
hana – work
haole – foreigner, sometimes Caucasian
hau – breeze, dew; a king of tree
heiau – temple, church, worship ground
hilo – twisting, braiding
hoaloha – a friend
hoku – a star
holua – a sled, or sliding place
honi – to touch, taste, kiss
hono – bay
honu – a turtle
huhu – angry, offended
hui – group, meeting
hukilau – group net fishing
hula – dance that enacts
   the stories that
   become myths
huli huli – barbecue
iki – small, little
ipo – sweetheart, darling
ka'a – cart or car
kahuna – teacher, expert, priest

KING KAMEHAMEHA'S KONA BEACH HOTEL
LUAU CEREMONY

kai – the sea
kama'aina – native born, or longtime resident
kanaka – the people
kane – man
kapa – tapa, bark cloth
kapu – forbidden, no trespassing
kapuna – older, wise person
keiki – child, or young banana plant
keiki pond - beach or swimming area for children
ki'i – image, statue
ki'i pohaku – etchings made in rock, petroglyphs
kiawe –the algaroba tree from South America, has long thorns
kipuka – a portion of native forest surrounded by a lava flow
koa – largest of the native forest trees
kona – leeward
kokua – help
kopa'a – sugar
Ku – god of war
kukui – a type of tree; lamp or torch
lanai – deck, porch, patio
laulau – fish, pork, sweet potatoes, and taro leaves in steamed pouch
lei – garland of flowers, vines, or beads worn around the neck
lolo – dumb
lomi lomi – a traditional massage

Lono – god of peace and fertility
luau – feast
mahalo – thank you
mahina – lunar month
makahiki – fall celebration of return of peace and fertility; a year
makai – toward the sea
mana – spiritual power in all things
mauka – toward the mountain, inland
mauna – mountain
Mele Kalikimaka – Merry Christmas
menehune – dwarf person; legendary first settlers
moana – ocean
moku – island
Na Ala Hele – 'trails for walking'
nalu – surf breaking on the beach
nani – pretty, beautiful
nene – Hawaiian goose
niu - coconut
o'ne – sand
ohana – family
ohia – mountain apple, lehua blossom bearer
oluolu – please
opala - rubbish
pahoehoe – smooth, undulating lava
pali – cliff, precipice
paniolo – Hawaiian cowboy
Pele – the goddess of volcanoes
peleleu – a large, double canoe
piko – umbilical cord or, figuratively, a blood relation
pohaku – stone
poi – pasty food made from taro
pono – good, blessed; in balance with nature
pu'u – hill or cinder cone
pu'uhonua – a place of refuge
puka – a hole
pupu – snack or hors d'oeuvres
tsunami – tidal wave (Japanese)
tutu – grandmother, old woman, term of   endearment
ula - red
ulu – the breadfruit tree
wahine – woman, girl
wai – fresh water

Notes

FOR PUBLISHER-DIRECT SAVINGS TO INDIVIDUALS AND GROUPS,
AND FOR BOOK-TRADE ORDERS, PLEASE CONTACT:

DIAMOND VALLEY COMPANY
89 LOWER MANZANITA DRIVE, MARKLEEVILLE, CA 96120

Phone-fax 530-694-2740
www.trailblazertravelbooks.com
www.trailblazerhawaii.com (blog site)
trailblazertravelbooks@gmail.com

All titles are also available through major book distributors, stores, and websites. Please contact the publisher with comments, corrections, and suggestions. We value your readership.

DIAMOND VALLEY COMPANY'S
TRAILBLAZER TRAVEL BOOK SERIES

ALPINE SIERRA TRAILBLAZER
Where to Hike, Ski, Bike, Fish, Drive
From Tahoe to Yosemite
ISBN 13: 978-0-9786371-3-2
"The best and most attractive guidebook for the Sierra."—Tahoe Action

GOLDEN GATE TRAILBLAZER
Where to Hike, Walk, Bike
In San Francisco and Marin
ISBN 13: 978-0-9670072-7-4
ISBN E-book: 978-0-9829919-7-8
"Makes you want to strap on your boots and go!"—Sunset Magazine

KAUAI TRAILBLAZER
Where to Hike, Snorkel, Bike, Paddle, Surf
ISBN 13: 978-0-9786371-4-9
ISBN E-book: 978-0-9829919-0-9
"Deserving of ongoing praise. You are guaranteed a unique experience.
— Midwest Book Review.

MAUI TRAILBLAZER
Where to Hike, Snorkel, Surf, Drive
ISBN 13: 978-0-9829919-8-5
ISBN E-book: 978-0-9829919-2-3
"Recommended for places off the beaten path"—New York Times

HAWAII THE BIG ISLAND TRAILBLAZER
Where to Hike, Snorkel, Surf, Bike, Drive
ISBN 13: 978-0-9786371-8-7
ISBN E-book: 978-0-9786371-9-4
"Essential for a trip to Hawaii"—About.com

OAHU TRAILBLAZER
Where to Hike, Snorkel, Surf
From Honolulu to the North Shore
ISBN 13: 978-0-9829919-9-2
ISBN E-book: 978-0-9829919-1-6
"Marvelously flexible. A well-marked trail of tropical adventures."
—San Francisco Chronicle

NO WORRIES HAWAII
A Vacation Planning Guide for
Kauai, Oahu, Maui, and the Big Island
ISBN 13: 978-0-9670072-9-8
ISBN E-book: 978-0-9829919-4-7
"Really a travel planning guide without peer. If only other travel destinations had something this good."—Guide to Travel Guides

NO WORRIES PARIS
A Photographic Walking Guide
ISBN 13: 978-0-9786371-6-3
ISBN E-book: 978-0-9829919-5-4
"Making Paris trouble free"
—Chicago Tribune

"Long story told short—there are no guidebooks for Hawaii that begin to compare to the Trailblazer books."—Maui Weekly